rary of Congress Cataloging-in-Publication Data

mpbell, Lisa D.
    Michael Jackson : the king of pop! / by Lisa D.
ampbell.
        p. cm.
    Includes bibliographical references and index.
    ISBN 0-8283-1957-X
    1. Jackson, Michael, 1958-
    2. Rock musicians--United States--Biography.
    I. Title.
ML420.J175C3 1993
782.42166'092--dc   92-43018
[B]   CIP
                                                      M N

BRANDEN BOOKS

Branden Publishing Company, Inc.
17 Station Street
Box 843 Brookline Village
Boston, MA 02147

MICHAEL JACKSON

The King of Pop

by
Lisa D. Campbell

BRANDEN BOOKS
Boston

CONTENTS

INTRODUCTION

Since the release of his *Thriller* album in late 1982, there has been no shortage of publicity on Michael Jackson. Unfortunately, there has also been no shortage of rumors, inaccurate statements of fact, and deliberate lies invented to increase circulations of newspapers and magazines. A great deal of this material has been made up of half-truths, or just made up!

This onslaught of fictitious publicity has not been confined to supermarket tabloids. Many books purporting to review Jackson's life and career contain several errors. Sometimes it's relatively trivial things like spelling his brother's name, Jermaine, with a "G". The well worn story of how the Jackson Five were discovered by Diana Ross is getting tired. Authors tell of Michael winning eight Grammys for his *Thriller* album in 1984, when actually seven of his Grammys were for *Thriller*, the remaining one being for his narration of the children's storybook album, *E.T.: The Extra Terrestrial*. A noted rock critic, in his book on Jackson, reviewed Michael's career, often erroneously, and even offers psychological insights into Michael Jackson that it is very doubtful any rock critic is qualified to make. Other publications however, are accurate, having been verified by additional sources and personal inspection, and I have used many of these sources in completing this book.

6 MICHAEL JACKSON: THE KING OF POP

I hope to present here a clearer picture of the world's most successful entertainer. Previously published untruths and misconceptions will be exposed and explained helping the reader recognize Jackson for what he is, an endlessly talented singer and dancer who has no peer. I also hope to present the most thorough and detailed review of his already long and amazing career.

One publication devoted entirely to Michael Jackson, described him as follows:

To describe this fragile, delicately framed young man as a singer would be an injustice. To call him a dancer would be an understatement. Call him a one man entertainment sensation and you'll be nearer the truth. Michael Jackson is a self contained PERFORMANCE. He is mesmeric. He commands one hundred percent attention, and receives it.

After researching his career, reading hundreds of newspaper and magazine articles, dozens of books, watching hours of news stories, viewing every video and TV performance, and attending several concerts on both the Victory and Bad tours, I couldn't agree more!

CHAPTER ONE

IN THE BEGINNING

Hundreds of fans stood shivering outside New York's Metropolitan Museum of Natural History on a cold February night in 1984 hoping for a glimpse of a famous face. Inside, CBS Records International President, Allen Davis read from a long, impressive list of awards and record breaking sales figures of his label's biggest selling artist. The occasion? *The Guiness Book of World Records* had stopped their presses to include the new record holder for the biggest selling album of all time, Michael Jackson's *Thriller*. This is only one of endless accomplishments in a career that began when five year old Michael Jackson began singing with his four older brothers in Gary, Indiana.

Katherine Scruse was born on May 4, 1930 near Russell County, Alabama to Martha Upshaw and Albert Scruse. Martha and Albert had a second daughter, Hattie, a year later. Albert worked as a Pullman porter for the Illinois Central and was also a cotton farmer, as was his father and grandfather. Katherine's great grandfather was once a slave. His name was originally Screws, but he later took the name Scruse from the family for whom he had been a slave.

Katherine was stricken with polio at a very young age, before she was two years old. Then polio was commonly fatal, or crippling. Katherine was more fortunate than others, but today she still walks with a limp.

When Katherine was four year old, the family moved from Alabama to East Chicago, Indiana. Not long after the move, Martha and Albert divorced. Katherine and her sister Hattie continued to live in Indiana with their mother. Each of them loved music and often listened to country and western songs on the radio.

At the age of nineteen, Katherine met and married Joe Jackson. Joseph Walter Jackson was born on July 26, 1929, in Arkansas to Samuel J. Jackson and Chrystalee King. Samuel, born in Mississippi in 1903, attended Alcorn College and later got a teaching job in Arkansas. There he married one of his students, Chrystalee. Joseph was their first of five children. One daughter, Verna, died at age seven of polio.

Samuel Jackson was said to be a very strict and unfeeling man, rarely letting his emotions show even to his family. He would pass these traits onto his oldest son.

Samuel and Crystalee divorced when Joe was a teenager. Samuel took Joseph and moved to Oakland, California. The other children lived with their mother in East Chicago, Indiana. Even though he liked California, Joe later went to live with his mother in Indiana after his father remarried. There, for a brief time, he became a boxer in the Golden Gloves. He then got a job working as a crane operator in a steel mill.

At age nineteen Joe married. It didn't last long, they were divorced after one year. He then met Katherine Scruse, and they fell for each other instantly. They were married on November 5, 1949. Joe would often tell Katherine of living in California and they dreamed of someday being able to move there. But for now, they settled in a small two bedroom house in Gary, Indiana, a dark, dingy, industrial town, and began to raise a family.

Their five oldest sons developed an early interest in music and soon formed their own group, The Jackson Five. This group's lead singer, the seventh of Joseph and Katherine's nine children was to go beyond the group and become the greatest entertainer of the world.

Joseph and Katherine Jackson actually had ten children, Marlon had a twin, Branden, who died about eight hours after birth. Their first child was Maureen Reilette (Rebbie), born on May 29, 1950. She was followed by their first son, Sigmond Esco (Jackie) one year later on May 4, 1951. Toriano Adaryl (Tito) followed on October 15, 1953. Jermaine LaJuan was born on December 11, 1954. Their second daughter, LaToya Yvonne, was born exactly six years after their first, on May 29, 1956. Marlon David was next, born on March 12, 1957. On August 29, 1958, Michael Joseph took his place in the growing Jackson clan. Michael was followed by Steven Randall (Randy) on October 29, 1961. The youngest Jackson, Janet Damita, was born on May 16, 1966.

The continually growing Jackson family still lived in the same small house in Gary, coincidentally on the corner of 23rd Avenue and Jackson Street, at 2300 Jackson Street. Roosevelt High School's football field lay directly behind their house.

Music has always played an important role in the Jackson household. Early in his marriage, Joe Jackson played guitar in a band called The Falcons. The band played cover versions of songs in local bars and colleges but only enjoyed limited success. As his family steadily grew Joe eventually quit the band. Katherine went to work part-time, at Sears.

Joe and Katherine still made time to enjoy music at home. The children would often join in on sing-a-longs at home with their parents on country and western songs while Joe played his guitar.

Father Joe's guitar was strictly off limits to the children. However, when he was away, Tito would get the guitar out and practice playing. Katherine was aware they were playing with the forbidden instrument but didn't enforce the ban figuring it was helping to keep her boys off the streets of Gary. When a string was accidentally broken, Father Joe threatened to punish his son unless he could show that he could play the instrument. Tito surprised and amazed his father with his talent. Joe was equally impressed with the talent of his other sons.

Joe eventually bought Tito his own, bright red guitar. Later, a bass was purchased for Jermaine and microphones were added to the boy's growing equipment collection. The three oldest boys, Jackie, Tito, and Jermaine had formed their own group, with Jermaine as lead singer. Not long after the formation of the group, little brothers Marlon and Michael joined with Michael on bongos. The brothers voted that Michael, who at age five had been imitating Jermaine's lead vocals, should be the group's new lead singer.

Michael made his first public performance at age five for his Kindergarten class at Garnett Elementary School when he participated in a school pageant. His performance of "Climb Every Mountain" was so emotional it moved his teacher and his mother to tears. Michael recalls in his autobiography, *Moonwalk*, how he felt at being able to touch people with his performance. He must have somehow known it was what he wanted to do because it has been told that later when he was having trouble with his arithmetic, he told his teacher that he didn't need to learn math anyway because his manager would handle all of his money!

Living out his dream of making it big through his children, Joe was determined that his sons would be their absolute best. He insisted they put in long hours of rehearsal everyday after school while still completing homework assignments and keeping grades up, leaving very little time for any other activities. In *Moonwalk*, Michael remembers working much too hard for a child, missing out on normal childhood activities we all take for granted.

Michael also recalls the strictness with which daily rehearsals were held. According to Michael, if one of them messed up at rehearsal, missed a step or forgot a lyric, they were beaten. While each of the children received their share of the beatings, Michael was the only one who ever fought back, one time heaving one of his shoes at his father. Because of Joe's need to control the lives of his sons and his strictness, Michael has never enjoyed a close relationship with his father.

The group soon began entering local talent contests using their new name, The Jackson Five, suggested by a neighbor. They performed cover versions of songs by Motown artists and anything by Michael's idol, James Brown. Joe would visit clubs in Chicago to check out other performers to get ideas for his sons' act. They were soon winning every contest they entered and became quite well known around Gary.

The Jackson Five were performing regularly during the week at a club in Gary, Mr. Lucky's, when Michael was six years old. On weekends they began travelling to Chicago, New York, and Philadelphia, entering and winning more talent contests. They travelled in a Volkswagon van with their equipment in a second van that they had borrowed. They would often leave for home late Sunday night and the boys would sleep in the van, and would not return home until 3:00 or 4:00 a.m. They would still be up early Monday morning for school.

Katherine was not happy with some of the clubs where her sons were performing. They would often perform among several different types of acts, including strippers. In some clubs, holes were drilled in the walls dividing the men's and women's dressing rooms. Katherine was concerned about the effect this exposure to such things would have on her sons, especially Michael, her youngest. Michael explains in *Moonwalk* that she needn't have worried. He wasn't about to get into trouble, especially at only nine years old!

Katherine, a devout Jehovah's Witness, passed her strong religious beliefs onto her son. This solid religious background gave Michael then, and continues to give him today, a strong moral character that has long made him a standout in his field. He continues to be one of the relatively few to fall prey to the many temptations of fortune and fame. He rarely, if ever, drinks alcohol and has never experimented with drugs. He even normally refuses to take over the counter drugs or those prescribed by physicians.

In between their club dates, Joe was working on getting his sons a record contract. The boys made two records with a local record label in Gary, Steeltown Records in 1968. The first release, "I'm a Big Boy Now"/ "You've Changed", gained a certain level of popularity in the Midwest, but never made it nationally. The second release from Steeltown Records was "You Don't Have To Be Over 21 (To Fall In Love)"/ "Jam Session". This second single was less successful than "Big Boy", but both singles did help increase the group's popularity locally.

In 1968 came the group's biggest challenge to date. They were invited to perform at amateur night at the Apollo Theater in Harlem. Amateur night at the Apollo had long been regarded as the proving ground for amateurs. It was common for some acts to be booed by the audience or be literally pulled off the stage by a giant hook. The Jackson Five took the tough crowd by storm, they not only won amateur night at the Apollo, they received a standing ovation and were invited back as paid performers.

It was while performing at the Apollo that Michael got to watch his idols perform. He always stood backstage and watched the other acts, like Jackie Wilson and the Godfather of Soul, James Brown. Michael studied Brown's moves, committing every turn and glide to memory. He studied and practiced the steps of James Brown until he could duplicate them perfectly. These two performers, along with Sammy Davis Jr., had an especially influential impact on Michael.

The same year they won the talent contest at the Apollo, the group was signed to appear on a TV show in New York, their first television appearance. The boys were ecstatic. On the afternoon after school when they were scheduled to leave, Joe announced he had cancelled their appearance in New York and that they would be going to Detroit instead. The boys were crushed until Joe gave his reason. He had received a call from Motown Records. This was the big break they had been hoping and praying for. Phone calls in the Jackson household had been limited to five minutes in case a record company was trying to call.

How this call from Motown came to be has three different versions, each crediting someone else with "discovering" the Jackson Five. In any case, the group's television debut was postponed until 1969 when they performed on the Miss Black America Pageant.

CHAPTER TWO

MOTOWN CALLED

Contrary to popular belief, Diana Ross did not discover the Jackson Five. In an attempt to generate stronger, more widespread, attention to the newly signed group Motown chose Diana Ross, their greatest star, to present the group to the public. Motown created the now well known tale of how Diana Ross discovered the Jackson Five at a "Soul Weekend" held in Gary for Mayoral candidate Richard Hatcher. Both the Supremes and the Jackson Five performed as part of the festivities. According to the legend, when Diana Ross watched the Jackson Five perform she was so impressed she took them to Motown and introduced them to Berry Gordy, President and founder of Motown Records.

Early in the group's existence, Joe added two other members to the group. Randy Rancifer and Johnny Jackson played organ and drums. Later Motown, wanting to present the group as one big happy family, would create another story that these two boys were also part of the Jackson family, reporting that they were cousins of the Jackson brothers. Actually, neither boy was related to the Jacksons.

Another often told story credits Gladys Knight with discovering the Jackson Five. After seeing the group perform at the Apollo Theater, she brought them to the attention of Berry Gordy at Motown. Actually, she did see them perform and was impressed, but being new to Motown and yet to have any hits, she carried little clout with Berry Gordy. Gordy then took little, if any, notice.

A third story, which is most widely accepted as being the true version, has Bobby Taylor of Bobby Taylor and the Vancouvers discovering the Jackson Five. Bobby Taylor first became aware of the Jackson Five when the two groups were both appearing at the Regal Theater in Chicago, after which Taylor arranged for them to audition at Motown. Tommy Chong, of the comedy duo Cheech and Chong, was a member of the Vancouvers at the time. Tommy Chong and Marlon Jackson have each confirmed this version of how the Jackson Five were discovered.

Berry Gordy was not present at the Jackson Five's audition for Motown. He did however have the audition video taped to view later. Michael's early mastery of the moves of James Brown

is incredible in this film. He duplicates his idol's steps perfectly.
Other acts performing in the same small clubs as the Jackson Five
during this time were constantly amazed at Michael's dancing
ability and the emotion with which the ten year old sang. This
gave rise to ridiculous stories that the Jackson Five's lead singer
was actually a midget, much older than he appeared. Unfortunately, having such ludicrous rumors spread about him is something he
would have to live with for the rest of his life.

When the group signed with Motown, the record company
was in the process of relocating its headquarters from Detroit to
Los Angeles. Berry Gordy moved the family from Gary to Los
Angeles, fulfilling a lifetime dream for both Joe and Katherine.
Until Joe and Katherine could settle affairs in Gary and settle in
California, the children were temporarily split up. Half of the
family lived with Berry Gordy, the other half, including Michael,
lived with Diana Ross.

Michael lived with Diana for nearly a year and a half.
During this time their relationship grew to be a very close one,
and although she did not discover him, Diana would go on to have
a profound influence on Michael's life. They spent hours together
going to Disneyland, and she taught him to draw and paint,
instilling in him an appreciation for art. He still carries a deep
love for art. He also still carries a deep love for Diana, often
describing her as his mother-lover-sister. In his autobiography,
Moonwalk, Michael describes how hurt he felt when Diana
announced she was to marry Arne Naess, "I have to admit that I
was a bit hurt and a little jealous because I've always loved Diana
and always will."

There were conflicting stories about Michael being a part
of Diana's wedding. Some stated he was asked to be best man,
others said Diana asked him to give her away. Both instances
seem shaky. Arne Naess had never met Michael before, why
would he ask him to be his best man? Also, why would Diana ask
Michael to give her away when her father is still alive? In any
case, Michael declined whatever invitation he received and skipped

the ceremony completely. Later when Diana gave birth to her and Arne's first child in October, 1987, Michael was asked to be godfather. It is not clear whether or not he accepted.

After signing the Jackson Five, Motown immediately began grooming the boys for their soon to be success. They were taught how to carry themselves, how to respond to interviewers questions, and they were taught the story of how they were discovered by Diana Ross. And rehearsals continued. Many of the group's early routines were choreographed by a young new Motown executive, Suzanne de Passe. She too became close to the boys, especially Michael.

Berry Gordy took direct, personal control of the group as soon as they were signed to Motown which didn't go over too well with Joe Jackson. He had personally managed his sons up to this point with New York lawyer Richard Aarons and was now downgraded to making sure his boys were at the studio on time. Berry Gordy decided which songs the Jackson Five would record and who would produce them. A trio of songwriters, Freddie Perren, Deke Richards, and Fonce Mizell made up a song writing team referred to by Motown as "The Corporation". The Corporation had written a song for Gladys Knight, entitled, "I Want To Be Free". Berry Gordy asked that the song be rewritten to make it more appropriate for kids to sing. They rewrote the lyrics and returned to Gordy with "I Want You Back", the Jackson Five's first single with Motown from their debut album, *Diana Ross Presents the Jackson Five*. The album contains cover versions of Motown hits, most notably Stevie Wonder's "My Cherie Amour". Michael's soulful deliverance of Smokey Robinson's "Who's Lovin' You" makes it impossible to believe he's only ten years old.

"I Want You Back" was released in late 1969 and the week of January 31, 1970, became their first number one hit single on *Billboard's* pop singles chart. It spent one week at number one replacing B.J. Thomas' "Raindrops Keep Falling On My Head". The single also went to number one on *Billboard's* black singles chart. Their debut album peaked at number five on the pop album chart and went to number one on the black album chart. And this was only the beginning.

To promote their new single, the Jackson Five appeared on the *Ed Sullivan Show* in December, 1969. They performed "I Want You Back" and "Who's Lovin' You". In 1988, Michael narrated a collection of film clips covering his career for *Entertainment Tonight* which included a clip of this performance. "I remember this was the *Ed Sullivan Show*. As young as I was, I never felt shy while performing. It was what I did and what I came into the world to do."

The group was now professionally known as the Jackson Five. However, the spelling and logo of the group varied between projects. Their name was sometimes spelled out, "The Jackson Five", or the number "5" was used, "The Jackson 5", other times these two were combined, "The Jackson 5ive". However you spell their name, Jackie, Tito, Jermaine, Marlon, and Michael were on their way to enormous success.

If Jackie hadn't been a member of the Jackson Five, he may have had a career, instead of in the music field, on a baseball field. Jackie was the athlete of the family, and was offered a contact with the major leagues.

Jackie married Enid Spann in November, 1974. It has been reported that the ceremony was informal, to say the least. Jackie was dressed in jeans and tennis shoes. Enid is a fashion designer and has designed costumes for the group. They have two children, Sigmund Jr. and Brandi. Jackie and Enid divorced in 1987 after Enid filed charges of abuse from Jackie. In 1989, Jackie released his second solo album, *Be The One*. His first solo effort was a self titled album.

Tito, the brother who most resembles his father, developed an interest in cars and now has an extensive collection of antique automobiles. Like Jackie, he also enjoys sports and has coached little league baseball. At age 18, Tito married Delores (Dee Dee) Martes. They have three sons, Taryll, Tito Jr., and Taj. Tito is the only brother yet to release any recordings independent of his brothers.

Jermaine was the original lead singer of the group when they first began performing at home in Indiana. He was later the brother chosen by Motown to be promoted as the group's sex symbol. Michael was too young to be considered in that light, though he was a favorite of their very young fans. Jermaine married Hazel Gordy in 1973 and they divorced in 1987, after which he returned to the family home in Encino with his girlfriend, Margaret Maldonado. Jermaine and Margaret later married. Jermaine is the father of five children, three with Hazel and two with Margaret; Jermaine Jr., Autumn, Jaimy, Jourdyn, and Jeremy. Jermaine made several solo albums with Motown before signing with Arista in 1984, where he has had even more success with his solo career.

Marlon was the brother who had to work the hardest at mastering the group's choreography. Ironically, he was originally singled out by the press as the brother having great dancing talent. He did contribute to the group's choreography early in their career, but was soon overshadowed by you-know-who.

As seemed to be the tradition for Jackson males, Marlon married at a young age. At eighteen, he secretly married Carol Parker. They supposedly kept the marriage secret for months, without even Joe knowing for sure. They now have three children, Valencia, Britany, and Marlon Jr. Marlon released his first solo album, *Baby Tonight* in 1988.

The youngest member of the original Jackson Five was Michael. He quickly took over the position of lead singer from Jermaine and contributed to the group's choreography. After the success of the Jackson Five with Motown, Michael made a few forgettable solo albums for Epic Records and eventually faded into oblivion having never made any real contribution to the music world...NOT!!!

Randy officially joined the group when they moved from Motown to Epic. He had played bongos for the group much earlier though. He played on albums and even played with his brothers in concert, but with little or no recognition. In the late 1980's, Randy formed his own band, Randy and the Gypsies. The group released their debut album and single, "Love You Honey" in 1989.

Randy is one of two Jackson brothers not to marry at a young age, waiting until his mid twenties before marrying. Randy and his wife Eliza have one daughter, Steveanna. Eliza filed for divorce from Randy in 1990 charging Randy with abuse.

The eldest Jackson is daughter Maureen, nicknamed Rebbie. Rebbie married Nathaniel Brown at age eighteen. They then moved from Gary to Kentucky and now have four children, Stacee, Yashi, Nathaniel Jr., and Austin. Rebbie has released three solo albums, *Centipide, Reaction,* and *R U Tuff Enuff.*

LaToya studied business law before starting a recording career. She has released four albums, *LaToya Jackson, Heart Don't Lie, Imagination,* and *LaToya.* Her first album includes the single, "Night Time Lover" written by LaToya and Michael, and produced by Michael. LaToya has also been the spokeswoman for Mahogany, a line of cosmetics.

Janet has become the second most successful solo Jackson. Janet started her career as an actress at age ten playing Penny Gordon on the television series, *Good Times.* She also portrayed Willis Jackson's girlfriend, Charlene, on *Diff'rent Strokes.* Later, she played Cleo on *Fame.*

Janet's recording career was relatively unsuccessful until the release of *Control* in 1986 and *Janet Jackson's Rhythm Nation 1814* in 1989. Only half heartedly committed to a singing career, her first two albums, *Janet Jackson* and *Dream Street* failed. Janet was briefly married to James DeBarge of the Motown family group DeBarge.

Shortly after the Jacksons signed with Motown, they met and became friends with the president of their fan club, Steve Manning. Manning later worked as a publicist for the Jacksons. In 1976, he wrote a book about them entitled, *The Jacksons.*

The follow up single to "I Want You Back" was "ABC", off of their second album of the same name. The week of April 25, 1970, "ABC" became the Jackson Five's second number one single, replacing the Beatles' "Let It Be" at the top of the pop chart, where it stayed for two weeks. "ABC" was also their second number one hit on the black singles chart. The *ABC* album reached number one on the black album chart and number four on the pop album chart. The single was nominated for a Grammy award for Best Pop Song, but didn't win. In February, 1970, the Jackson Five made their first appearance on *American Bandstand*. They performed both of their number one hit singles, "I Want You Back" and "ABC".

"ABC" would be revived twenty years later by rap group Naughty By Nature. Michael's line, "C'mon, C'mon, tell me what it's all about" is sampled in their hit "O.P.P."

The week of June 27, 1970, the Jackson Five again topped *Billboard's* pop singles chart and again knocked out the Beatles. "Long and Winding Road" was replaced as the number one song in the country by "The Love You Save" off of the *ABC* album. Their third single stayed at number one for two weeks and also hit number one on the black singles chart. This third number one single fulfilled the prophesy made to them by Berry Gordy that their first three singles would all be number one hits. But the Jackson Five did him one better.

The Jackson Five's *Third Album* yielded their fourth number one single. It was quite a change of pace from the singles that had been previously released. "I'll Be There" is a touching ballad with Michael and Jermaine trading lead vocals. "I'll Be There" gave the Jackson Five their longest stay at number one, entering the number one position the week of October 17, 1970 and remaining at the top of the chart for five weeks, replacing Neil Diamond's "Cracklin' Rose". It also became their fourth number one hit on the black singles chart. The Jackson Five became the first group ever to have their first four singles become number one hits. "I'll Be There" became Motown's third biggest single of all time behind Marvin Gaye's "Heard It Through the Grapevine" and Lionel Richie and Diana Ross' duet, "Endless Love". A remake of "I'll Be There" by Mariah Carey went to number one on the pop singles chart for one week in June, 1992.

Other notable tracks on *Third Album* include "Goin' Back To Indiana", "Mama's Pearl", and a cover version of "Bridge Over Troubled Water." The album peaked on the black and pop album charts at numbers one and four respectively.

Billboard's year-end singles chart for 1970 showed the Jackson 5's first four singles all in the top twenty. "I Want You Back" was the number nineteen song of the year, "The Love You Save" was number fourteen, "ABC" was number thirteen, and the number two song of 1970 was "I'll Be There".

With their fourth single climbing the charts, the Jackson Five set out on their first American tour in the fall of 1970. Earlier in the spring, many of Motown's artists were embarking on tour in England as part of Motown's tenth anniversary. The Jacksons were not allowed to accompany their fellow Motowners to England because of legal complications. Minors must be at least twelve years of age to rehearse long hours or appear on English television after 8:00 p.m. and Michael was only eleven at the time. The Jackson Five's first performance in England didn't happen until late 1972 when Michael was an old man of fourteen.

To help keep their grades up while on tour, a tutor, Rose Fine, travelled with them. When they weren't touring they attended a private school with other young performers and children of performers. After the move to California, they were initially enrolled in public school, but fans would wait for them outside or barge into their classrooms. Michael attended Gardner Elementary School for a few months in sixth grade before it became necessary to arrange for private tutoring.

The Jackson family moved into their own home on Hayvenhurst Avenue in Encino, California, in late 1970. The brothers gradually all moved out as they got older and got married. Only Michael and LaToya remained, living with their parents until the spring of 1988.

For the first time since they moved to California, the Jackson Five returned to Gary in January, 1971. They played two benefit concerts for the re-election campaign for Mayor Richard Hatcher. In return, January 31, 1971, was declared "Jackson Five Day" in Gary. A ceremony was held in front of the family's old home to officially rename their street from Jackson Street to Jackson Five Street, and Mayor Hatcher awarded the Jackson Five with the keys to the city. As part of the homecoming, a plaque was placed at the University of Indiana stating that the Jackson Five gave "Hope to the Young". Their Congressman then presented them with the flag from the top of the State Capital.

These award presentations and performances were filmed and later used in their TV special, *Goin' Back to Indiana*. The special aired on September 19, 1971, and featured guest appearances by Tom Smothers and Bill Cosby. The Jackson Five performed their biggest hits and acted in skits with their guests. A soundtrack album of the special made it to number sixteen on *Billboard's* pop album chart and number five on the black album chart.

The day following the airing of their first TV special, the Jackson Five received commendations for "contributions to American youth." On September 20, 1971, the Congressional Record read as follows:

The Jackson Five
Mr. Bayh, Mr. President, I desire to pay tribute to a family of five young black musicians and singers from Gary, Indiana, who have made a large contribution to music in the past few years.

The Jackson Five, young men ranging in age from 12 to 20, have captured the imagination of today's youngsters, especially black youth, as no musical group since the Beatles in 1964. The Jackson Five have become a symbol of pride among black youth, who can readily identify and relate to them. As special tribute, the

Grambling University Marching Tigers, a predominately black university in Louisiana, saluted the Jackson five in their half-time performance during Saturday's Morgan State-Grambling University NCAA football game.

Last year the group had four hit singles, and they have had two more already this year. In the words of 12 year old Michael Jackson, the lead singer:

'We started singin' together after Tito started messin' with Dad's guitar and singin' with the radio. It was Tito who decided we should form a group and we did, and we practiced a lot, and then we started entering talent shows and we won every one we entered.'

On Septmeber, 19, the Jackson Five starred in their first television special, 'Goin' Back to Indiana,' on ABC-TV, with athletes Elgin Baylor, Ben Davidson, Rosey Grier, Elvin Hayes, and Bill Russell, and comics Tom Smothers and Bill Cosby as their guests. In addition, the Five were featured on September's cover of 'Ebony' Magazine and this fall will have a Saturday morning animated TV series modeled after them.

Group members include Jackie, who is 20, Tito, 17, Jermaine, 16, Marlon 14, and Michael 12. They started singing for fun and soon became known around Gary. Papa Joe, a crane operator, played the guitar and wrote songs to relax away from the job. Their mother, Catherine [sic], sang blues and as they became old enough, the kids joined in the family music sessions. As Joe Jackson says:

'It was fun, the kids liked it and it was one sure way of keeping them home and not roaming in the streets of Gary.'

Motown Records recording star, Diana Ross, heard them during a benefit for Gary Mayor Richard Hatcher and the rest is history.

Despite their fantastic commercial success, members of the Jackson Five are continuing their education. Jackie has started college as a business administration major; the rest are still in secondary school and follow a rigorous schedule of homework, group practice, and classes. On weekends, holidays and during vacations the group makes recordings and gives concerts around the country.

I think it is important to recognize and pay tribute to the family unity that has made the Jackson Five the No. 1 soul group in the country. Indiana and the Nation are proud of the Jackson Five.

The Jackson Five set out on their second American tour in the spring of 1971. One especially noteworthy item about this tour was their opening act. A group of musicians from Tuskegee, Alabama known as the Commodores, toured with the Jackson Five. The Commodores doubled as victims of practical jokes. Former Commodore Lionel Richie recalled some of these antics years later to an interviewer. While staying in the same hotel as the Jacksons, the Commodores would leave their shoes outside their rooms to be polished. The Jacksons would get to them first and fill them with ice cubes! Other times one of the Jackson boys would rush in to the Commodores' room proclaiming someone was after them in the hallway. When the targeted victim opened the door to check out the situation, he was immediately drenched by a pail of water by another brother waiting in the hall!

As the group's popularity soared, so did the need for increased security. For this tour, a retired Los Angeles police officer, Bill Bray, was hired as security chief for the boys. Bray has been with the family or with Michael ever since. He has spent several years as Michael's personal security chief. They have grown very close, Bray often being described as Michael's confidant or as his second father.

Their next two singles just missed adding to their string of number one hits. "Mama's Pearl", the second single from *Third Album*, peaked at number two on both the pop and black singles charts in the spring of 1971. "Never Can Say Goodbye" from their next album, *Maybe Tomorrow*, spent three weeks in the number two spot on the pop singles chart, but made it to number one on the black singles chart. *Maybe Tomorrow* peaked at number eleven on the pop album chart. In 1988, "Never Can Say Goodbye" was re-recorded by The Communards. The title song from the *Maybe Tomorrow* album was much more disappointing, only making it to number twenty on *Billboard's* Hot 100. It did much better on the black chart, making it to number three. The Jackson Five would never have another number one song.

An animated cartoon series based on the Jackson Five began airing in the fall of 1971. At age 13, and a huge fan of cartoons, Michael especially enjoyed being depicted in the series. The speaking voices used in the cartoons were not the real Jacksons, but the singing voices were. "Mama's Pearl" was used as the series' theme song.

A few episodes of the cartoon series were based on real life experiences of the Jackson Five. Their homecoming ceremony in Gary to rename their street after them, their performances for the Queen in England, and their discovery by Diana Ross were all made into cartoon episodes. When trying to make it in time for the ceremony in Gary, Michael thinks they will miss it and they will rename the street, "Anybody But the Jackson 5 Street"! While in England to perform for the Queen, Michael inadvertently starts a clothing fad, with everyone dressing exactly like Michael Jackson, something not to different from what would be happening in a few years.

Other things in the series mirrored the group's real life also, such as their pets. In the series they had two mice, Ray and Charles, and a snake named Rosie. Michael did keep rats as pets and Rosie was a snake given to Jermaine by Hazel Gordy.

All of these back to back hit singles, tours, TV specials, and awards being bestowed on the Jackson Five began to spawn other family singing groups, most notably the Partridge Family and the Osmonds. The Partridge Family, whose members weren't really related, featured teen heartthrob David Cassidy. The Osmonds had a young cute lead singer in little brother Donny. Even though both of these acts had successful TV shows and hit records, their success never matched that of the Jackson Five. Geoff Brown, in his book, *Michael Jackson: Body and Soul*, commented: "Neither Cassidy nor Donny Osmond were able to compete in any real sense with the singing of Michael and Jermaine Jackson... One hugely significant fact remained after all the teenmania surrounding the Osmonds died down. They had sold more photographs of themselves than records."

On the heels of Donny Osmond, Motown prepared Michael to begin a solo career in addition to his role as lead singer of the Jackson Five. Michael recorded his first solo single, "Got To Be There" in 1971, from his first solo album of the same name. "Got To Be There" is a touching ballad in the same vein as "I'll Be There". The *Got To Be There* album includes Michael's version of "Rockin' Robin", a remake of Bobby Day's 1958 hit, and covers of Bill Withers' "Ain't No Sunshine" and Carol King's "You've Got A Friend". "Got To Be There" made it to number four on both the pop and black singles charts. "Ain't No Sunshine" was released as a single only in England where it went up the British singles chart to number eight in September, 1972.

Michael recorded his second solo album in 1972. It featured the theme song to a movie, a tender ballad of friendship. What really made this song different was that it was about a rat. A rat named Ben. *Ben*, the sequel to *Willard*, is a horror movie about a young boy's affection for rats, one named Ben in particular. Don Black, who wrote "Ben" with Walter Scharf, suggested Michael Jackson to sing it. Michael's emotion filled performance of "Ben" makes you forget it is a ballad to a rodent:

> *Ben, most people would turn you away*
> *I don't listen to a word they say*
> *They don't see you as I do*
> *I wish they would try to*
> *I'm sure they'd think again*
> *If they had a friend like Ben*

"Ben" was released as a single and became Michael's first number one hit as a solo artist. It peaked at number five on the black singles chart. The song went on to earn an Academy Award nomination for Best Song and Michael performed the song at the Academy Award presentation, but it didn't win the Oscar. The song however, did win a Golden Globe award.

The *Ben* album cover was originally issued with a photograph of Michael with a horde of rats superimposed on the lower half of the picture. A revised cover with just the photo of Michael was soon used instead when it was decided the rat cover was too graphic for children. The original rat cover of *Ben* has today become a rare collectible among fans.

Michael actually did like rats. At one time he kept them as pets, until the adults began to eat the young. This repulsed him. He left the cage outside overnight, it got unexpectedly cold, and the remaining rats froze to death.

The Jackson Five set out on a tour of England in 1972, where they gave a command performance for Queen Elizabeth at Kings Hall in Glasgow, Scotland. They also played in Liverpool, where their opening act was a British rocker who was just getting his start on what was to become a very long, flamboyant and successful career, Elton John.

Later in 1972, the Jacksons made their second TV special. *The Jackson 5 Show* aired in November on CBS. This second TV Special, the group's and Michael's records, TV appearances, and concerts fueled their fans continued fascination with the Jacksons and Michael. *Right On!*, a teenage fan magazine created in 1973, featured Michael and/or the Jackson Five on the cover of every issue during its first year of publication. During the magazine's second year of publication, the Jackson Five or Michael alone were featured on eleven of the year's twelve issues.

By the age of fourteen, Michael Jackson had become a millionaire. It was only the first in a very long line of millions yet to come.

Although each tour continued to attract hordes of fans, the albums the Jackson Five were turning out weren't matching the sales and chart success of their early releases. In 1973, *Get It Together* and *Skywriter* were released and each met with disappointing sales. A third solo album for Michael, *Music and Me* also failed to match the success of his earlier solo albums. One possible factor contributing to these albums' failure is that Berry Gordy had become preoccupied. Gordy, who had always taken a personal role in producing the Jackson Five's albums had now become involved in Motown's first movie project, *Lady Sings the Blues*, the story of Billie Holiday starring Diana Ross. This preoccupation kept Gordy from supplying the Jackson Five with the big hits they had been getting from Motown. The Motown production line formula of producing hits was beginning to fail. One bright spot however, was the release of "Dancing Machine" from their album, *Get It Together*. The single became the group's biggest hit single since "Never Can Say Goodbye" three years earlier, peaking at number two on the pop chart and making it to number one on the black chart. "Dancing Machine" had a more mature sound that their other records lacked, helping to bring the Jackson Five out of the "bubblegum pop" sound.

Michael recorded one more solo album for Motown, *Forever, Michael*. Later Motown releases were compilations of earlier recordings. The last Jackson Five album to be recorded for Motown was *Moving Violation*. Later Jackson Five album releases were also comprised of earlier recordings.

In 1974, with no input from Motown, Joe Jackson organized performances for his children at Las Vegas' MGM Grand Hotel. The brothers were joined by their three sisters and youngest brother Randy. Randy and Janet teamed up to do impersonations of Sonny and Cher. While these performances were well received by their audiences, they did not get favorable reviews from critics.

On December 13, 1973, Jermaine Jackson married Hazel Gordy, daughter of Berry Gordy. Gordy spent an enormous amount of money on the wedding which had a winter wonderland theme that included mountains of artificial snow and live doves. Smokey Robinson performed "The Wedding Song" which he wrote especially for the occasion. It appeared as though the Jacksons and Motown were closer than ever before, but just the opposite was true.

CHAPTER THREE

"UNEASY LIES THE HEAD THAT WEARS A CROWN.
W. Shakespeare."

THE SCARECROW FROM "THE WIZ"

As the Jackson boys got older, they began to write songs on their own. Motown however did not allow them to record any of their own songs. As with most Motown artists, the Jackson Five were required to record songs written and produced by Motown's staff of writers and producers. While this formula of producing hits worked for the group initially, Motown's production line methods were no longer as successful as they once were. The Jacksons continually fought to gain more artistic control over their careers which Motown denied. Even though the Jacksons had grown and matured, they weren't allowed to record their own songs that reflected this growth.

While the Jackson Five resented this lack of control over their music, Joe Jackson resented the amount of authority Berry Gordy exercised over his sons. Once the manager of the group, Joe's role was diminished to practically nothing. Their contract with Motown called for Berry Gordy and Motown to make all decisions affecting the group and their music.

Another factor of dissatisfaction with Motown was the low royalty rate the group was paid. Standard Motown contracts called for a 2.7 percent royalty to be paid on every album sold, based on the wholesale price. It has been written however, that the Jacksons, in their contract, were paid 6 percent of 90 percent of the wholesale price of each album. Regardless of which was actually stated in their contract, they were paid just over five to ten cents per album sold, assuming a wholesale price of $2.00 per album. This then had to be split five ways, making each group member's earnings between one and two cents per album. They were also responsible for paying all of their recording expenses for all the songs they recorded, regardless if they were ever issued as a single or included on an album.

The royalty rate paid to the group was low, but not considered unusual for a new group. However, they continued to receive the same amount of royalties well after they had had several hit records and were a firmly established act at Motown. Michael especially learned from this experience. In later years he would sign several contracts for recording and commercial endorsements making him the highest paid entertainer in the world.

His contract with Epic Records in the eighties earned him in excess of $2.00 per album, with this rate increasing with sales. With over 43 million copies of *Thriller* sold, he has earned well over $86 million in royalties from his *Thriller* album alone. His next contract would top that.

All of these objections as to how Motown was managing their careers contributed to the announcement made in July, 1975, that the Jackson Five were leaving Motown when their contract expired on March 10, 1976. In the summer of 1975, they signed a new contract with Epic Records, a division of CBS Records.

With the switch from Motown to Epic, the group suffered two emotional and crushing blows. The least of which was the loss of their name. Motown fought back by filing a $20 million lawsuit against Joe Jackson and CBS Records for influencing the group into breaching their contract with Motown. Motown claimed the Jackson Five breached their contract when they signed with Epic before their contract with Motown had expired. The Jacksons countersued for back royalties that Motown still owed them. When the suit was finally settled, Motown received $100,000 cash and other items worth $500,000. Motown was also awarded the right to re-release Jackson Five songs, and they maintained the right to the name, "Jackson Five". This meant a certain loss of identity for the group. They had become known as the Jackson Five well before signing with Motown. They then changed their name to "The Jacksons".

The second, and most painful, loss for the group was the loss of Jermaine. Joe Jackson had each of his sons sign the new contract with Epic Records before even mentioning it to Jermaine. He was then shown that each of his brothers had already signed, and was told to do the same. Jermaine had a very difficult decision to make. He was faced with choosing between signing with Epic and staying with his brothers, or staying with Motown, his father-in-law's company. Jermaine elected to stay with Motown and pursue a solo career.

The loss of Jermaine hit the group hard. He was especially missed by his partner on stage, sharing lead vocals, and his partner off stage, pulling practical jokes and fooling around. Michael missed Jermaine deeply. In *Moonwalk*, Michael explains how strange and alone he felt on stage without Jermaine in his usual spot, to Michael's left. Randy officially joined the group after Jermaine's departure.

Shortly before the release of their first album with Epic, the Jacksons had their own TV variety series, *The Jacksons* which aired during the summer of 1976. Michael hated doing the weekly series, and generally any TV. He hated not having the time to perfect performances, being forced to sacrifice quality to meet deadlines. He also hated the silly comedy routines that were included in each show.

After the move to Epic Records, Joe Jackson regained control over his son's careers, becoming the group's manager once again. In 1977, he hired Freddy DeMann and Ron Weisner as partners in managing the group. The management team of DeMann/Weisner would manage the group as well as Michael on his solo projects for several years.

While the move from Motown to Epic proved to be successful in regaining control over the management aspect of their careers, the artistic control they longed for was a little longer in coming. They were given little more freedom to record their own music, continuing to record songs written and produced by others. They were assigned producers Kenny Gamble and Leon Huff, who had been very successful in producing hits for other artists. Gamble and Huff had become known for producing the "Philadelphia Sound". Their first album for Epic did, however, include two songs written and produced by the Jacksons.

Their first album with Epic was released in November, 1976, and was titled with the group's new name, *The Jacksons*. Two singles were released from the album. "Enjoy Yourself" went to number six on the pop chart and peaked at number two on the black chart. "Enjoy Yourself" became the group's first single to be certified gold. They had had other gold singles, but "Enjoy Yourself" was the first to be certified by the Recording Industry Association of America because Motown didn't participate in the RIAA. They refused to allow the RIAA to audit their books.

The second single didn't fare as well. "Show You The Way To Go" only made it to number twenty eight on the pop chart, but did go to number six on the black chart. *The Jacksons* also did much better on the black chart than on the pop chart, peaking at number thirty six on the pop album chart and at number six on the black album chart.

The two songs included on the album written and produced by the Jacksons were "Blues Away", written by Michael, and "Style of Life", written by Michael and Tito. Neither of these songs were released as singles, but Epic was impressed enough with Michael's song writing abilities to allow them to contribute two more Jackson originals on their next album.

The Jacksons wrote and produced "Different Kind of Lady" and "Do You Wanna" for their next album, *Goin' Places*, released in October, 1977, and again produced by Gamble and Huff. Although titled *Goin' Places*, the album went nowhere on the pop album chart, making it as high as number sixty three. On the black album chart, *Goin' Places* just missed the top ten, peaking at number eleven. The album's two singles did just as poorly on the pop chart. "Goin' Places" only went as high as number fifty two, and "Find Me a Girl" never made the Hot 100. The two singles did significantly better on the black chart, "Goin' Places" became a top ten hit, peaking at number eight, and "Find Me a Girl" reached number thirty eight.

In between the releases of their first two albums for Epic, the Jacksons gave a special performance in England. In May, 1977, the Jacksons were invited for the second time to perform for Queen Elizabeth II, at King's Hall in Glasgow, Scotland, as part of the Queen's Silver Jubilee.

This time surrounding the group's move from Motown to Epic Records was an especially difficult period for Michael. On one hand he was being forced to grow up much too quickly, having much of the group's business responsibilities put on his shoulders at the age of eighteen. He was representing his brothers in their fight for more artistic input in their music, for the freedom to write and produce their own albums. Yet publicly, their audiences still wanted to see cute, "little" Michael Jackson who was now approaching 5'10". Michael was waging another battle as well, this one with his mirror. In *Moonwalk,* Michael reveals how troubled he was by his complexion. His bad complexion through his teenage years caused him to shy away from other people and made him feel extremely self-conscious.

He was also being plagued by rumors in the press that he and singer/songwriter Clifton Davis, who wrote "Never Can Say Goodbye", were lovers. The tabloids went so far as to claim that Michael was undergoing a sex change operation and the two were planning to marry. These difficult situations eventually did clear up, along with his skin, with the exception of the continued speculation by the press as to Michael's sexual preference.

At age nineteen, Michael helped to change the group's "destiny". He accompanied his father to a meeting with CBS Records' Ron Alexenburg, who had signed the Jacksons to the Epic label. They convinced him that the brothers should be given an opportunity to write and produce an entire album on their own. Alexenburg agreed stipulating that an executive producer be involved as an overseer of the project. Bobby Colomby and Mike Atkinson were chosen as the album's executive producers. This album, the first to be written and produced by the Jacksons, was *Destiny*.

The Jacksons then formed Peacock Productions, their own publishing company. This name was chosen out of Michael's love of animals. At one time, he owned two peacocks but had to get rid of them because of the noise they made when mating. On the back covers of *Destiny* and its follow up, *Triumph*, Michael and Jackie wrote the following words to express how they felt about their music:

Through the ages, the peacock has been honored and praised for its attractive, illustrious beauty. Of all the bird family, the peacock is the only bird that integrates all colors into one, and displays this radiance of fire only when in love. We, like the peacock, try to integrate all races into one through the love of music.

Michael and Jackie Jackson for
Peacock Productions

Today, Michael has several different companies to handle his own productions, publishing, copyrights, and other business interests. MJJ Productions, Optimum Productions, Ultimate Productions, and MIJAC Music have been established for the administration of his publishing and video interests. Triumph Merchandising, Inc., and Triumph International, Inc., have been established to handle the lines of authorized Michael Jackson merchandise. Michael hired Bob Jones as vice president of communications of MJJ Productions. Jones had formerly worked in public relations for Motown and had handled the publicity for the Jackson Five.

One very important contribution that the executive producers of *Destiny* would make is in suggesting Greg Phillinganes as keyboardist and to aid in arrangements for the album. Phillinganes would go on to play an important role in future Jackson albums, and especially Michael's solo albums.

Destiny, released in December, 1978, was the most successful album the group had had in several years and became their first album ever to go platinum. A party was held to celebrate the album's success and to present the group with a platinum copy of *Destiny.* Los Angeles mayor Tom Bradley declared "Jacksons Day" and a celebration was held in a bank vault specially equipped with a dance floor at the City National Bank of Beverly Hills. Michael's date for the occasion was Tatum O'Neal, his first real love, as Michael says, "after Diana."

All of the songs on *Destiny,* with the exception of one, was written by the Jacksons, or by Michael and Randy. Michael and Randy wrote together most often because they were the only two brothers still living at home. The only song on the album that was not written by the Jacksons was the first single, "Blame it on the Boogie", which was co-written by Michael Jackson. This Michael Jackson however, is white and from England. Despite its catchy disco beat and lyrics, "Blame it on the Boogie" reached only a disappointing number fifty four on the pop singles chart. The single did however, reach number three on the black singles chart.

The most successful single from *Destiny* was the second release, "Shake Your Body (Down to the Ground)". This infectious dance tune peaked at number seven on the pop singles chart and number three on the black singles chart. Michael, in a rare interview for a radio program, recalled writing the song with Randy. "Randy was going around the house humming a tune and I liked it. I asked him what it was and he said, 'It's nothing.' I said, 'No, it's something.'" Michael went on to write the melody and lyrics for "Shake Your Body". "I don't know where it came from. God, I say."

Other excellent tracks on *Destiny,* and there are plenty, include "Things I Do For You", "Bless His Soul", "That's What You Get (For Being Polite)", and the title track. "Things I Do For You" deals with Michael's feelings of being used, the beginnings of his distrust of others except those very close to him, similar feelings to those he expressed in "Heartbreak Hotel" and "Wanna Be Startin' Somethin'":

Always wanting something for nothing
Especially what they don't deserve
Reaching in my pocket
I just got to stop it
Even though they got a lot of nerve

The Jacksons set out on a world tour in 1979, to promote the album. Several of the concerts on the tour however were cancelled when Michael's voice became strained.

Just prior to the release of the *Destiny* album, in October, Michael's first project without his brothers since leaving Motown was released. Ironically, this project was a production of Motown.

Michael first fell in love with movies while visiting Diana Ross on the set of *Lady Sings The Blues*. Michael went on to star with Diana Ross in another Motown movie project, even after the Jacksons had left Motown. Michael played the Scarcrow to Diana's Dorothy in *The Wiz*, an updated version of *The Wizard of Oz*, featuring an all black cast. Directed by Sidney Lumet, *The Wiz* also starred Nipsey Russell as the Tinman, Ted Ross as the Cowardly Lion, Lena Horne as Glenda the Good Witch, and Richard Pryor as the Wiz.

Michael truly loved portraying the Scarecrow. He spent four hours every morning for five months getting into his costume and makeup to be transformed into his character. He loved being the Scarecrow so much, he often wanted to wear the makeup and costume home at night. It was while portraying the Scarecrow in *The Wiz* that Michael decided films would play a definite role in his future career.

While filming the movie, Michael lived in an apartment in New York for six months. LaToya also went to New York and stayed with Michael to keep him from getting lonely. Not one for going out to nightclubs, or anywhere for that matter, Michael would become very lonely living by himself. Fear of being lonely is one of the reasons he lived with his parents for so long.

Making *The Wiz* was not without problems for Michael. Just before filming was scheduled to begin, Michael spent the fourth of July holiday at Jermaine's beach home. Relaxing on the beach, suddenly he couldn't breathe. He ran to the house and Jermaine rushed him to the hospital. One of Michael's lungs had collapsed. Tests revealed he suffered from pneumothorax, which occurs most often in people with a slim build.

Another, though much less serious, problem occurred during filming of the movie. In one scene the Scarecrow had to pick up Dorothy, who had fainted. Michael later recalled the rather humorous incident: "The funniest thing was a scene we were doing on the rooftop. Diana was supposed to faint, and I had to pick her up. But she was too heavy. I kept puffing away on the dialogue while I tried over and over again to lift her, until I finally made it."

The Scarecrow was the most lovable of the misfits trying to meet the Wiz to have their needs and wishes fulfilled. As in the original, Dorothy was lost and wanted desperately to find her way home. The Tinman needed a heart. He was convinced he was just an empty shell, completely devoid of any feelings. The Cowardly Lion, of course, needed courage. He was posing as a statue outside the public library when the others spotted him. He was hiding, hoping no one would ever discover his terrible secret. The Scarecrow needed a brain. He had been teased by crows, who told him he was unable to get down from his post in the garden and walk. They made him repeat the crow commandments and sing the crow anthem, "You Can't Win", to further erode any confidence in himself. After being rescued from the pole by Dorothy, they set off together to find the Wiz to get Dorothy home and get the Scarecrow a brain.

While these characters very closely resemble their counterparts in *The Wizard of Oz, The Wiz* does differ in some respects. Instead of Kansas, it takes place in New York, and it has updated music and dance sequences. "Follow the Yellow Brick Road" is replaced by the more refreshing duet with Michael and Diana, "Ease On Down The Road". Released as a single off the soundtrack album, the duet peaked at number forty one on the pop chart and number seventeen on the black chart.

The Wiz is much more comical than the original. Instead of being stuffed with straw, the Scarecrow is stuffed with garbage, mostly shredded newspaper. He pulls scraps of newspaper from his stuffing to "lay appropriate quotes" on others to help offer advice with their problems. These quotes are more appropriate at some times than others. After meeting the Lion on their search for the Wiz, and learning that the king of the jungle has no courage, the Scarecrow reaches inside his stuffing, retrieves a scrap of paper and reads, "Uneasy lies the head that wears a crown. W. Shakespeare." Later, the Lion, thinking Dorothy is dead and that he is responsible, decides to end it all and leap off a rooftop. The Scarecrow quickly pulls out an "appropriate quote" and reads, "Showers expected late tomorrow."!

The Wiz was a tremendously elaborate production costing over $30 million to produce. The Coney Island Amusement Park was used as the deserted carnival where Dorothy and the Scarecrow discover the Tinman. The 42nd Street library was the location used for the scene where the Lion is discovered posing as a statue outside the building. The Emerald City scenes were filmed at the World Trade Center, using 650 dancers and requiring 385 crew members.

Reviewers panned *The Wiz*, criticizing the movie as being over-produced and many felt Diana Ross was too old to play Dorothy. Diana, then thirty two, played a twenty four year old Dorothy. The one bright spot most critics mentioned was the acting ability of Michael Jackson. While *The Wiz* is generally considered to have been a flop, it did show that Michael has genuine acting talent.

After *The Wiz,* it was reported that Michael had been offered a role in another film also directed by Sydney Lumet. He was offered the role of Paul in *A Chorus Line*. Michael, according to the rumor, turned the role down. Paul was the role of a young dancer who was gay, and Michael did not want to be associated with the homosexual aspect of the character, considering the stories already being circulated concerning his sexual preference.

Michael's desire to make more movies was deepened in 1980 when he spent time with Jane Fonda on the set of *On Golden Pond*. During the month he spent on the movie set, he became close friends with the movie's other stars, Katharine Hepburn and

Henry Fonda, who had taken Michael fishing. Later, when Henry Fonda died, Michael spent the evening with the Fonda family.

The main reasons Michael wanted to do *The Wiz* were his love for the movies, *The Wizard of Oz* being one of his favorites, and especially the opportunity to work with Diana Ross. However, it was the musical director of the film that would later join with Michael and together they would make music history. The musical director of *The Wiz* was Quincy Jones.

CHAPTER FOUR

OFF THE WALL

After completing *The Wiz,* Michael began work on his first solo album for Epic Records. He wanted his solo album to have a different sound than his work as part of the Jacksons, so he first looked for an outside producer. He called Quincy Jones to ask for any suggestions he may have, Jones suggested himself and a great team was formed.

Quincy Jones had been working in the music industry for over thirty years. He has worked with, among several others, Billie Holiday, Frank Sinatra, and Count Bassie. Jones produced Leslie Gore's 1963 hit, "It's My Party".

Michael's first solo album with Epic Records was *Off The Wall.* Greg Phillinganes was again chosen as keyboardist and arranger. Phillinganes told how Michael and Quincy, "Q", worked together, "Their ideas just blend into each other. You see, Michael is not like a lot of other singers who come around just to add a vocal. Michael is involved in the whole album. 'Q' is basically an overseer, who runs the show without really running the show. The icing he adds to the cake can be the difference between a good tune and a great one."

Off The Wall is basically a collection of the best dance songs ever included on one album. Three of the album's tracks were written and co-produced by Michael. "Working Day and Night" told of his suspicions that his girl, "must be seeing some other guy instead of me." "Get On The Floor" has him trying to get his girl to join him on the dance floor:

So get on the floor
And dance with me
I love the way you shake your thing
Especially

"Don't Stop 'Til You Get Enough", another of Michael's compositions, was the album's first single and became one of the album's biggest hits. The week of October 13, 1979, it held the number one spot on the pop singles chart, Michael's first number one hit since "Ben" in 1972. "Don't Stop" spent one week at the top of the pop chart and five weeks at the top of the black singles chart.

Michael told Dick Clark's *National Music Survey* how he wrote "Don't Stop 'Til You Get Enough" with help from Randy. "I was walking around the house and I just started singing, 'da-da--da-da-da-da-da', and said, 'Ah, that sounds kinda nice.' I kept singing it and gradually it came about. I went into the studio, we have a studio at home, a 24 track studio. Randy and I, I told Randy what to put down, what to play on the piano, and we did some percussion and some clapping and it turned out real funky. I played it for Quincy Jones and he loved it."

Rod Temperton, a songwriter from Germany, made substantial contributions to *Off The Wall,* as he would later do on *Thriller.* Temperton penned "Rock With You", the album's title track, and "Burn This Disco Out". Although never released as a single, "Burn This Disco Out" measures up splendidly against the latter two, which both became top ten hits. "Rock With You" became the album's second number one single, reaching the top of the pop singles chart the week of January 19, 1980 and remaining for four weeks. "Rock With You" was also the album's second single to reach the number one position on the black singles chart. "Rock With You" isn't as fast paced as "Don't Stop", but the beat is definitely just as infectious:

> *Girl, close your eyes*
> *Let that rhythm get into you*
> *Don't try to fight it*
> *There ain't nothing that you can do*

"Off The Wall", Temperton's other composition, gave Michael his third top ten hit from the album. The single peaked at number ten on the pop singles chart and number five on the black singles chart.

Many other established songwriters contributed to *Off The Wall* in addition to Temperton. "I Can't Help It" was written by Stevie Wonder with Susaye Greene. Greene was a member of The Supremes in one of their many configurations after the departure of Diana Ross. Carole Bayer Sager and David Foster contributed "It's The Falling In Love".

Besides Quincy Jones and Michael Jackson, *Off The Wall* marked the beginning of another partnership that would go on to produce more hits. It was the first time Michael worked with Paul McCartney. McCartney wrote a song called "Girlfriend" which he thought would be perfect for Michael to sing. He told Michael about the song at a party, but they never managed to get together to record the song. McCartney ended up putting the song on his own album, *London Town.* Quincy heard the song and told Michael he thought it was perfect for him to do. Michael was shocked because Quincy never knew McCartney made the offer earlier. So, Michael finally did record "Girlfriend" and included it on *Off The Wall*.

While most of the album does consist of catchy dance tunes, one song definitely stands out as the most moving and most emotional track on the entire album. Michael himself is so moved, he cries at the end. Michael cried when they first recorded the song. So, they did it again. And again Michael cried. Quincy Jones later recalled recording the song, "I had a song I'd been saving for Michael called, 'She's Out Of My Life'. Michael heard it and it clicked. But when he sang it, he would cry. Everytime we did it, I'd look up at the end and Michael would be crying. I said, 'We'll come back in two weeks and do it again, and maybe it won't tear you up so much.' Came back and he started to get teary. So we left it in."

She's out of my life
She's out of my life
And I don't know whether to laugh or cry
I don't know whether to live or die
And it cuts like a knife
She's out of my life

This would not be the only time Quincy Jones would experience Michael being brought to tears while recording.

"She's Out Of My Life" was the fourth single from *Off The Wall* to become a top ten hit, peaking at number ten on the pop charts. The ballad only made it to number forty three on the black singles chart. Michael became the first solo artist in history to have four top ten hits from one album. In England, "Girlfriend" was released as a single making Michael the first artist there to ever have five singles from one album.

Promotional videos were made of Michael performing his biggest hits from *Off The Wall*. Michael performs "Rock With You" dressed from head to toe in silver sequins, including silver sequin covered boots. For "She's Out Of My Life", Michael puts away his dancing shoes and sits solemnly on a stool. In the video clip for "Don't Stop 'Til You Get Enough", Michael dons his then trademark tuxedo, as on the album's cover. The idea of having him wear the tux in the album's cover photo was to emphasize that he had grown and matured. The glowing socks were Michael's touch.

Off The Wall became CBS Records' biggest selling album ever. It spent a year and a half on *Billboard's* pop album chart, eight months of which were spent in the top ten, peaking at number three. *Off The Wall* went to number one on the black album chart. The album re-entered the album charts during "Michaelmania" in 1984.

Despite the album's enormous sales success, it failed to garner a Grammy nomination for Album of the Year. Michael was crushed when he received only one Grammy nomination, even though he won. Michael's first ever Grammy win was for Best R&B Vocal Performance-Male for "Don't Stop 'Til You Get Enough". Feeling that he had been overlooked, Michael skipped the award presentation and vowed that his next album would not be ignored. It wasn't.

Off The Wall was not overlooked at the American Music Awards, however. Dressed in his trademark tux with a sequined shirt, Michael took home the awards for Best Soul Album, Best Soul Male Vocalist, and Best Soul Single for "Don't Stop 'Til You Get Enough".

Off The Wall also received recognition from music industry publications. *Cashbox* magazine chose *Off The Wall* as the most popular soul album of the year. The year end issue of *Billboard* recapped the year in music with Michael, and his *Off The Wall* album and singles, placing high on several charts, often competing with Jermaine and his hit single and album, "Let's Get Serious". Michael was named the number two Top Pop Male Artist, and the number one Top Black Artist, with Jermaine placing at number eight on the latter chart. *Off The Wall* was ranked as the third Top Pop Album of the year and as the number one Top Black Album. Jermaine's *Let's Get Serious* album placed at number five on the black album chart. "Rock With You" placed at number four for the year on the Top Pop Singles chart and at number two on the Top Black Singles chart, just behind "Let's Get Serious".

Off The Wall earned awards in many other countries as well. The album was certified triple platinum in Britain, seven times platinum in Australia, triple platinum in Canada, and it went gold in Holland.

This was not the end of the awards, however. Later, in 1980, the Hollywood Chamber of Commerce honored the Jacksons with a star on Hollywood's Walk of Fame. The Jackson's star is located on Vine Street in Hollywood. This was just a taste of the increased attention the group, and especially Michael, would receive during the next few years.

With this heightened level of interest in Michael's life and career, his distrust of the press began to intensify. He hated being misquoted, having his words distorted to change their meaning. He began to give fewer and fewer interviews, isolating himself from the public. His already extreme shyness began to deepen as his popularity began to soar.

Motown attempted to cash in on this renewed popularity of Michael Jackson, releasing a Jackson Five album in 1979, *Boogie*.

Since only a limited number of copies were made, today it is a valuable collectors item. *Boogie* includes several songs which were never before released.

Michael also used his talents at this time to help choose hits for other artists. In 1980, Queen released their album, *The Game*. After hearing the album, Michael suggested to the group's lead singer, Freddie Mercury, that one particular track be released as a single. "Another One Bites The Dust" spent three weeks at number one in October of 1980, and it is one of Queen's biggest hits ever.

Then it was back to work on the next Jackson album, the follow up to *Destiny*. Again the Jacksons would write and produce their entire album. As with *Destiny,* the Jacksons struck gold. Then platinum. *Triumph* went to number twelve on the pop album chart and number two on the black album chart. Although *Triumph* matched *Destiny's* chart performance it pales, albeit slightly, when compared to the strong tracks on *Destiny*.

Triumph produced four singles, each of which were only moderately successful on the pop charts, but which did much better on the black charts. The album's first single was the album's biggest hit, "Lovely One", written by Michael and Randy. "Lovely One" was the only top ten hit from the album, peaking at number ten on *Billboard's* Hot 100 and going to number two on the black singles chart.

The second single released off of *Triumph* was "Heartbreak Hotel", written by Michael. The song's title was changed to "This Place Hotel" on some copies of the album to avoid confusion with the Elvis Presley song of the same name. Although the songs share the same title they are otherwise very different. Michael has said that he didn't have the Presley song in mind at all when he wrote it. Michael's song is a dark, foreboding tale of impending doom, opening with a blood curdling scream courtesy of LaToya. Michael sings of his feelings that people are after him, watching him and that "hope is dead":

As we walked into the room
There were faces staring, glaring
tearing through me
Someone said 'Welcome to your doom'
They all smiled with eyes that looked
as if they knew me
This is scaring me

"Heartbreak Hotel" made it to number twenty two on the pop singles chart, and number two on the black singles chart.

Michael created and produced a short promotional film based on the single, "Can You Feel It", entitled, "The Triumph". The video includes some impressive special effects well ahead of its time, including animated images of fire and water symbolizing the creation of the world. One of the first times the film was broadcast was on *American Bandstand,* which didn't normally show films. Despite the elaborate video to promote it, "Can You Feel It" did surprisingly poor on the pop and black singles charts, peaking at numbers seventy seven and thirty respectively.

"Walk Right Now" was the fourth single released off of *Triumph.* It also had very disappointing chart success, only making it to number seventy three on the Hot 100 and number fifty on the black singles chart. This was surprising for "Walk Right Now" is a catchy tune telling the story of a girlfriend being told to hit the road.

Triumph, like *Destiny,* was dedicated by the brothers to their mother. "A mother is a gift from God. For ours, we are most thankful and we dedicate this album to our beautiful mother, Katherine Jackson." Michael also dedicated *Off The Wall* to his mother. "I dedicate this to the year of the child & my mother. Love M.J." Conspicuously absent is any mention of their father.

In 1981, the Jacksons set out on tour to support their *Triumph* album. It was a huge production and was, Michael said, the last time he would tour. (In case you're keeping track, this is his first of four "last" tours.) Because Michael hates to tour, the

1981 tour was nearly cancelled. While Michael does love to perform for his fans live, he hates the other things that go along with touring, the constant travelling and being cooped up in hotel rooms, unable to go out without fear of being recognized and mobbed. Concerts scheduled for Florida and Alabama were cancelled when Michael collapsed due to exhaustion while the tour was in New Orleans.

One of the reasons Michael did consent to do the tour was because of one of the performances scheduled for July at the Omni Auditorium in Atlanta, Georgia. The concert there was a benefit performance that raised $100,000 for the Atlanta Children's Foundation. This was in response to the series of kidnappings and murders that had been plaguing the children of Atlanta.

Randy nearly missed being included on the tour. On March 3, 1980, he was in a serious car accident. His car went off the road and hit a post, he was almost killed. He had crushed both of his legs, broken both ankles, and suffered internal injuries. Initially, it was feared that he may lose both of his legs, or be permanently paralyzed. Randy refused to accept this grim prognosis and not only fully recovered, but he recovered in time to join his brothers on tour.

Their performance at New York's Madison Square Garden was attended by one of Michael's close friends, Katharine Hepburn. It was the first rock concert she had ever attended. Michael had been pen pals with Hepburn and they had became friends when he visited the set of her movie, *On Golden Pond*, a year earlier.

The Jackson's 1981 U.S. World Tour was chosen by *Rolling Stone* magazine as one of the greatest live performances of the seventies and eighties. The spectacular lighting, pyrotechnics, and choreography helped to show skeptics that the Jackson boys had grown up to be one the best bands around. Michael, Marlon, and Jackie each contributed to the choreography. Jackie, Tito and Randy directed the band. While each contributed to the production, "Michael, who had just turned twenty-three, was unquestionably the star of the Jackson's '81 shows... For disco dynamite like his *Off The Wall* smash 'Don't Stop 'Til You Get Enough', Michael literally turned into a dancing machine, executing split-second kicks and dizzying spins with smooth precision."

The group performed their greatest hits from their early years at Motown and their hits from *Destiny* and *Triumph* as well as Michael's solo hits from *Off The Wall*. A live album was released following the tour. *Jacksons Live* had very disappointing sales. It peaked at number thirty on the pop album chart and at number ten on the black album chart. While it does give a taste of what a Jacksons concert is like, it is a very small taste. The spectacular effects, costumes, and especially choreography must simply be seen to fully appreciate a live performance of the Jacksons.

In 1981, Michael made a TV appearance, something that was becoming increasingly rare. He was a guest on Diana Ross' special "Diana". They performed "Ease On Down The Road" together in look-a-like white tuxedos, and Michael performed "Rock With You".

It was around this period that Michael's appearance began to change. His complexion had cleared up, thanks in large part to a drastic change in his diet. He had become a vegetarian. Although he was never really overweight, this change in eating habits caused him to lose quite a bit of weight. His facial features became more prominent, he now had more defined cheekbones and jawline. He no longer wore the huge afro hairstyle the Jacksons had become know for. He had also had the first of his soon to be widely speculated about nose jobs.

Triumph didn't have the impact that Michael had with *Off The Wall*, but it did rank as the number ten Top Black Album of 1981 on *Billboard's* year end charts. The Jacksons also ranked at the number ten position on the Top Black Artist chart of 1981, and at number four for Top Dance Artist. "Can You Feel It"/"Walk Right Now" was number four for Top Audience Response Single for the year. Years later the Jackson's *Triumph* album was named by *Spin* magazine as one of the ten most underrated albums of all time.

After completion of the *Triumph* album and tour, Michael started to work on his next solo album and other solo projects. He was now faced with the pressure of topping the success of *Off The Wall*. Nineteen eighty two was going to be a busy year for Michael Jackson.

CHAPTER FIVE

1982

In 1982, Michael released a number of new projects. He wrote and produced a song for Diana Ross, titled, "Muscles"; he narrated a children's storybook album, *E.T.: The Extra-Terrestrial;* and he released his second, moderately successful, solo album for Epic Records, *Thriller.*

It was on a flight returning to Los Angeles from England, after working with Paul McCartney on "The Girl is Mine", that Michael came up with a song that he thought would be perfect for Diana Ross. "Muscles" was named after Michael's pet boa constrictor. Michael wrote the song for Diana because he wanted to do something to thank her for all she had done for him. It was a very big thank you. "Muscles" became a top ten hit for Diana and earned a Grammy nomination.

Steven Spielberg, producer and director of the blockbuster movie *ET: The Extra-Terrestrial,* and Quincy Jones produced a children's storybook album which tells the story of E.T. Michael Jackson was chosen to narrate the story. While recording the narration for the album, Michael became so emotional, he cried at the part where E.T. is dying. Steven Spielberg and Quincy Jones decided to leave it in. Trying it again wouldn't lessen Michael's emotions. Quincy Jones learned this from the recording sessions for "She's Out Of My Life."

E.T.: The Extra-Terrestrial was released in November, 1982 on MCA Records. CBS Records, Michael's record company, filed a $2 million lawsuit against MCA for releasing the album before Christmas. The agreement between the two record companies stipulated that RCA was not to release the E.T. album before Christmas, so it wouldn't draw sales away from Michael's newly released solo album with Epic, *Thriller.* The ensuing litigation resulted in the New York Supreme Court prohibiting sales of the album's single, "Someone in the Dark". A few promotional copies of the single were already distributed to radio stations before its release was prohibited. Those promotional copies of "Someone in the Dark" are collectors items today.

Several contributors to the E.T. album had also worked with Michael on his solo projects. The music for "Someone in the Dark" was written by Rod Temperton, who had written several songs for Michael on his *Off The Wall* and *Thriller* albums. Freddy DeMann and Ron Weisner, former managers of Michael and the Jacksons, served as production coordinators for the E.T. album. The album was engineered by Bruce Swedien, who has also engineered Michael's albums *Off The Wall, Thriller, Bad,* and *Dangerous*. Quincy Jones was one of the album's narrative writers. Dick Zimmerman photographed Michael for the album's cover and the included poster, he also photographed Michael for the *Thriller* album cover.

It was during this same period in late 1982 when Michael had the family's Encino home completely razed and rebuilt for his mother. This was an especially hard time for Michael's mother. Just one year earlier, Katherine Jackson had filed for divorce from Joseph in response to his many infidelities. It received very little attention by the press. Joe refused to move out of the house, so they continued to live under strained conditions. Eventually, Katherine withdrew her petition for divorce and it was never finalized.

Michael contributed heavily to the design of the beautiful tudor style mansion. He had virtually everything he needed and wanted built into the house, creating his own private world and giving him fewer and fewer reasons to ever have to leave. He has his own arcade, complete with all kinds of pinball and video games, a private screening room with seating for thirty five people, and a candy room, a sweetshop with a peanut stand, an ice cream fountain, a popcorn machine, and an impressive variety of chocolate bars. The trophy room houses many of his awards, in the center of the room is a terrarium depicting a scene from *Snow White and the Seven Dwarfs,* which was delivered to Michael's home in person by actual Disneyland characters. Along with rooms filled with things to play with, there are also rooms for Michael to work in. He has his own recording studio and dance studio.

Just as it seemed Michael was trying to seal himself off from the rest of the world, his new album and videos would soon constitute the beginning of the world's renewed and intensified fascination with him to be referred to as "Michaelmania".

The *Thriller* album was released on December 1, 1982, and was an instant smash, selling one million copies before the end of the year. By November, 1983, it had sold ten million copies and was a hot seller for that Christmas season too.

The first single off of *Thriller* was "The Girl is Mine", a duet with Paul McCartney. Paul and Michael fought over the affections of the same girl all the way to number two on *Billboard's* Hot 100, and to number one on the black singles chart:

Paul: *Michael, we're not going to fight about this, ok?*

Michael: *Paul, I think I told you, I'm a lover, not a fighter.*

Paul: *I've heard it all before, Michael, she told me that I'm her forever lover, you know, don't you remember?*

Michael: *Well, after loving me, she said she couldn't love another.*

Paul: *Is that what she said?*

Michael: *She said it, you keep dreaming.*

The second single became one of *Thriller's* two number one songs. With "Billie Jean", Michael Jackson became the first performer ever to hit number one on the pop singles and album chart, and the R&B singles and album charts, simultaneously. The week of March 15, 1983, "Billie Jean" began its seven week stay at number one on the pop singles chart, while *Thriller* topped both the pop and black album charts. "Billie Jean" accuses Michael of fathering her child, and Michael denies it:

> *Billie Jean is not my lover*
> *She's just a girl*
> *Who claims I am the one*
> *But the kid is not my son*

A video for "Billie Jean" was made for the then relatively new music television channel, MTV. The video, directed by Steve Barron, shows Michael being followed by a detective. The detective, however, never succeeds in catching him. Michael doesn't even show up on film when several rigged cameras all snap photos of him at the same time. Michael dances his way to Billie Jean's hotel room, with each segment of the sidewalk lighting up at his touch. It is here that Michael shows how his dancing abilities have advanced. He performs lightening quick spins and then freeze frames poised up on his toes. Arriving at the hotel, he climbs the staircase to her room, each stair lighting up as he steps, even the burned out "HOTEL" sign lights up letter by letter as he passes. The police and the detective arrive at the scene only to see Michael disappear beneath the sheets of Billie Jean's bed.

For his new album and videos, Michael had a new and different look than that he sported on the cover of *Off The Wall*, and its videos. He now had jeri curled hair, and he had had his nose surgically reshaped. He had also adopted a new style of dress. He appears in the "Billie Jean" video in a black leather suit with a pink shirt and a bow tie. From now on, whatever Michael wore would be copied from elementary school playgrounds to college campuses, except in New Jersey where single white gloves were banned at Bound Brook High School. In response, the student held protests.

While "Billie Jean" was one of MTV's most popular and successful videos, CBS Records did have some difficulty in getting the video aired on the music network, as MTV's video playlist consisted mainly of white rock bands. CBS threatened to withhold all videos from their company's artists if MTV refused to play more videos by black artists. "Billie Jean" helped to break MTV's predominately white programming.

Another interesting note about "Billie Jean" is the way in which it was recorded. To get the exact sound that Quincy and Michael were looking for, the instruments were played and recorded many times over until both were finally satisfied. Then it was time for Michael to add the vocals. All of the vocals for "Billie Jean" were recorded in one unbelievable take.

Thriller's third single, and second number one hit was "Beat It". "Beat It" is the hardest rock song on *Thriller,* featuring a guitar solo by guitar great Eddie Van Halen. Eddie Van Halen's contribution, for which he received no money, brought Michael's music to a whole new audience: white kids who liked hard rock music. It had similar affects for Van Halen, their latest album, *1984,* made it to the black album charts!

Usually, a record company waits for a song to peak on the music charts and fall, before releasing another single from that same album. It is generally thought that if a another single is released prematurely, it will kill the first single. However, while "Billie Jean" was still at number one on the singles chart, "Beat It" was released as the follow up single. A few weeks later, "Beat It" and "Billie Jean" were both in the top five, "Beat It" occupied the number one spot and "Billie Jean" was at number five. In fact, only one week separated the two songs' stays at number one. When "Billie Jean" fell from number one after seven weeks, "Beat It" became the new number one song one week later, the week of April 30, 1983, where it stayed for three weeks. Dexy's Midnight Runners' "Come On Eileen" separated "Billie Jean" and "Beat It" as the country's number one pop single. This was the shortest amount of time between number one singles by the same artist since the Beatles replaced themselves at number one in 1964. "She Loves You" was knocked out of number one by "Can't Buy You Love". "Beat It" was the third single from *Thriller* to hit number one on the black chart.

In "Beat It", Michael expresses his views against violence, that if at all possible, fighting should be avoided:

> *You better run, you better do*
> *what you can*
> *Don't wanna see no blood,*

don't be a macho man
You wanna be tough, better do
what you can

The video for "Beat It" was directed by Bob Giraldi, and choreographed by Michael Peters, choreographer of the broadway hit *Dreamgirls*. Peters also appears in the video as a gang leader. Genuine Los Angeles street gang members were used in the video along with professional dancers, to make the gang scenes look authentic.

At the start of the video, the members of two rival gangs emerge from the streets, pool halls, and even the sewers to face each other in an empty warehouse. Michael shows up just in time to prevent the possible bloodshed. Instead of battling, Michael convinces the opposing sides to join him in dance. "Beat It" features some of his best moves ever, and has become a classic video.

Shortly after "Beat It" topped the charts, "Weird Al" Yankovic recorded a song and made a video parodying "Beat It". "Weird Al's" version was titled, "Eat It" and was a hilarious reworking of Michael's lyrics:

Eat a banana
Eat a whole bunch
It doesn't matter
What you had for lunch
Just eat it!

The video for "Eat It" was equally as comical. "Weird Al", dressed in short black pants and red zippered jacket, just as Michael wears in "Beat It", mimics Michael's moves in a clumsy, uncoordinated manner. Michael enjoyed the parody of himself, giving Yankovic permission to use the music from "Beat It".

Following "Beat It", "Wanna Be Startin' Somethin'" was released as a single. It made it to number five on both the pop and black singles charts with no video to promote it. The song emphasizes Michael's hatred of how rumors and lies are made up from nothing. In the song's lyrics, he describes himself as being a vegetable and buffet others eat off of:

> *I took my baby to the doctor*
> *With a fever, but nothing he found*
> *By the time this hit the street*
> *They said she had a breakdown*
> *Someone's always tryin' to start*
> *my baby cryin'*
> *Talkin', squealin', lyin'*
> *Sayin' you just wanna be startin'*
> *somethin'*

The next two singles from *Thriller* both made it to the top ten. "Human Nature" peaked at number seven, and "PYT (Pretty Young Thing)" went to number ten on the pop singles chart. They peaked at numbers twenty seven and forty six respectively on the black singles chart. Neither single had a video to promote them.

The seventh single from *Thriller,* released in early 1984, was the album's title track. "Thriller" features the eerie sound of creaking doors and a ghoulish rap by horror film star Vincent Price. "Thriller" debuted on *Billboard's* Hot 100 at number twenty, making it one of the highest debuting singles ever. "Thriller" entered the top ten in its second week on the charts, and peaked at number four. It went to number three on the black singles chart.

For the seventh and final single from *Thriller,* Michael went all out to create his most elaborate video to date. Costing $1 million to produce, it was the most expensive video ever. It was also the longest video, running 13 minutes, always being broadcast with an opening disclaimer and closing credits.

After seeing the film, *An American Werewolf in London,* Michael decided he wanted that film's director, John Landis, to direct the "Thriller" video. Rick Baker, who did the makeup for *An American Werewolf in London,* was chosen to do the makeup for "Thriller", transforming Michael into a werewolf right on camera. Michael's co-star was Ola Ray.

The story for the "Thriller" video was written by John Landis and Michael Jackson. Running out of gas on their date, Michael starts to walk Ola home. After telling her, "I'm not like other guys", he transforms into a werewolf in front of her eyes. He chases her through the woods when suddenly the scene switches to Michael and his date watching the scene in a movie theater. Ola, too scared to watch, leaves the theater with Michael following her out. On their way home, they find themselves surrounded by dead, or rather undead, zombies. Michael becomes one of them and joins them in one of his most dazzling dance routines ever.

The "Thriller" video was released on video cassette along with a brief documentary on the behind the scenes making of the video. *The Making of Michael Jackson's Thriller* was produced by John Landis, George Fosley Jr., and Michael Jackson. The director for the documentary was Jerry Kramer. Included on the tape is Michael and John Landis discussing how they came up with the ideas for the video, and what each wanted to achieve with it.

Makeup artist Rick Baker shows how he made Michael's face gradually transform into a werewolf. Plaster was applied to Michael's entire face, allowed to harden, and then removed, forming several plaster casts of his face at various stages of the transformation. The preparation of the costumes and makeup for the "dead" people emphasizes the painstaking measures taken to make every detail as lifelike, or unlifelike, as possible.

Several clips included in the documentary from Michael's already long career show the Jackson Five's performance of "Who's Lovin' You" from the *Ed Sullivan Show* and the film, *The Triumph*, which Michael had produced for the single, "Can You Feel It". Major portions of the "Beat It" video and Michael's performance of "Billie Jean" from the Motown 25 special are also included.

The most enjoyable portions of *The Making of Michael Jackson's Thriller* are scenes of Michael at dance rehearsals with Michael Peters and with Ola Ray. Although Michael Peters had worked with Michael before on "Beat It", he was still impressed with his talent while working on the choreography for "Thriller":

Michael is quite amazing to me because he's working with these people that have made a living at this, I mean, have studied this for a greater portion of their lives, and he'll walk into a studio and purely on rhythm, I mean I purely give him a rhythm of a step and he does it. It's fascinating because here are these people who have spent X amount of thousands of dollars training, studying to be dancers all their lives and this kid walks into the room and you say this is the beat - da-dat-da-dat- and he does it. It's really wonderful to watch because it's an innate gift that he has. He's a dancer in his soul.

Other fun peaks behind the scenes show the occasional silliness breaking out while working on the video. John Landis lifts Michael up and hoists him over his shoulder, calling to the crew, "Let me know when you need Jackson!" Landis later lifts Michael up and turns him completely upside down during rehearsals with Ola. Other quick funny moments have Michael smashing something over John's head. The tape concludes with Landis revealing to the world that "Michael Jackson is extremely ticklish." He removes Michael's shoe and tickles the bottom of his foot, in a rare shot of Michael wearing argyle socks instead of white ones. Landis and Jackson are seated in directors chairs with their names lettered on the backs, only they are sitting in each other's chairs.

The documentary was made to help offset the production costs of the video, which Michael was paying for himself. The documentary certainly more than paid for the cost of the video.

The Making of Michael Jackson's Thriller sold one million copies, making it the best selling music video ever. It was ranked as the third best selling videocassette, of all types, of 1984 by *Billboard* and it was the tenth most rented video cassette of 1984.

While each of the singles from *Thriller* stormed the singles charts, the album continued to do likewise on the album charts. When considering all of the "firsts" that were achieved, along with the simple sales figures, *Thriller's* success is truly astounding. *Thriller* spent all fifty two weeks of 1983 in the top ten on the pop album charts, thirty seven of which were spent at number one. It was the first album to ever start and end a year at number one on the album chart. In March, 1983, *Thriller* topped the album charts in England, and was still number one in the U.S., marking the first time an artist held the number one album in both countries at the same time.

Thriller, to date, has sold in excess of 43 million copies, making it the best selling album in history. To better comprehend this phenomenal figure, consider these facts: *Thriller* has surpassed the sales of the previous best selling album, the soundtrack album, *Saturday Night Fever* by at least 18 million copies! Forty three million is greater than the entire population of several third world countries. *Thriller* has sold more copies than the Beatles' *Sgt. Peppers Lonely Hearts Club Band,* Elvis Presley's *Blue Hawaii,* the Rolling Stones' *Exile on Main Street,* and Stevie Wonder's *Song's in the Key of Life* combined! Sales of one million copies, to be certified platinum, is quite an accomplishment for any album, *Thriller* has sold over one million copies just in the city of Los Angeles. At one point, *Thriller* was selling one million copies *every four days!*

For the year-end recap for 1983, *Billboard* named Michael Jackson the top artist in pop, black, and dance/disco music. *Thriller* was named the number one album for the year on the pop and black charts. "Billie Jean" and "Beat It" shared the number one spot on the dance singles chart for the year. "Billie Jean" was the number two single on both the pop and black singles charts.

"The Girl is Mine" was the sixth top black single, and the ninth top adult contemporary single.

Thriller held on to again top the pop album chart for 1984, and it was the number two black album for the year. Michael Jackson was the number two top pop artist and the number six top black artist. "Say Say Say" was the number three top pop single of 1984.

The U. S. and England weren't the only countries swept up in Michaelmania. He received several other titles and awards from many other countries. In Japan, *Thriller* was named Album of the Year in 1983, and Michael Jackson was named Best Artist and Best Male Vocalist. Australia named *Thriller* Album of the Year and Single of the Year. Michael Jackson was named Artist of the Year in Italy, he had the Record of the Year in Greece, and the Album of the Year in Holland. *Thriller* was named the Most Important Foreign Album of the Year in Spain and Michael was named the International Artist of the Year in Brazil, just to name a few!

One of the several factors contributing to the phenomenal success of *Thriller* was Michael's appearance on a TV special commemorating the twenty fifth anniversary of Motown Records. *Motown 25: Yesterday, Today, and Forever* aired on May 16, 1983 and featured vintage clips of Motown's biggest stars along with reunion performances from the company's biggest groups. All of Motown's greatest performers came together to pay tribute to Motown and to the man who started it all, Berry Gordy. The Temptations and the Four Tops performed together again. Smokey Robinson was reunited with the Miracles, and Motown's brightest star, Diana Ross, performed once again with Cindy Birdsong and Mary Wilson, the Supremes.

One other great Motown group reunited that night in May, the original Jackson Five. For the first time in eight years, Jackie, Tito, Jermaine, Marlon, and Michael were performing on stage together again. They performed a medley of their biggest hits they enjoyed at Motown as the Jackson Five, including "I Want You

Back", "The Love You Save", and "Never Can Say Goodbye". During the medley they were joined on stage by Randy. The last song the group performed was "I'll Be There". For the first time since the Jackson Five left Motown, Michael seemed happy to have his old partner back. For Jermaine's turn in singing lead, instead of using his own microphone, Michael put his arm around Jermaine and held his mike out for his brother to use. At the finish, the brothers all embraced each other. Michael immediately went to Jermaine and hugged him first.

The brothers then left the stage to Michael alone, speaking to the audience:

Those were the good old days. I love those songs. Those were magic moments with all my brothers, including Jermaine. But, those were good songs, I like those songs a lot, but especially, I like the NEW songs.

While Michael was speaking, the stage was cleared of the six microphone stands, leaving one stand left, with something lying on the floor behind it. A black fedora. Michael reached down for the hat, perched it on his head, down over his eyes, and went into an absolutely breathtaking performance of "Billie Jean".

He was dressed in short black pants, up around his ankles with white sequined socks and black loafers. He wore a silver sequined shirt with a black jacket also covered in sequins. And one white sequined glove. Michael later gave the black jacket to Sammy Davis Jr. after he had admired it.

It was during this performance that Michael first dazzled America with his now signature dance step, the moonwalk. Even his brothers, watching from backstage, were surprised at how Michael's dancing had advanced. His moves seemed to defy the law of gravity. He glided backwards, unveiling the moonwalk, went into a lightening quick spin, then froze for a few seconds up on his toes. He received a standing ovation at the end of his performance.

With this single TV appearance, Michael managed to reach a whole new audience and sales of *Thriller* were again sent into orbit. The Motown special was seen by an audience of forty million viewers. People who didn't hear his music on the radio, or see his videos on MTV or *Friday Night Videos*, became new fans of Michael Jackson and charged into record stores to buy a copy of *Thriller*.

An issue of *Rolling Stone* devoted to a review of the music industry during the eighties examined the impact of Michael's *Motown 25* performance and that of his *Thriller* album. Record sales in the early part of the decade were down noticeably due in part to the poor economy and to the increasing popularity of video games as an alternate form of entertainment. The review credits Michael's electrifying performance of "Billie Jean" on the *Motown 25* special as rejuvenating the music industry, sending record buyers back into record stores, where they picked up a copy of *Thriller,* and often a second album or two, giving the record industry a badly needed boost. *Thriller* was deemed by the review of the eighties as redefining the standards of success. With *Thriller* selling over 40 million copies, sales of 500,000, a gold album, no longer seemed as impressive. Sales of one million copies, a platinum album, was now the revised benchmark for success.

Considering the tremendous impact of Michael's appearance on *Motown 25,* it seems ironic that he was at first reluctant to appear on the special. While he did want to take part in a tribute to Motown and Berry Gordy, he does not like to make TV appearances. Michael agreed to perform on the special with his brothers only after he was allowed to perform "Billie Jean", the only non-Motown song performed throughout the entire show.

After finally agreeing to perform on the show, Michael spent many hours rehearsing with his brothers for their medley of Motown hits, so much so, he found himself rehearsing for his "Billie Jean" solo the night before the taping of the show! Michael describes in *Moonwalk* that he went to his kitchen the night before the taping, with the spy hat he had requested, and played "Billie Jean", LOUD. Then and there he created his dance routine, deciding he would perform his moonwalk for the first time in public on the special. His brilliant performance earned him an Emmy nomination. Michael lost the Emmy to Leontyne Price, but the Motown special did win an Emmy for Outstanding Musical Special. Even though award nominations, and especially winning awards are very important to Michael, he was most honored by the phone call he received the next morning from one of his idols, Fred Astaire, commending him on his performance. *Motown 25: Yesterday, Today and Forever* was later released on videocassette and was ranked by *Billboard* as the number two Top Music Videocassette of 1986.

Nine years after it was first broadcast, *Entertainment Weekly* magazine included Michael's performance on *Motown 25* as one of the twentieth century's greatest entertainment moments:

... a delicate young man with a choked voice, a white glove, and magic shoes took the microphone and began to write the next chapter of American music history. The moment Michael Jackson ripped into his single, 'Billie Jean' - squealing, moaning, spinning, and finally taking viewer's breath away with his moonwalk -the music industry had to throw away its old yardsticks of success.

"Billie Jean" was of course only one of Michael's many hits he enjoyed throughout 1983, but not all of his hit singles during the year came from the *Thriller* album. Michael's seventh single to reach the top ten in 1983 was "Say Say Say". With "Say Say Say" becoming his seventh top ten single in 1983, Michael broke records previously held by Elvis Presley and the Beatles for the most top ten singles in one year. The single went to number one on the Hot 100 the week of December 10, 1983, and stayed for six weeks. It peaked at number two on the black chart. This duet with Paul McCartney is included on McCartney's album,

Pipes of Peace. McCartney's album also includes another duet with Michael, "The Man". A photo of Michael was included on the inside cover of the album among photos of other contributors to the album.

Paul McCartney flew to California to film the video for "Say Say Say" with Michael because Michael's schedule wouldn't allow him the time to fly to England. The video was filmed in the Santa Ynez Valley, about 100 miles North of Los Angeles. Paul and Michael pay con men selling a miracle potion "guaranteed to give you the strength of a raging bull." Paul poses as a salesman and Michael, pretending to be a customer, tries the potion and challenges a very large man, also in on the scam, to arm wrestle. When Michael wins, the gathering crowd rushes to buy a bottle of the magic potion. "Mack and Jack" then give all of the money raised in the scam to an orphanage. Changing their trade from salesmen to vaudevillians, they put on a show in a saloon, where Michael catches the eye of a beautiful saloon girl, played by LaToya. Paul McCartney's wife, Linda, also appears in the video as part of the conning crew.

Nineteen eighty three wasn't all hit records for Michael however. It was also when his management contract with Weisner/DeMann Entertainment expired. A few months later, the management contract with his father also expired. Neither contracts were renewed. Michael had fired his father. Although Michael was never close to his father, he explains in *Moonwalk* that it was a business decision, that he and his father were worlds apart when it came to creativity. Joe would come up with ideas that Michael totally disagreed with, because he felt they weren't right for him. This started an extremely rare public battle between Joe Jackson and Michael, and between Joe and Weisner and DeMann. In the June 25, 1983, issue of *Billboard* magazine, Joe Jackson, in regards to Weisner/DeMann Entertainment, was quoted as saying:

They have been put on notice and it (their contract) will not be renewed. As far as I'm concerned, it's over. They will not have a contract and my boys are not re-signing them...A lot of people have been whispering in Michael's ear but they know who they are. They're only in it for the money...Weisner\DeMann were needed because there was a time when I felt I needed white help in dealing with the corporate structure at CBS.

Michael responded to his father's remarks in the same issue of *Billboard:*

I don't know what would make him say something like that. To hear him talk like that turns my stomach. I don't know where he gets that from. I happen to be color blind.

Ron Weisner and Freddy DeMann said of Joe:

The problem seems to be with their father more than anybody...we have no problem with Michael or the Jacksons...I don't think he (Joe) enjoys a good relationship with anyone whose skin is not black.

Joe Jackson would later be fired by two other of his children. At age 19, Janet changed managers just before recording *Control*, her first multi-platinum album. Still later, in the spring of 1988, Joe was replaced by Jack Gordon in managing LaToya's career. Again, there were bitter words exchanged in the press between Joe and his replacement. Joe remarked, "I make 'em, and they take 'em...Gordon is a mooch." Gordon responded, "I love Joe like poison." LaToya later married Gordon in September, 1989, though she denied it publicly.

Until Michael could select a new manager, his personal lawyer, John Branca, aided Michael in handling his business affairs. Michael always has and still does maintain an amazing level of control over his business affairs, down to every decision and detail. He learns every detail of his contracts, and although professionals, lawyers, managers, and accountants are consulted, all decisions are ultimately made by Michael himself. John Branca told *Billboard*:

> *The genius in his artistry speaks for itself. His business acumen isn't necessarily as obvious because it is conducted behind closed doors. But he is equally brilliant in running his career as he is in recording his music.*

CBS Records President Walter Yetnikoff also told *Billboard* of Michael's keen business sense in the July 21, 1984, issue which included a large section dedicated to Michael Jackson:

> *He has made observations to me about things like promotion, which indicate he would be totally qualified to run a record company if he so desired. He has assembled a terrific team of advisors, but he makes his own decisions in the end. He's not one those artists who reacts blindly to what the last person tells him. He's got a great sense of where he is going and what he wants to do. But he's also got a way of making things happen. He's reached his goals so many times that I've come to believe that if Michael wants something to happen, it'll happen.*

It was nearly a year later, in 1984, when Michael signed a new manager. He had selected Frank Dileo, who was then vice president of promotion at Epic Records. Dileo was responsible in large part for the promotion of *Thriller*. Frank Dileo and Michael soon became very close personal friends as well as manager and client. They would often play practical jokes on each other. While on the road with the Victory tour, Michael pulled $4,000 out of Frank's pocket, threw it in the bathtub and turned on the water to see Frank scramble to retrieve it. Another time, Michael threw Frank's money out of a car window!

While Michael spent most of 1983 enjoying one hit single after another, he spent 1984 collecting one award after another. *Thriller* definitely made up for Michael's feeling that his *Off The Wall* album had been ignored at award time.

CHAPTER SIX

AND THE WINNER IS...

January, 1984, brought Michael an avalanche of awards, and it was only a taste of what was to come throughout the year. Michael received a record breaking ten nominations for the American Music Awards. *Thriller* was nominated for Best Pop Album, and Best Soul Album. "Billie Jean" was nominated for Best Pop Single and Best Soul Single. "Beat It" and "Billie Jean" were both nominated for Best Pop Video and Best Soul Video. And Finally, Michael was nominated for Best Pop Male Vocalist and Best Soul Male Vocalist. Michael attended the award ceremony accompanied by *Webster* star Emmanuel Lewis and his date for the evening was Brooke Shields. He was dressed in cropped tuxedo pants and military style jacket covered with red sequins with a single black sequin glove and dark sunglasses.

Michael approached the podium eight times that night to accept awards, a new record. *Thriller* was named Best Pop Album and Best Soul Album. "Billie Jean" won as Best Pop Single, and "Beat It" was named Best Pop Video and Best Soul Video. Michael took top honors as Best Pop Male Vocalist and Best Soul Male Vocalist.

In addition to these awards Michael was honored for his lifetime career achievements as the year's recipient of the Award of Merit. The Award of Merit was presented to Michael by Diana Ross and by the previous year's winner, Kenny Rogers. Barry Manilow also took part in the tribute, singing "Ben" and a medley of Jackson Five hits. The presentation featured video taped messages from Michael's closest friends, including Liza Minnelli, Katharine Hepburn, and Jane Fonda, who had this to say:

Michael, I can't tell you how many times I've studied your tapes, trying to figure out what it is you do. I've decided you are a miracle. You have so much talent, the more you give of it, the more you seem to have. I'm so proud of you...and so proud to be your friend.

Winning the award at age 25, Michael is the youngest performer to ever receive the Award of Merit.

Michael's next armload of awards came the following month at the Grammys. The Grammys are the music industry's equivalent to the Oscars. Michael again received a record breaking number of nominations. He was nominated for twelve Grammys in ten different categories, he was competing against himself in two categories. Both "Beat It" and "Billie Jean" were nominated for Song of the Year, and "Billie Jean" and "Wanna Be Startin' Somethin'" were both nominated for Best R&B Song. *Thriller* was nominated for Album of the Year, "Beat It" was nominated for Record of the Year. Michael received nominations for Best Pop Male Vocalist for *Thriller*, Best R&B Male Vocalist on "Billie Jean" and Best Rock Male vocalist for "Beat It". Michael shared a nomination with Paul McCartney for Best Pop Vocal Duo or Group for "The Girl is Mine". Michael shared two other nominations with Quincy Jones for Producer of the Year, and for Best Recording for Children for *E.T.: The Extra-Terrestrial* storybook album.

Again, Michael attended the award presentation with Emmanuel Lewis and Brooke Shields. He was dressed in tuxedo pants and a sapphire blue sequined military jacket, this time with a single white glove. Uncomfortable in situations where so much attention is focused on him, he again wore sunglasses so dark you could not see his eyes.

Michael was seated in the front row of the Los Angeles Shrine Auditorium and rose to approach the podium to accept one award after another so often, it became a popular joke the evening. Joan Rivers appeared on the program to read the rules:

I think that the reason we should read the rules is mainly because every one of the nominees out there should know exactly why they lost out to Michael Jackson, okay! ... You shouldn't all think Michael Jackson is going to get it, because Michael Jackson may not get everything... And just one more thing though, just in case, Tito!, please back up the truck!

Later, presenter Mickey Rooney commented, "It's a pleasure doing the Michael Jackson show!"

Tito hauled home eight Grammys for his little brother that night, setting a new world record. Michael won in eight of the ten categories in which he was nominated. The two categories in which he lost both went to the same group. Song of the Year went to The Police for "Every Breath You Take". The Police also picked up the tiny gramophone for Pop Vocal Duo or Group for "Every Breath You Take". While it would seem that having two nominations in the same category would increase the chances of winning, actually just opposite is true. Having both "Beat It" and "Billie Jean" nominated for Song of the Year served to divide the Jackson vote. Division of Jackson fans between favorites didn't hurt in the R&B category though, "Billie Jean" was chosen over "Wanna Be Startin Somethin'" for Best R&B Song. All of his other nominations earned Michael another Grammy.

After winning the first of his awards, Michael ascended the stairs to the stage, said his quick thank yous, and quickly returned to his seat. As the evening went on however, Michael seemed to become more comfortable and started to enjoy himself more. He began making lengthier acceptance speeches, which is quite unusual for him. Quincy Jones and Michael were chosen as Producers of the Year, and they also shared the Grammy for Best Recording for Children for the E.T. storybook album. Michael was especially pleased with this honor:

Of all the awards I've gotten, I'm most proud of this one, honestly. Because I think children are a great inspiration, and this album is not for children, it is for everyone. And I'm just so happy and I'm so proud, and I'd just like to say, thank so you so much.

Michael's seventh Grammy of the night was for Best Pop Vocal Performance Male. This win broke a record for the most Grammys won in a single year, set in 1965 by Roger Miller.

Michael was aware he had just set a new record and was visibly elated. He called each of his sisters on stage to share his moment. "When something like this happens to you, you want those who are very dear to you to be with you." Then Rebbie, LaToya and Janet joined their brother on stage. Michael continued:

My mother's very shy, she's like me, she won't come up. I'd also like to thank all my brothers whom I love dearly, including Jermaine. I made a deal with myself. If I win one more award, which is this award, which is seven, which is a record, I would take off my glasses. Katharine Hepburn, who is a dear friend of mine, she told me I should and I'm doing it for her, okay?

Over the deafening screams of the fans, he added, "And for the girls in the balcony." He removed his sunglasses for a few seconds, giving the first glimpse of his eyes all evening. He blew kisses to the girls in the balcony and put his glasses back on where they remained for the rest of the night.

When *Thriller* was named as Album of the Year, Michael became the third youngest artist, at age 25, to win the award. Barbra Streisand was 22 when *The Barbra Streisand Album* won as Album of the Year, and Stevie Wonder was 23 when his album *Innervisions* was given the honor. Michael dedicated his Grammy for Album of the Year to Jackie Wilson, his idol who had recently passed away:

Some people are great entertainers, some people make the path and are pioneers. I'd like to say Jackie Wilson was a wonderful entertainer. He's not with us anymore, but Jackie, where you are, I'd like to say I love you and thank you so much.

Along with eagerly anticipating each award category, the audience was also looking forward to the commercials, but not to run to the kitchen for a snack. The Pepsi commercials Michael had made with his brothers were premiering during the Grammy telecast. The premiere of the pair of Jackson Pepsi ads were promoted as heavily as the Grammy telecast itself. These Pepsi ads were regarded as news items so heavily that several of their first broadcasts were free of charge. They are the first and only commercials to ever be included in the *TV Guide* listings. While it was great knowing which programs would air the Jackson Pepsi ads, it could also cause the most diehard Jackson fan severe torment, having to, at times, sit through almost an entire episode of *Hart to Hart* just to see one commercial! It could put Jackson starved fans in the awkward position of leaving the room during a program and rushing back when commercials came on!

A new Pepsi jingle was written for the commercials, putting new lyrics to "Billie Jean". Michael lent his music to "Billie Jean" for use in the commercial, helped write the Pepsi lyrics, and agreed to perform the new jingle in the ads, but had it stated in his contract with Pepsi that he would not be filmed drinking, or even holding a bottle of Pepsi. It became a well known fact that Michael doesn't even drink Pepsi. He has long been a vegetarian and only eats and drinks natural foods. Bottled water, fruit juice, and carrot juice being among the few things he does drink. Michael exercised a great deal of control over the making of the commercials, having a hand in choosing the director and the choreographer. The director was Bob Giraldi, who directed the "Beat It" video and the choreographer was Michael Peters, who had worked with Michael on the videos for "Beat It" and "Thriller". Michael also had control over the editing. One of the commercials includes a close up of Michael which was edited down to last only three seconds.

The first commercial shows a group of children playing and dancing in the street. One of the children is dressed as Michael from his "Beat It" video and is imitating his moves when he moonwalks into the real thing. Young Alfonso Ribeiro looks absolutely astonished as he looks up into the eyes of the real Michael Jackson. The commercial ends with Alfonso and his friends joining Michael and the rest of the Jackson brothers in song and dance:

> *You're a whole new generation*
> *You're dancin' through the day*
> *You're grabbin' for the magic*
> *on the run*
> *You're a whole new generation*
> *You're lovin' what you do*
> *Put a Pepsi into motion*
> *The choice is up to you*
>
> *Hey Hey you're the Pepsi Generation*
> *Guzzle down and taste the thrill*
> *of the day*
> *And feel the Pepsi way*
> *Taste the thrill of the day*
> *And feel the Pepsi way*
> *You're a whole new generation*
> *You're a whole new generation*
> *You're a whole new generation*

Alfonso Ribeiro is also known for his work on Broadway. He starred in *The Tap Dance Kid* and was already quite an accomplished dancer. Following his exposure in the Jackson Pepsi commercials, Alfonso later appeared as a regular with Ricky Shroeder on *Silver Spoons*. Michael and Alfonso became friends while working together and their friendship continued after the completion of the commercials. When Alfonso released his first single, "Dance Baby" in 1984, he dedicated it to Michael Jackson. Alfonso landed a second role on a TV series in 1990 playing nerdy Carlton Banks on *The Fresh Prince of Bel Air*, the series' producer is Quincy Jones.

The second Pepsi commercial shows the Jacksons in concert. It begins with scenes of the brothers in their dressing room preparing for the concert. There's a shot of Michael's gloved hand and his sequined socks, while Tito finishes off a Pepsi. They hit the stage singing the new Pepsi lyrics to "Billie Jean" and Michael dances down a flight of stairs with flash bombs going off behind him, to join his brothers on stage. They finish the song, we see the three second close up of Michael and it's over. Seems simple enough, but it wasn't.

Two accidents occurred during the making of the Pepsi commercials. One only minor and rather humorous, the other very serious, nearly fatal. Just before hitting the stage to continue filming, Michael stayed behind to use the restroom. A few seconds later, the others hears him scream. Worried that perhaps a fan had hidden in there to catch a glimpse of one of the brothers, they rushed in to find that Michael had dropped his glove in the toilet! While somebody searched for a coat hanger to fish it out, Michael pulled it out himself. It was rinsed out and dried and good as new in minutes. Unfortunately, the second incident wasn't as trivial or solved as easily.

Filming on the second commercial concluded on January 27, 1984, at the Los Angeles Shrine Auditorium. At 6:00 PM, director Bob Giraldi called for another take of the scene with Michael dancing down the staircase. This was the last scene to be shot after four days of filming. Michael stood at his spot at the top of the stairs, and was told to stand there until the bombs went off this time, then make his descent. So after the pyrotechnics went off, Michael began to dance down the stairs. Suddenly he cried out in pain. A spark from the lighting effects had set his hair on fire. He pulled his jacket up over his head to try to put out the flames. Mass confusion followed. Fans and extras used in the audience were horrified as were his brothers and the crew. Jermaine initially thought Michael had been shot! The first to reach Michael to help was his security aid, Miko Brando, Marlon Brando's son. Miko suffered burns on his own fingers trying to put out the flames in Michael's hair. A fan from the audience applied an ice pack on the burn.

Michael was rushed to the emergency room of Cedars Sinai Medical Center. Having been told a barrage of reporters and photographers awaited his arrival at the hospital, Michael told the ambulance attendants that he wanted to wear his glove when he was wheeled into the hospital.

Michael had suffered a palm sized second degree burn on the back of his head with a smaller third degree burn the size of a half dollar at the center. It was a serious burn that reportedly could have burned through his scalp and killed him. Michael at first refused any pain killers due to his strong disapproval of any drugs. Later, he did give in to the extreme pain and accepted medication.

Shortly after the accident, Michael's personal physician, Dr. Steven Hoefflin arrived. "It was quite a shock for Michael, and when I got there he was in a daze. After I examined him and told him he would be fine, he felt a lot better." Dr. Hoefflin, the surgeon who reshaped Michael's nose, decided then to transfer Michael to the burn center of the Brotman Medical Center in Culver City. He arrived at 8:15 PM with his parents, Randy, and two bodyguards. He was admitted and occupied room 3307. His nurses later recalled that "he was still pretty shaken up and cold, so we put about five blankets on him." Instead of the usual, and embarrassing hospital gown, he wore a blue scrub outfit with a small cap covering the bandage on the back of his head.

Security at the hospital had to be increased, with a guard stationed at every entrance of the burn center. The emergency room became packed with fans and the phone lines were jammed. Among the callers were Liza Minnelli and Diana Ross.

During his stay at the hospital, Michael asked for a video cassette player. Unable to unlock an equipment cabinet, the nurses broke the padlock and got Michael the player with about ten tapes. He watched Steven Speilberg's *Close Encounters of the Third Kind* until 1:00 AM. He accepted a sleeping pill then rested for the night. By the time his doctor arrived the next day, Michael had watched *American Bandstand* and according to one of the his nurses, "was bebopping in bed while the doctor examined him."

Before being released, Michael visited the other six burn patients who, coincidentally, he had visited just one month earlier. He posed for pictures and signed autographs for the burn center staff. After his release, his doctor wanted Michael to rest and not to dance for a while, but, "telling Michael not to dance is like telling him not to breathe."

People magazine's next issue featured Michael on the cover. The issue informed worried fans of all the details of Michael's accident and his stay in the hospital. That February 13, 1984, issue of *People* became the publication's third best selling issue ever.

Later in the spring, in April, Michael had laser surgery to burn off the scar tissue on his scalp to allow his hair to grow back. Again, the hospital was deluged with phone calls on the day of his surgery, receiving over 5,000 calls.

Although he could have, Michael did not sue Pepsi. However, Pepsi did give Michael $1.5 million in damages. Michael used the money to establish the Michael Jackson Burn Center in Los Angeles.

These Jackson Pepsi commercials' success in selling Pepsi and popularity with fans was unprecedented. In *The Other Guy Blinked: How Pepsi Won The Cola Wars,* Pepsi president Roger Enrico told how he saw the enormous impact of these commercials:

> *Why did Coke decide to change its formula after ninety-nine hugely successful years? In two words: Michael Jackson. And I'm the man who signed him up to make commercials for Pepsi.... On November 11th, 1983- my thirty-ninth birthday- I signed the most expensive celebrity advertising contract in history: $5 million for the privilege of making two commercials and sponsoring a tour featuring a talented but shy young man who sang in a high-pitched voice and danced backward.*

The signing of Michael Jackson to make commercials for Pepsi's Choice of a New Generation campaign and the debacle of new Coke are not unrelated events.

In February, 1984, Michael received yet another honor. CBS Records hosted a party at New York's Metropolitan Museum of Natural History to honor Michael Jackson. There were 1,500 invitations mailed out on white cloth gloves, which were required to gain admittance into the museum. Michael was being honored for earning two entries in the *Guiness Book of World Records*. *Thriller* had surpassed the twenty five million mark in sales, making it the most successful album in history. It had outsold the soundtrack album for *Saturday Night Fever* to take over the top spot. Michael's recent domination of the Grammy Awards earned him another entry in the *Guiness Book of World Records* as the artist to win the most Grammys in a single year. His eight Grammys broke the previous record of six Grammys in one year.

At the party, CBS Records president Walter Yetnikoff presented Michael with a new copy of the *Guiness Book of World Records,* who had stopped their presses to include Michael's new record setting feats. Allen Davis, president of CBS Records International, presented Michael with the honor:

*Tonight, Michael, your international milestones for the album, **Thriller** are a total of 67 gold awards, 58 platinum awards in 28 countries on 6 continents. And the singles with 9 million in sales have earned 15 more awards, bringing the total to 140 gold and platinum awards.*

Then Michael spoke:

*I've always wanted to do great things and achieve many things, but for the first time in my entire career, I feel like I have accomplished something because I'm in the **Guiness Book of World Records**.*

A letter from an admirer who was unable to attend was read to Michael:

I was pleased to learn that you were not seriously hurt in your recent accident. I know from experience that these things can happen on the set, no matter how much caution is exercised. All over America, millions of people look up to you as an example. Your deep faith in God and adherence to traditional values are an inspiration to all of us, especially young people searching for something to believe in. You've gained quite a number of fans along the road since 'I Want You Back', and Nancy and I are among them. Keep up the good work, Michael. We're very happy for you. Sincerely, Ronald Reagan.

Although Michael did not meet President Reagan at this ceremony, they did meet soon after when Michael visited the White House to receive, you guessed it, another award. Michael left the party at the museum a couple of times during the night to go outside and wave to the crowds of fans waiting outside to catch a glimpse of him.

For the third award ceremony in less than two months, Michael's date was Brooke Shields. Michael wore jeans, a silver sequined shirt, and a black military jacket. He wore a single white glove, and notably, no sunglasses. (Nobody ever noticed what Brooke was wearing.)

Consistently appearing in public wearing the single sequined glove helped cement the glove as Michael's trademark. Although he became known for wearing one white glove he actually owns several different colors, though none have mates! Bill Whitten, a costume designer for the Jacksons since 1976, designed several gloves for Michael in white, black, red, blue, and one in red, white and blue. Each glove is covered with approximately 1,200 round Austrian crystal rhinestones each sewn on individually, taking up to 40 hours to complete. Estimates put the value of each glove at five figures.

Michael's wide ranging appeal was illustrated by the results of *Rolling Stone's* annual readers and critics poll, a publication which focuses primarily on white, hard rock artists. *Rolling Stone* readers voted Michael Jackson as the number one artist of the year, the number one soul artist, the number two male vocalist, and the number four songwriter. "Beat It" and "Billie Jean" were chosen as the number two and number three singles of the year respectively. *Thriller* was chosen as the second best album of the year. Quincy Jones tied for number one producer with Steve Lillywhite.

The critics voted Michael Jackson as the number one artist of the year, male vocalist, and soul artist of the year. "Beat It" and "Billie Jean" were the critics picks for the number two and number three singles of the year and the first and third best videos respectively. *Thriller* was chosen as the second best album of the year. Quincy Jones was the critics fifth choice for producer of the year.

Michael met President Reagan in May, 1984. Michael had donated the use of his song, "Beat It" to an advertising campaign aimed against drinking and driving. For his contribution to the campaign, Michael received a Special Achievement Award presented to him at the White House by President Reagan. With Michael's visit, chaos set in at the White House offices. The staff, all eager to meet Michael, left offices empty with phones ringing. The presentation was held on the White House lawn and a large sound system was set up so the huge crowds gathered at the gates of the White House could hear the ceremony. President Reagan remarked, "We haven't seen this many people since we left China!" The plaque presented to Michael by President Reagan was engraved with these words:

To Michael Jackson, with appreciation for the outstanding example you have set for the youth of America and the world. Your historic record-breaking achievements and your preeminence in popular music are a tribute to your creativity, dedication, and

*great ability. The generous contribution of your time and talent to
the National Campaign Against Teenage Drunk Driving will help
millions of young Americans learn that drinking and driving can
kill a friendship.*

Michael and his party of eight were then given a tour of the
White House. Michael especially liked a portrait of Andrew
Jackson wearing a blue military jacket very similar to the one
Michael was wearing, the same one he had worn to the Grammys
a few months earlier. During the tour, Michael stopped at the
East Room and sat at the piano to play. He was then to meet
President Reagan in the Diplomatic Reception Room where he was
told there would be a few children of staff members present
waiting to meet him. Upon reaching the room, Michael discovered there was in fact a room packed with adults waiting to meet
him. Uncomfortable with facing all of these people, Michael
reportedly avoided them by slipping into the mensroom off the
Presidential Library. He locked the door and refused to come out
until he was told the crowd had been dispersed and he could meet
the staff and their children in smaller groups.

In between award presentations, Michael still found time to
work. He sang background vocals on a single by Kennedy Gordy,
a.k.a. Rockwell, a Motown artist and son of Berry Gordy.
Michael sang one line, "I always feel like somebody's watching
me" repeatedly in Rockwell's hit single, "Somebody's Watching
Me". The single peaked at number two on the Hot 100.

Michael also lent his magical touch to the recordings of two
of his siblings. In 1984, Rebbie released her first album, *Centi-
pede*. Little brother Michael wrote and produced the title track.
He also co-wrote "Come Alive It's Saturday Night" with three of
his brothers. Jermaine also released an album in 1984, *Jermaine
Jackson* which included "Tell Me I'm Not Dreamin'", a duet with
Michael. Although it was never officially released as a single
because of legal difficulties between Michael's label, Epic, and
Jermaine's label, Arista, the song did receive a lot of airplay. The

song was re-recorded in 1989 by Robert Palmer. Besides these projects, Michael spent much of 1984 planning and embarking on a U.S. tour reuniting himself with his brothers, the Jacksons Victory tour.

CHAPTER SEVEN

VICTORY

A press conference was held at New York's Tavern on the Green in November 1983, to announce the Jackson's plans for a major U.S. tour. The press conference was hosted by tour promoter Don King. The brothers, all wearing sunglasses, sat quietly at a table while King did most of the talking. Michael spoke only to introduce his parents and sisters who were seated in the audience, after all, this was a press conference and the last thing he wanted to do was answer a lot of questions! The tour was to be called Victory, and was to be sponsored by Pepsi. The tour would promote the group's new album, also to be called *Victory*.

The *Victory* album was released July 2, 1984. Great anticipation surrounded the album's release and sales were expected to skyrocket. *Victory* is the first album ever to be shipped double platinum. The album was disappointing however, consisting mainly of songs written, produced and performed by each of the brothers individually. Failing to follow their previous format of having Michael and Jermaine sing the lead vocals weakened the album dramatically. *Victory* seems like a thrown together piece of work lacking the great dance tracks that make earlier Jackson albums great. Even the album's packaging seems hurried, with the song titles listed on the back cover in a different order than they appear on the record.

David Smithy, a fourteen year old fan of Michael's had a wish to meet his idol. David's wish was granted to him by the Brass Ring Society, who fulfills the wishes of terminally ill children. David was dying of cystic fibrosis. He was invited to Michael's Encino home where he had lunch, visited the animals, beat Michael at video games, and watched a movie in the private screening room. Michael gave David his red leather jacket from the "Beat It" video, and the black sequined glove he had worn to the American Music Awards. Seven weeks later, David Smithy died. The *Victory* album is dedicated to the brothers' mother, Katherine Jackson, the late Marvin Gaye, Teddy Pendergrass, and David Smithy. David is also included among the long list of names to be thanked on the inside sleeve of Michael's *Bad* album.

The best offerings from *Victory* are the album's first two singles. "State of Shock", released on June 13, was written by Michael and Randy Hansen, with lead vocals by Michael and Mick Jagger. No video was made to accompany the single, but nothing else was really needed to promote the single any further. Anticipation for anything new from Michael Jackson reached such a feverish pitch, that a Los Angeles radio station, K-IQQ, played the brand new single for twenty two hours straight. The Jackson/Jagger duet peaked on the Hot 100 at number three.

Originally, the duet was to be with Queen frontman Freddie Mercury, but Mercury never had to time to record the single. Michael supposedly recorded three other songs with Mercury that have never been released.

The second single off of *Victory* was "Torture", the only song on the entire album to feature lead vocals by Michael and Jermaine. While it doesn't measure up to previous Jackson singles from *Destiny* or *Triumph*, "Torture" clearly stands out among the album's other weak selections.   "Torture" peaked at a very generous number seventeen on *Billboard's* Hot 100.

A video was made for the second single but it has one big problem, it lacks an appearance by either of the two lead singers! Only Jackie, Tito, Marlon and Randy appear in the "Torture" video. All six brothers were in New York to film the video when a disagreement broke out between the brothers, and Michael and Jermaine each refused to be a part of the video. Michael took off for Disney World, leaving the other brothers to finish the filming without him. While Michael does not appear in the video at all, there are still many strong references to him. Skeletons moonwalk across the screen, there's a close up shot of a gloved hand, and a wax figure of Michael, borrowed from a museum, is even substituted for the real thing in a brief shot of all the brothers. The choreography for the video was done by Laker girl turned choreographer Paula Abdul.

The third single from *Victory* was Marlon's contribution, "Body". Even though the single features background vocals by the

Jackson brothers, it is not enough to help this indistinct dance song. "Body" peaked at number forty seven on the Hot 100.

The video for "Body" has the brothers holding auditions for dancers. Each brother arrives at the studio one by one. Marlon arrives first, riding in on a motorcycle. Driving closely behind Marlon is Tito. Randy drives up next in his Jeep. Jackie arrives a bit late, rushing in the doors of the studio. Suddenly, a huge crowd of fans gather outside as a helicopter makes it landing. Those viewers expecting Michael's arrival were disappointed to see all of the brothers disembark, dressed in stage costumes, ready to film their finished performance with the chosen dancers. Again, Michael does not appear in the video.

Michael did not want to do the Victory tour. He did not feel it was a wise choice following the success he had enjoyed with his *Thriller* album. He wanted to concentrate on his other love, films. He was persuaded to join his brothers on the tour by his parents, especially his mother who he adores. It was reported that some of the brothers were having financial problems and needed the income from the tour. Having Michael participate in the tour would dramatically increase the tour's earning potential. Another motivator for Michael to join his brothers on tour is his love of performing.

From the very beginning, the Victory tour was greeted by as much anticipation and excitement as bitter criticism and controversy. Because Michael didn't tour with his *Thriller* album, the Victory tour would be his fans' first chance to see Michael perform live his monster hits from *Thriller*. The criticism of the tour arose from its poor management and organization. Michael quickly became dissatisfied with the leadership of tour promoter Don King. He wrote King a letter informing him that he had no authority to speak or deal for Michael. It stated that King was:

...not to communicate with anyone on Michael's behalf without prior permission,

that all moneys paid to Michael for his participation in the tour would be collected by Michael's personal representatives, not by Don King,

that King did not have permission to approach any promoters, sponsors, or any other persons on Michael's behalf,

that King was not to hire any personnel, any local promoters, book any halls or, for that matter, do ANYTHING without Michael Jackson's personal approval.

Shortly thereafter, King was fired as tour promoter and replaced by Chuck Sullivan. King remained on the tour as a figurehead only. The entire tour was marked by constant management changes. One promoter, Frank Russo, lasted only three weeks.

Ticket prices, set at $28.00 with a $2.00 service charge, were among the first items to come under fire from the press and from fans, all claiming Michael was greedy and wanted to get as much money from the tour as possible. Only Michael was mentioned in this charge, not any of his brothers, or the tour's managers or promoters. What these fans didn't know, and what most of the press didn't bother to print was that Michael vehemently fought to keep ticket prices down, wanting them no higher than $20.00, the current going price for concert tickets. With each brother and possibly their parents and promoters each having equal say in how the tour was managed, Michael was outvoted. He even offered to perform on the entire tour for free to keep ticket prices down. Again, he was outvoted and ticket prices were set at $30.00. But only Michael took the heat for the high prices, it was as though everyone forgot it was a Jacksons tour, not a Michael Jackson tour.

The system by which tickets were sold also came under fire from the press and from fans. The tickets were sold by a mail order system and only in lots of four. A lottery system was used to determine which orders were filled first, and which ones would be filled at all if orders exceeded the quantity of tickets available for sale. Regardless of how many tickets were wanted, you had to order four, for a total cost of $120.00, with no guarantee of even receiving any tickets. If orders exceeded the number of tickets for sale, you could very well end up empty handed after mailing in $120.00. This money was then held for long periods before being returned with promoters pocketing the interest made on short term investments.

To request tickets, a coupon order form was needed from the local newspaper. For the tour's first stop, Kansas City, the *Kansas City Times* printed an additional 20,000 copies to meet the expected demand for the Victory tour ticket order forms. Again Michael, and only Michael, was unjustifiably the aim of an avalanche of criticism against the ticket order system.

Michael stepped in to correct the situation after an open letter to Michael appeared in a Dallas newspaper from a young fan, Ladonna Jones, complaining the ticket order system was unfair and that she couldn't afford $120.00. Michael then had the mail order system abolished. It was ended after the first three cities on the tour.

Chris Bliss, a juggler, opened each night for the Victory tour. He juggled mirrored glass balls to the beat of pop music. As a further example of the tour's management problems, Bliss was chosen as the opening act just two days before the opening date.

While all of these problems continued to plague the management and organization of the tour, Michael and his brothers were hard at work on the shows themselves. Rehearsals began in February, and lasted five hours a day, six days a week. As opening night drew closer, rehearsals began lasting eighteen hours a day, to get every detail of the show, as Michael would say, "perfect". Just before the start of the tour, the brothers rehearsed in Birmingham, Alabama. Despite the city's efforts, however, no concert was ever scheduled there.

Besides rehearsing their performances the brothers worked behind the scenes in bringing Victory to the stage. Tito and Randy chose the band for the tour. David Williams and Gregg Wright were each chosen as guitarists. Pat Leonard and Jai Winding were chosen as keyboardists along with Rory Kaplan, who would also play on Michael's Bad tour. Jonathon "Sugarfoot" Moffett was hired as the drummer for the Victory tour. Moffett had played with the Jacksons before on their 1981 concert tour. Jackie, Marlon and Michael choreographed the show. The Victory tour concerts were written and designed by Michael. Michael served extra duty as the tour's stage designer. A stage specialist was hired to help Michael bring his ideas into reality, but the staging for the Victory tour was Michael's concept. Michael also contributed to the design of the lights for the robotic contraptions in the show and he designed the specialty costumes with Ted Shell. The opening sequence of the show was written by Michael with Jai Winding and Pat Leonard, it was produced by Michael and Jai Winding.

Bill Whitten designed the Jacksons costumes for the tour, and Tito's wife, Enid, designed the costumes for the musicians. The costumes worn by the brothers were valued at $500,000. Michael's black jacket worn for "Billie Jean" and "Shake Your Body", covered entirely with sequins, weighed in at forty pounds.

In May, the brothers did take time out from rehearsing to throw their mother a birthday party. She was given a Rolls Royce from all of her sons, though newspapers later reported it was Michael alone who gave her the elaborate gift.

Meanwhile, cities around the country were hopeful they would be chosen to host the Victory tour. Many cities tried to improve their odds of being chosen. In Boston, *The Boston Herald* printed coupons for fans to fill out asking the Jacksons to perform in Boston. The Herald received thousands of the coupons which were forwarded to the Jacksons. In Iowa, Iowa State

University collected signatures on petitions urging the Jacksons to include Iowa on their tour. The Governor of Iowa even contacted then tour promoter Don King to urge him to have the Jacksons perform in Iowa. Detroit Mayor Coleman Young tried to attract the Jacksons to his city's Joe Louis Arena. The largest and most impressive efforts to attract the Jacksons came from their home town, Gary, Indiana. The Mayor of Gary circulated "please come back" letters from school children. The city even sponsored a "Michael Jackson Come Home" event which included Michael Jackson look-a-like contests.

The day before opening night of the tour, Michael held a press conference to announce the changes being made to the ticket mail order system. He also made one other important announcement:

We're beginning our tour tomorrow and I wanted to talk to you about something of great concern to me. We've worked a long time to make this show the best it can be. But we know a lot of kids are having trouble getting tickets. The other day I got a letter from a girl in Texas named Ladonna Jones. She'd been saving her money from odd jobs to buy a ticket, but with the current tour system she'd have to buy four tickets and she couldn't afford that. So I've asked our promoter to work out a new way of distributing tickets, a way that no longer requires a $120.00 money order.

There has also been a lot of talk about the promoter holding money for tickets that didn't sell. I've asked our promoter to end the mail order system as soon as possible so that no one will pay money unless they get a ticket.

Finally, and most importantly, there's something else I am going to announce today. I want you to know that when I first agreed to tour, I decided to donate all the money I make from our performances to charity.

Three charities benefitted from Michael's extraordinary generosity. The United Negro College Fund used Michael's contribution to establish the Michael Jackson Scholarship fund. The other two recipients were Camp Good Times for terminally ill children, and the T.J. Martell Foundation for Leukemia and Cancer Research.

On July 6, 1984, all of the tour planning and management problems disintegrated before a sold out crowd of 45,000 fans packed into Arrowhead Stadium in Kansas City. This opening of the Victory tour was one of three sold out shows in Kansas City and was included in all major newscasts that evening. ABC's *Nightline* even broadcasted two songs live from the concert, "Human Nature" and "Off the Wall". Jackie appeared live on the program as he was unable to join his brothers for the tour due to recent knee surgery.

After what seemed like an endless wait after Chris Bliss' performance, the house lights finally went down, and huge muppet-like creatures crossed the stage. At the center of the stage was a large stone with a sword sticking out from it. Five knights in armor appeared and each attempted to pull the sword from the stone. The first four failed. The last knight appeared and successfully pulled the sword from the stone, and proclaimed, "Arise all the world, and behold the kingdom." He removed his helmet to reveal that he was Randy Jackson. After Randy saved the world from the creatures, stairs slowly arose from beneath the stage. The five brothers descended the stairs in unison, to the pounding beat of "Wanna Be Startin' Somethin'". All of the brothers were wearing sunglasses. Michael was in the middle, dressed in black and white stripped pants, a white sequined military jacket with a red banner across his chest, white sequined socks and black loafers, and one white sequined glove.

Michael's solo hits were intermixed with Jackson hits, with "Things I Do For You" sandwiched between "Wanna Be Startin' Somethin'" and "Off The Wall". "Human Nature" was next, followed by "Heartbreak Hotel". Michael really tore the house down with "She's Out of My Life", complete with the tears at the end. Then Michael left the stage for a solo set by Jermaine.

Initially, an argument was staged between Michael and Jermaine over what to perform next, ending with Michael leaving the stage. This argument was dropped after a few performances when fans took the cue that Michael was leaving the stage, and headed to the restrooms and snack counters during Jermaines solos. Jermaine performed "Let's Get Serious", and "Dynamite" then Michael joined him for their duet, "Tell Me I'm Not Dreamin'".

The concert continued with Jackson Five oldies, "I Want You Back", "The Love You Save", and "I'll Be There". Following the Jackson Five medley was "Rock With You" then "Lovely One". Then Michael changed into a bright red jumpsuit for "Working Day and Night". At the end of which Randy chased Michael around the stage, Michael fell to the ground, and was engulfed by a huge brightly lit spider-like contraption. His body was covered with a cloth and raised up on a pedestal. When Randy jerked away the cloth, Michael disappeared. Seconds later, Michael reappeared on a platform, dressed now in black pants and red sequined zippered jacket as the first distinctive sounds of "Beat It" rang out. Screams rose from the audience as they recognized the choreography from the song's video.

Following "Beat It" in the show was "Billie Jean", for which Michael recreated his unforgettable performance from *Motown 25*. His moonwalking during "Billie Jean" brought the loudest cheers of the night. After singing the song's last words, "Billie Jean is not my lover", Michael whipped his fedora into the crowd to the delight of that single fan who managed to snatch up the prized hat. Inside each fedora was a label that read, "Made Expressly For Michael Jackson by Maddest Hatter/100% Genuine Fur". The concerts were closed with "Shake Your Body (Down to the Ground)". No encore was performed.

Conspicuously absent from the show containing several of Michael's solo hits from *Off The Wall* and *Thriller* was one of his biggest hits, "Thriller". The elders of the Jehovah Witness' thought the song was offensive and endorsed a belief in the occult. Even though Michael included a disclaimer at the beginning of the song's video stating that the video, "in no way endorses a belief in the occult", the Witnesses still objected to it. Michael decided not to include the song in the Victory tour performances to please the church elders. Also conspicuously absent were any songs from the *Victory* album. It seemed strange that a tour named "Victory" after their latest album contained no songs from that album. Although it was said more songs would be added later, no songs from *Victory* were ever performed on the Victory tour.

There were, of course, several Jackson souvenirs for sale at each stop on the tour. Jackson buttons, bandannas, t-shirts, and tour programs were available along with Michael-only t-shirts and sunglasses.

While the Victory tour may have been haunted by management, organizational and planning problems, the shows themselves were nothing short of spectacular. The special effects, lighting, and especially choreography and singing were unsurpassable. Even the staging was impressive. Weighing in at 375 tons, it stood five stories high and was 160 feet wide, and ninety feet deep. It used seven computers, several elevators, and required twenty two men to operate it. Speakers numbered 120, and there were 2,200 lights. All of this equipment was carried in twenty two semitrailers. Actually, there were two stages, with one being set up in the tour's next stop.

Two chefs travelled with the Victory tour. Cy Kosis furnished food for the brothers. Mani Khalsa travelled as Michael's personal chef. After a performance, Michael would eat watermelon to replace water lost while performing. He would lose as much as four pounds after one performance. Another favorite food of Michael's in addition to fruits and vegetables, is Mexican food, especially cheese enchiladas.

Most of the shows on the Victory tour went smoothly. However, performances in Knoxville, Tennessee were nearly cancelled due to death threats directed toward Michael. The University of Tennessee and the Knoxville newspaper, *Sentinel,* received the death threats in the mail. Tour promoters wanted to cancel the three performances, but Michael insisted the shows go on as planned, he hated to disappoint his fans. So, the shows went on as scheduled with increased security. Fans were screened with metal detectors, and purses and bags were physically searched. Airplanes and helicopters were banned from flying overhead Heyland Stadium during the shows. Fortunately, there were no incidents.

When the Jacksons arrived at the airport in Dallas for their performances there, they were stranded at the airport when their limousine failed to show up for them. They hitched a ride in a van with Robert King, maintenance director of Muse Air. For their performance in Dallas on July 14, Eddie Van Halen joined the Jacksons on stage to perform his guitar solo on "Beat It".

Another superstar Michael met while on the road was Elton John. Both were in Denver for concerts. Michael tried on one of Elton's jackets, an elaborate gold number, and asked if it was one of his stage costumes. Elton replied, that it wasn't, it was just for everyday!

While Victory was in Detroit, Michael had film of himself shot with the Pontiac Police Department. Dressed in dark blue pants and a dark blue sequined military jacket, shades, and the single glove, the footage shows Michael running with a large group of police officers behind him. The footage later was included in a video of a live performance of "Billie Jean".

In New York, the Jacksons stayed at the Helmsley Palace Hotel. An elevator operator from the hotel gave one of his uniform jackets to Michael after he had admired it.

In between performances, many hours were spent cooped up in hotel rooms, one of the things Michael hates most about touring. Inevitably, it was let out where they were staying, making it nearly impossible for them, especially Michael, to leave. Never completely satisfied with his performance and wanting every detail to be perfect, Michael would study tapes of Victory tour concerts and fine tune his performance. He carried a portable dance floor with him to practice on. He did manage to sneak out

a few times.   He attended services at the Jehovah Witness'
Kingdom Hall regularly and he snuck out in Kansas City to see
Ghostbusters. But he mostly waited for the next performance. He
loves to be on stage. Frank Dileo said at the time, "Michael is
very happy when he's on stage. Everynight before the show, he's
the first one dressed and ready to go."

There were also awards to be accepted along the way.
Michael and Tito accepted an award from the NAACP, the 1984
Dr. H. Claude Hudson Medal of Freedom Award.   They also
accepted the 1984 Olympic Medal of Friendship Award on behalf
of the entire Jackson Family.

During breaks in the tour, Michael spent a lot of time at
one of his favorite places, Disney World. Disney's Hotel Royal
Plaza had renamed a set of rooms, "The Michael Jackson Suite".
Michael kept his eight Grammys in the suite, protected in a glass
showcase.

It was while the brothers were still on the road with
Victory that they learned of Janet's marriage to James DeBarge.
They were married on September 7, 1984, in Grand Rapids,
Michigan. None of the Jackson family attended the ceremony.
This news hit Michael especially hard. He had always been very
close to Janet. This made him feel as though he had lost one of
his best friends. The couple filed for an annulment, and eventual
divorce, four months later.

With *Thriller* breaking all previous sales records and with
the Victory tour playing to unprecedented crowds, a flood of
Michael Jackson merchandise hit the market.   There were
numerous books published on Michael and the Jackson family,
Michael Jackson t-shirts, buttons, posters, notebooks, keychains,
puzzles, Colorforms, record players, bubblegum, picture discs,
bumper stickers, watches, and of course, sequined socks and single
white gloves. For 1985, there was the Official Michael Jackson
calendar.

Replicas of Michael's jackets were also popular. Copies
of his red, multi-zippered jacket from the "Beat It" video and the

red and black jacket he wore in the "Thriller" video were big sellers along with a copy of the black and white leather jacket he wore in one of the Pepsi Commercials and in the dance rehearsal portions of "The Making of Michael Jackson's Thriller".

Four Michael Jackson dolls were also marketed, authorized by Michael. They came in four different, supposedly "authentic stage outfits", from the videos of "Beat It" and "Thriller", and from the American Music Awards and the Grammys. However, the doll dressed in the Grammy outfit is wearing a blue military style jacket with gold metallic pants. It's difficult to say what Grammy telecast the creator of this outfit saw, but Michael never wore gold pants to the Grammys, or probably anywhere else for that matter, save his days with the Jackson Five. The Barbie sized dolls each came with a stand, a microphone, a glove, and a tiny pair of sunglasses.

Some of this Michael Jackson merchandise was authorized by Michael, a great deal of merchandise, however, was being sold with Michael's name or likeness that was not authorized by him. In 1984, Michael filed a lawsuit in New York to prevent further sales of this unauthorized Michael Jackson merchandise. Official Michael Jackson merchandise carries the name of one of Michael's companies, MJJ Productions, Inc., Triumph Merchandising, Inc., Triumph International, Inc., Ultimate Productions, Optimum Productions, TTC Touring, Peacock Productions, The Jacksons Entertainment Inc., or EMMC, Entertainers Merchandise Management Corp.

During this period of "Michaelmania" there was, to say the least, a great deal of publicity about Michael. During the first eight months of 1984, Michael appeared on the covers of over 170 magazines. *Time, Newsweek, Ebony, Life, Rolling Stone,* and several issues of *People* all featured Michael Jackson on their covers during the year. *Time* broke a long standing policy of not featuring a person on the cover without an interview. The portrait of Michael that appears on the March 19, 1984 issue of *Time* was painted by Andy Warhol. There was no interview with Michael for the accompanying article. The author of the article, Denise Worrell, did talk with Joseph and Katherine Jackson, and she did meet Michael briefly. During a tour of their home, Joseph took her to Janet's and LaToya's bedrooms where they each said hello. Then Joe knocked on another door at the other end of the hall and went in. Michael and a friend were there watching TV in the dark. Michael stood up to say hello to Worrell, she shook hands with him and his friend. That was the extent of her meeting with Michael.

Besides stories dealing with actual events concerning Michael, the press also published an enormous number of stories filled with rumors and outright lies accusing Michael of being gay, having extensive plastic surgery, and taking hormones to maintain his high voice. After these lies persisted for some time, with no response from Michael, he finally decided to answer the accusations with a press statement released through his manager, Frank Dileo:

For some time now, I have been searching my conscience as to whether or not I should publicly react to the many falsehoods that have been spread about me. I have decided to make this statement based on the injustice of these allegations and the far-reaching trauma those who feel close to me are suffering.

I feel very fortunate to have been blessed with recognition for my efforts. This recognition also brings with it a responsibility to one's admirers throughout the world. Performers should always serve as role models who set an example for young people. It saddens me that many may actually believe the present flurry of false accusations:

No! I've never taken hormones to maintain my high voice.

No! I've never had cosmetic surgery on my eyes.

Yes! One day in the future I plan to get married and have a family.

Any statements to the contrary are simply untrue.

I have advised my attorneys of my willingness to institute legal action and subsequently prosecute all guilty to the fullest extent of the law.

As noted earlier, I love children. We all know that kids are very impressionable and therefore susceptible to such stories. I'm certain that some have already been hurt by this terrible slander. In addition to their admiration, I would like to keep their respect.

When the Victory tour winded down it had grossed $90 million and had played to over three million fans, setting a record for the largest audience for a tour. The spectacular performances of Michael and his brothers overshadowed all of the surrounding controversy and management problems, and it was definitely worth the $30 price tag. Mark Bego, author of *On the Road With Michael*, dedicated solely to the Victory tour, was also truly impressed with Michael:

Throughout these past two years of intense Michael Jackson-mania, I can honestly say that I have nothing but admiration for his talent, his creativity, and his undefatigable energy. On these pages I feel I have faithfully paid tribute to the number-one superstar of the decade and the most successful personality in the history of show business. As a journalist, I have also presented many of the negative aspects of the Victory tour. These tour-planning troubles have in no way altered my respect or admiration for Michael Jackson. My respect for him is not only intact, it has been enhanced. Anyone who would donate 100 percent of his profits from the Victory tour to charity truly has to have a heart as golden as his hit records.

After the conclusion of the Victory tour it was time Michael got on with what he was doing before the tour, winning awards and receiving honors. On November 20, 1984, The Hollywood Chamber of Commerce honored Michael with the 1793rd star to be placed on the Hollywood Walk of Fame. The star was placed, at Michael's request, directly in front of Mann's Chinese Theater on Hollywood Blvd. About 5,000 fans turned out for the presentation, the largest crowd to ever attend such a presentation. Michael appeared at the unveiling of the star for a full three minutes, then he was advised by security to leave as the crowd grew out of control.

Visitors to the Walk of Fame in Hollywood may have noticed another star for Michael Jackson. This second star is for another Michael Jackson, a radio broadcaster. Actually, this other Michael Jackson started in broadcasting before Michael Jackson from Gary started singing. The broadcaster is registered with the performers union as Michael Jackson. Since no two people can be registered using the same name, singer Michael Jackson is registered as Michael J. Jackson.

In 1984, Kim Fields, the young actress who portrayed Tootie on the television series, *The Facts of Life,* recorded a single about Michael Jackson titled, "Dear Michael". Kim was good friends with Janet and had met Michael before. Kim's character on her show was also a big Jackson fan. Jermaine even made an appearance in one of the series' episodes.

In November, 1984, *People* magazine published its first issue devoted entirely to one person, Michael Jackson. While it didn't include an interview with Michael, it did have interviews with his mother and Tito and Randy. Michael did have some input however. He offered his advice and suggestions and even helped set up a photo that appears in the issue of his dressing table backstage at one of the stops on the Victory tour. Besides his stage makeup, the table was covered with several other items of Michael's, a red tie, a belt, several pins, his sunglasses and glove, and two photos, Dopey, one of the seven dwarfs and the other of his favorite comedians, the Three Stooges.

The *People Extra* issue featured photos of stars that attended the Jackson concerts and met with Michael during the tour. Bruce Springsteen, Sugar Ray Leonard, Sean Lennon, Brooke Shields, Larry Hagman, New York Mayor Ed Koch, and

Elton John were all pictured in the special issue. Not to be outdone, *Ebony* named Michael Jackson one of the 100 Most Influential Black Americans, of 1984.

By the end of 1984 and early 1985, Michael was once again dominating award shows. For the American Video Awards, Michael had a whopping twenty four nominations in eight categories. Randy Newman's "I Love LA" was the only non Michael Jackson video nominated for Best Pop Video with "Beat It", "Billie Jean", "Thriller" and "Say Say Say" comprising the rest of the nominees in the category. "Beat It" and "Billie Jean" were both nominated for Best Soul Video and Best Editing. "Beat It", "Billie Jean", and "Thriller" were all nominated for Best Lighting Design, Choreography and Directing. "Beat It", Billie Jean", "Thriller" and "Say Say Say" were all nominated for Best Art Direction. Michael Jackson was nominated for Best Male Performance for "Beat It", "Billie Jean" and "Thriller". Michael won four awards out of the eight categories.

Michael's nominations for the MTV Music Video Awards included "Thriller" being nominated six times, for Best Video of the Year, Best Male Video, Best Concept Video, Best Overall Performance, Best Choreography, and the Viewers Choice Award. "Thriller" was chosen the winner in the latter three categories. Michael was further honored with four Black Gold Awards, and he walked away with the People's Choice Award for Favorite All-round Male Entertainer. He didn't attend any of these award presentations.

These awards were only a fraction of the recognition Michael's videos received. At year end, Billboard's America's Top 10 Videos compiled the top videos of the year. Not surprisingly, Michael Jackson dominated the chart. In fact, his four videos placed at the very top of the chart, one through four! His duet with Paul McCartney, "Say Say Say" placed at number four, "Billie Jean" placed at number three. The second favorite video in 1984 was "Thriller" and the number one video for the year was "Beat It". These videos continued strong throughout 1985, two years after their release, they again topped the year end video charts. "Billie Jean" was the sixth favorite video of 1985. "Beat It" and "Thriller" remained the top two favorites, but they switched places. "Beat It" was replaced at number one by "Thriller".

Besides the many awards and honors, there were also problems. A man named Fred Sanford claimed he wrote a song titled, "Please Love Me Now" which CBS Records stole from him. Sanford claimed his song was later recorded by Michael with the new title, "The Girl is Mine". Michael had to testify in a Chicago court on December 6, 1984, that the idea for the song was that of Quincy Jones, and that he wrote the song himself. The jury found in favor of CBS Records.

Around this same time, Michael had to answer charges that he had stolen the sketches that appear on the inside sleeve of *Thriller*. An artist had accused Michael of using the sketches without his permission. Michael had drawn the pictures himself. One is a sketch of Michael and Paul McCartney each pulling on the arms of a girl depicting a scene for "The Girl Is Mine". The other sketch is one depicting the single, "Thriller". It is of Michael and his date sitting in the front row of a theater watching the movie screen as a monster reaches out from the screen and surrounds Michael and his girl.

In March, 1985, Michael travelled to London for the unveiling of his wax likeness at Madame Tussaud's Wax Museum. Upon his arrival at London's Heathrow Airport, he was subjected to an extensive body and baggage search. The customs officials were concerned about the possibility of drug smuggling. Their search turned up nothing.

The street was packed with 8,000 fans each trying to catch a glimpse of Michael as he entered the building. His path from his car to the museum entrance was lined with rows of bobbies. The wax figure is dressed as Michael from the Victory concerts, in black pants and white sequined military style jacket, one glove and sunglasses. Michael stood next to his likeness and checked it out as dozens of flashbulbs went off one after another. Returning from his museum to his car, Michael climbed on the roof of the car to wave to his fans. He quickly climbed down and got immediately into the car, with Frank Dileo right behind him, to avoid being mobbed. Some of the fans even followed Michael to his hotel and waited outside all night. They were treated by the occasional sighting of a gloved hand reaching from behind the curtains to wave to the crowd.

An updated likeness of Michael was added to the museum's collection in the summer of 1990. The latest version copies Michael's costume from the Bad concerts, black pants and jacket lined with buckles.

Another visit Michael made in early 1985 was to a girl who was paralyzed in a car accident. Michael visited her in Miami. He later sent her a tape of the Victory tour concerts and a Jacksons Victory tour jacket.

One of two recordings Michael contributed to in 1985 was "Eaten Alive" by Diana Ross. Michael stayed at Barry Gibb's home in Florida while he worked with Barry and Maurice Gibb in writing and producing the title song for Diana Ross' album, *Eaten Alive*. Michael can be heard on the background vocals on the song. Written on the back cover of the album is a note to Diana from Michael in Michael's own handwriting: "You are truly supreme, good to be with you again. I love you, Michael 1998". An arrow and "1998" followed his signature and frequently still does.

The other recording Michael contributed to in 1985 was recorded on January 28, 1985, with forty four other recording artists, comprising USA for Africa.

CHAPTER EIGHT

"REMEMBER THE CHILDREN"

Following the Victory tour, Michael intentionally avoided the limelight. After two years of constantly being in the public eye, he stayed home. He released no new albums or videos and very rarely ventured out of Hayvenhurst, his Encino home. The awards, however, kept rolling in from the previous year's continued success of *Thriller*. In early 1985, *Making Michael Jackson's Thriller* captured the Grammy for Best Video Album. Michael also picked up two American Video Awards for Best Home Video and Best Long Form Video both for *Making Michael Jackson's Thriller*. He didn't attend either of the award presentations. One recording Michael did contribute to in 1985 was "We Are the World".

Harry Belafonte first contacted Ken Kragen, an entertainment manager, about starting a project for the relief of famine in Africa. After considering many different ideas, including an all-star concert, they finally decided on a recording involving several major artists. Kragen contacted two of his clients, Kenny Rogers and Lionel Richie, both of whom agreed to be involved. Lionel Richie then contacted Stevie Wonder. Quincy Jones was asked to produce the record. Coincidentally, at this same time, Michael Jackson happened to phone Quincy Jones. Jones told Michael about the project and Michael readily agreed to contribute, even volunteering to write the song with Lionel Richie. Originally, the song was to be written by Michael and Lionel with Stevie Wonder. But Stevie Wonder was rarely available to work on the project, so Michael and Lionel worked on the song together.

When they first began work on the project, they didn't get much done, they had dinner at each others homes, and reminisced about the early days of their careers when Lionel and his group, the Commodores, worked as an opening act for a group of brothers with a 13 year old lead singer, the Jackson Five. Then they got serious. LaToya told *People* magazine, "I'd go into the room while they were writing and it would be very quiet, which is odd, since Michael's usually very cheery when he works. It was very emotional for them. Some nights they'd just talk until two in the morning."

With the deadline for the song approaching, they finally got down to business. Lionel had taped two melodies. Michael took it from there and came up with music and words that same night: "I love working quickly. I went ahead without even Lionel knowing, I couldn't wait. I went in and came out the same night with the song completed- drums, piano, strings, and words to the chorus. I presented the demo to Quincy and Lionel, and they were in shock- they didn't expect to see something this quick. They loved it."

We Are the World, the book that chronicles the making of the famine relief single, reveals that the next meetings between Michael and Lionel didn't produce any additional lyrics. Everything was funny and no work got done. The rest of the song's lyrics didn't get written until the night before the all-star recording session was scheduled. They got down to work and in two and one half hours, the song was completed.

Michael and Lionel then recorded guide vocals for the other artists involved to learn the melody and the lyrics. These cassettes were delivered to the rest of the artists making up USA for Africa. These vocals were recorded, according to the *We Are the World* book, amidst some busy, and silly, conditions, "...the studio is swimming in musicians, organizers, techies, video crews, retinues, hangers on, assistants, and spilled popcorn from a fierce kernel shootout between Michael and his constant companion, Emmanuel Lewis, star of *Webster.*"

On January 28, 1985, Michael is the second artist to arrive at A&M's Lion Share Studios for the recording of "We Are the World". He arrived after Steve Perry of Journey, with manager Frank Dileo and his bodyguard, Bill Bray. Michael arrived at the studio early so he could record the chorus by himself, to be used as a guide for the other artists. It is Michael's vocals that the other artists are listening to in their headphones when learning the song.

Most of the other artists were scheduled to arrive at the studio following the American Music Awards. Michael skipped the awards where he had four nominations. For the second consecutive year, *Thriller* had been nominated for Favorite Album and Favorite Black Album. Michael had been nominated for Favorite Black Male Vocalist, and the Jacksons were nominated for Favorite Group. It was just as well he didn't go, he would have gone home empty handed.

The video cassette, *We Are the World: The Video Event* shows Michael leading the all-star group through the song, and offering individual help on the lyrics to Huey Lewis, a last minute soloist chosen when Prince failed to show up. Michael's shyness and discomfort around crowds is evident in this tape. When he's not directly involved in the activity at the moment, he can often be spotted standing alone quietly in the background.

Before the actual recording began, Ken Kragen, one of the organizers, spoke to the group about distributing the proceeds from the record sales, and the steps being taken to insure the money went directly to where it was needed. Bob Geldoff, organizer of Band Aid and Live Aid, also spoke to the group of artists. Finally, Michael addressed the group. He described the song he and Lionel Richie had written as "a love song to inspire concern about a faraway place close to home." The recording session began at 9:00 p.m., and lasted the entire night. Michael didn't leave until 8:00 a.m. the next morning.

Quincy Jones had posted a sign outside the studio reading, "Leave your ego at the door." The forty five artists who comprised United Support of Artists for Africa, and who left their egos at the door, included a wide range of artists, with at least one representative from various categories of music; pop, rock, R&B, and country. Dan Aykroyd, Harry Belafonte, Lindsey Buckingham, Kim Carnes, Ray Charles, Bob Dylan, Sheila E., Bob Geldoff, Daryl Hall and John Oates, and James Ingram were all part of USA for Africa. Perhaps the most widely represented music in USA for Africa was Jackson music, with Jackie, LaToya, Marlon, Michael, Randy, and Tito all contributing to the famine relief single. The balance of USA for Africa was made up of Al

Jarreau, Waylon Jennings, Billy Joel, Cyndi Lauper, Huey Lewis and the News, Kenny Loggins, Bette Midler, Willie Nelson, Jeffrey Osborne, Steve Perry, the Pointer Sisters, Lionel Richie, Smokey Robinson, Kenny Rogers, Diana Ross, Paul Simon, Bruce Springsteen, Tina Turner, Dionne Warwick, and Stevie Wonder.

The song was produced by Quincy Jones and the associate producer was Tom Bahler, who wrote "She's Out of My Life" from Michael's *Off The Wall* album. Keyboards on "We Are the World" are handled by another Jackson associate, Greg Phillinganes.

The recording session resulted in a single, a video and a video cassette documenting the making of the single, *We Are the World- The Video Event*. A double album made up of the "We Are the World" single, and previously unreleased material from some of the participating artists was also released. Michael did not have a song included on the album. The proceeds from the sale of these items along with proceeds from sales of books, shirts, buttons, posters, and other merchandise all went directly to the famine relief fund. *We Are the World - The Video Event* was the ninth best selling video cassette of 1985.

All members of the press were barred from reporting the happenings leading to the history making recording session, with the exception of *Life* magazine, who did a cover story on USA for Africa. Seven members of USA for Africa were pictured on the cover of the April, 1985, issue; Willie Nelson, Bob Dylan, Tina Turner, Cyndi Lauper, Bruce Springsteen, and the song's composers, Lionel Richie and Michael Jackson. Inside were photos of the participants working and taking breaks. One photo was particularly surprising, Mr. Health Food and Bottled Water holding a can of Budwiser! Michael had his representatives tell the press that he was just moving the can when the picture was snapped. I guess we'll never know for sure if it was indeed Michael's beer or not. It's not impossible though, Michael is a strict vegetarian and does only eat healthy foods, but he did once finish off an entire bag of potato chips while doing his last interview for *Rolling Stone*.

"We Are the World" became the first single ever to go multiplatinum. It debuted on *Billboard's* Hot 100 at number twenty one and three weeks later, the week of April 13, 1985, it was the number one song. The single stayed at number one for four weeks.

On Good Friday, April 5, 1985, "We Are the World" was broadcast simultaneously on thousands of radio stations around the world. It was a very special event. At 10:25 am, over 8,000 stations all played the touching anthem for the relief of famine in Ethiopia. This event was repeated one year later on Good Friday, when thousands of stations again simultaneously aired "We Are the World".

USA for Africa was possible because of the concern and dedication of all those who contributed. A few brain dead critics, however, singled Michael Jackson out as the sole artist who was unable to leave his ego at the door. These accusations were based on the shot of Michael in the video with the camera following him from a close up of his feet, with his sequined socks, up past his glove to his face. These few critics concluded that Michael didn't leave his ego at the door because he wore his sequined socks, glove and his sunglasses. It seems they only considered what he chose to wear to the recording session rather than recognize the tremendous contribution he made to the entire project. They certainly didn't have any first hand knowledge of the session, because no press was allowed with the exception of *Life* magazine. Michael co-wrote the song with Lionel Richie, and worked on his own to come up with the music and words to the chorus. He recorded guide vocals for the other artists to use to learn the song, and he served on the board of directors of USA for Africa. Just like everyone else involved in the project, Michael received NO compensation for his contribution of his time and talent. On the back cover of the *We Are the World* book are comments made by some of the members of USA for Africa, included are Michael's thoughts and feelings about the song, "When I was asked to write the song, I put my soul into it. That's really my statement."

Michael also describes in *Moonwalk* how honored and proud he felt to be a part of USA for Africa.

USA for Africa took top honors at the American Music Awards and at the Grammys. In 1986, the American Music Award of Appreciation went to the person who first conceived of the idea to create a project for the relief of famine in Ethiopia, Harry Belafonte. In accepting his award, Belafonte had these words:

I would like to take this opportunity to acknowledge four people who really made a great difference in this project. Two for moving it forward. One is our leader, Ken Kragen. Quincy Jones, who made us all leave our egos at the door. And the two artists who, without their great gift would not have inspired us in quite the same way as we were inspired, Mr. Lionel Richie and Mr. Michael Jackson.

These four were then called up on stage to share the award. Michael, who had showed up half way through the show with Elizabeth Taylor, ascended the stairs to the stage of the Shrine Auditorium dressed in a green khaki uniform that looked like a cross between a Canadian mountie and a school crossing guard. The show concluded with most of the stars reuniting together on stage to sing "We Are the World."

Following the awards presentation, Michael, with Elizabeth Taylor, joined Lionel and Brenda Richie for dinner. Michael took along his personal chef who prepared him steamed okra.

A few weeks later, USA for Africa was again honored at the Grammys with four wins out of five nominations. "We Are the World" lost in the race for Best Album to Phil Collins' *No Jacket Required,* but won with each of the other four nominations. Three of the awards went to the single, the remaining one was for the song's video. The "We Are the World" video took top honors as the Best Short Form Video. Among the single's awards, was the prize for Best Pop Group Performance.

Record of the Year and Song of the Year are considered two of the most prestigious honors of all the Grammys. Record of the Year goes to a record's artist and producer. Song of the Year goes to the songwriter. "We Are the World" was chosen as both the Record of the Year and Song of the Year. Quincy Jones was joined on stage by Michael Jackson, Lionel Richie, Stevie Wonder and Dionne Warwick to accept the Grammy for Record of the year. Jones thanked, among others, Richie and Jackson for writing the song.

Michael and Lionel accepted the award for Song of the Year together, with Lionel speaking first to thank the artists involved and the public for responding when the world needed their help. Michael then stepped to the podium, dressed in black pants and uniform jacket over a red shirt, with several gold pins. After the cheers from the audience subsided, he spoke:

First, I'd like to thank God. I'd like to say thank you for choosing Lionel and myself to write 'We Are the World'. I thank Quincy Jones who is the greatest producer to me. I'd also like to say when you leave here tonight, remember the children. Thank you.

"We Are the World" went on to pick up the People's Choice Award for Favorite New Song. The award was accepted by Kenny Rogers, neither Lionel Richie or Michael Jackson attended the ceremony.

For the Hands Across America project, which followed the USA for Africa project, Michael favored use of "We Are the World". He was out voted by the other board members and a new song was specially written for the event, "Hands Across America", with "We Are the World" as the B-side. "Hands Across America" didn't achieve near the degree of success that "We Are the World" had achieved. Michael's disagreement with the other board members is assumed to be what led to his decision in December, 1986, to resign from the board of directors of USA for Africa.

A second version of "We Are the World" was produced by George Duke with children singing the lyrics. Michael has always preferred this version to USA for Africa's, feeling the song was meant to be sung by children.

We are the world
We are the children
We are the ones who make a brighter day
So let's start giving
There's a choice were making
We're saving our own lives
It's true we make a better day
Just you and me

We Are the World
Michael Jackson and Lionel Richie

The copyright to the "We Are the World" single is owned by Brockman Music and MIJAC Music, Michael's own music publishing company. By this time, Michael had become intrigued by the publishing aspect of the music business. But co-owning the "We Are the World" copyright was not his most significant venture into the music publishing business.

In mid 1985, Michael purchased the ATV Music Publishing Company for $47.5 million. ATV holds the copyrights to approximately 4,000 songs, including works by Pat Benatar, the Pointer Sisters, the Pretenders, and two of Michael's idols, Little Richard and Sly and the Family Stone. Most importantly, ATV also includes a 251 song catalog of Lennon-McCartney Beatle songs.

Through ownership of these copyrights, Michael receives royalties everytime one these songs is heard on a TV show or in a film, a record is sold, or the song is recorded. It was estimated at the time of his purchase that Michael will have recovered his investment within five years, or possibly sooner with the introduction of Beatle albums on compact discs, and the eventual introduction of digital audio tape. The song, "Yesterday", a classic, is part of the catalog and holds the record as the most recorded song. It has been estimated that through ownership of its copyright, Michael Jackson earns in excess of $30,000 per year from that one song alone.

For their help in the negotiations for the ATV Music purchase, Frank Dileo and John Branca were both handsomely rewarded. Michael bought each of them a $120,000 Rolls Royce Silver Spur.

Although there are several ways in which to earn money through music publishing, selling a song for use in advertisements tends to be one of the most profitable. It can also be one of the most controversial as Michael soon discovered when he granted permission to Nike to use "Revolution" in their ads for sport shoes, for $250,000. The surviving Beatles claimed Nike did not have the right to use the original recording of their song in the commercial. The Beatles and their record company, Apple Records, sued the Nike Corporation.

Many others criticized Michael for only being interested in earning even more money and not being concerned with preserving the integrity of the Beatle's work. *Rolling Stone* magazine reported, "But confidants of the singer stress that Jackson went into that deal with Yoko Ono's consent and that his primary goal is to bring the Beatle's music to a new generation, not to turn a quick buck." Michael's lawyer, John Branca, added, "Michael is the world's number one Beatles fan, and he wanted to protect and cherish these songs just as the Beatles would. We're in constant touch with the representatives of Paul McCartney and the estate of John Lennon, and nothing is done without their knowledge." A representative of the company that administers Michael Jackson's publishing holdings reported to *Rolling Stone,* "that while Jackson is certainly interested in the financial aspects of owning the rights to the Beatles catalog, he is more concerned with the artistic value of the songs."

Michael has a list of approximately one hundred Beatle songs which are not to be used in any commercial endorsements. The remaining 150 songs are eligible to be used in commercials, to be recorded by other artists, or used in other projects, if the projects are tasteful. It was obviously this last requirement that prevented the white rap group, the Beastie Boys, from including a Beatle song on their album. They had planned to include a rap version of "I'm Down" on their album, *Licensed to Ill.* Michael, having ownership of this particular song, called the president of CBS Records and successfully prevented the group from including the song on their album.

Michael also denied permission to Phil Collins to include a Beatle song on the soundtrack album of his movie, *Buster.* No reason was given for the denial, but it may have been due to other projects planned for the song, as Michael is said to be interested in developing many projects based on the Beatle songs.

Michael's main objective in owning the Beatle catalog is to encourage new artists to record Beatle classics. To help meet this objective, Michael hired publisher Dale Kawashima as president of ATV Music. Kawashima had previously handled and promoted the works of Bruce Springsteen, Prince, and Bob Dylan. ATV Music Group, formerly administered by EMI Music Publishing, was switched to MCA Music Publishing in April, 1991.

Gaining control of the Beatle song catalog cost Michael more than $47.5 million, it also cost him the friendship of former Beatle Paul McCartney. At best, it strained their relationship. While working together on duets for each others albums, the two had become very close friends. Michael learned that Paul had the only cartoon collection larger than his own. They discovered many other common interests as well, one of them being the music publishing business. McCartney was very much involved in music publishing and Michael became an eager to learn student. Paul taught Michael a great deal about the business. Michael even told Paul he would someday buy his stuff. When Michael actually did buy the Beatle catalog, Paul resented it. When the rights were available for sale, Paul was outbid by Michael.   Michael's investment was financed by Columbia Records, a subsidiary company of CBS Records.

McCartney could have been out bid by anyone. It seems to have attracted so much attention because he happened to have been out bid by Michael Jackson, who he introduced to the music publishing business. Any other investor could have purchased the catalog and not received near the publicity, or accusations of greed. Ownership of the rights to the Beatle catalog have been out of the hands of Lennon and McCartney for several years with relatively little mention ever made of it. Lennon and McCartney, early in their careers, signed over ownership of their copyrights to publisher Dick James. James' Northern Songs made millions off of the copyrights, then, in 1967, he sold Northern Songs to Sir Lew Grade. Grade subsequently sold the song catalog to Robert Holmes a Court. When Michael Jackson purchased the catalog, it suddenly seemed unfair.

Paul McCartney said in one interview that he suspected a scheme between Yoko Ono and Michael Jackson to purchase the copyrights. Copyrights are issued for 28 years and can be renewed for an additional 28 years. If a composer dies during the first 28 year period, their heirs can claim ownership of the copyrights for the second 28 year period. Interested in buying the copyrights, McCartney visited Robert Holmes a Court and was quoted a price of $20 million. McCartney offered to split the price and ownership of the copyrights with Lennon's widow, Yoko Ono. She thought the price was too high and suspected if they waited, the price would come down. In the meantime, Michael Jackson purchased the rights for $47.5 million. McCartney charged that this deal was planned by Ono and Jackson, knowing half of the ownership rights would begin reverting to Ono and Lennon's sons Julian and Sean in five years. McCartney suspected further that Michael Jackson would then purchase the rights back from Ono.

Hardcore Beatle fans, and it seems the remaining Beatles themselves, resent the use of Beatle songs in commercials. Many feel it is degrading to have classic Beatle tunes turned into jingles. What isn't widely known is that Paul McCartney owns, among several others, the rights to many Buddy Holly songs, and these songs are licensed for use in commercials. It is hard to understand how this could be suitable for Buddy Holly songs, but is degrading for Beatle songs. What is clear is Michael's intention to preserve the integrity of the Beatle catalog and lend their use only to projects which he deems suitable, which does entail some commercial endorsements.   Michael, obviously, does not consider licensing pop songs for use in commercials as degrading, he has lent his own biggest hits to be reworked for commercials.

Many projects were reported to be in the works involving the Beatle catalog, all of which have yet to be seen, including a weekly television series based on Beatle songs, which is to be co-produced by Michael. Michael is also said to be interested in feature films based on Beatle songs. A soundtrack album was reported to be in the works that included cover versions of Beatle songs by several artists, including Michael himself with a cover of "Come Together", his favorite Beatle song.

When unauthorized copies of Beatle movies began to be sold in early 1989, Michael had his attorneys prosecute those distributing the bootlegged tapes. *The Beatles in Tokyo, The Beatles in the Magical Mystery Tour,* and *The Beatles at Shea Stadium* were being sold and distributed by Video Wholesalers, Inc. of Neptune, New Jersey. Michael was successful in obtaining a court order preventing further sales of the videos until the lawsuit was settled. The suit was filed by attorneys for Michael Jackson and the Beatles. It was the first time Michael Jackson and the Beatles joined together to protect the material of the Beatles. In the suit, Michael claimed he actually owned the copyrights to the songs performed in the movies, and the video distributors had no right to produce or distribute the tapes. Michael also claimed that the poor quality of the tapes could turn off fans, lowering his potential profits if he should decide to release the movies himself. The suit was settled in October, 1989, Michael Jackson was awarded $130,000 and Video Wholesalers were permanently barred from any further sales of the video cassettes.

Michael has since been involved in greatly expanding his publishing holdings. In the spring of 1989, Berry Gordy offered for sale Jobete Music, the publishing division of Motown Records. Estimates of the price were as high as $120 million. Among the parties interested were Warner Communications, Sony, and Michael Jackson. Jobete Music holds the copyrights to most of Motown's biggest hits by Motown's biggest stars, such as Stevie Wonder, the Supremes and the Jackson Five.

CHAPTER NINE

ANOTHER PART OF ME

Following his work with USA for Africa, Michael went to work on another project, one that involved two of his greatest loves; Disneyland and movies. When Walt Disney Company chairman Michael Eisner asked Michael Jackson if he would like to be involved in a special film project for Disney Michael accepted, asking that one of his favorite directors also be involved. According to Eisner, "Well, you know Michael Jackson is a Disney aficionado, knows more about Walt Disney than anybody. He surely knows more than I do. We called up and said, 'Michael, would you like to do something for the parks?' He said, 'Definitely, but only if you can get George Lucas to direct me.'" Done. George Lucas, director of *Star Wars,* would direct. Francis Ford Coppolla, of *The Godfather,* would produce. Anjelica Huston would co-star. The movie would star Michael Jackson as Captain EO.

Captain EO is a spectacular 3-D movie filled with incredible state of the art special effects. Specially constructed theaters were built at Disney World and Disneyland to house *Captain EO* to accommodate the movie's extravagant special effects. Asteroids float through the screen and throughout the theater. During a shoot out, lasers are shot from the action on the screen into the audience.

EO is the Captain of a spaceship manned with a crew of colorful characters. The Geex is a two headed character who often gets into arguments with itself. Major Domo is a robot with Minor Domo, a miniature robot, who rides on his back. Hooter is a green elephant who wears an undershirt and can play his trunk like a flute. The most lovable of the group is Fuzzball, an orange, winged monkey who rides on the shoulder of Captain EO.

Having bungled their last mission, EO and his crew need to redeem themselves in the eyes of EO's boss, Commander Bogg, played by Dick Shawn. EO's new assignment calls for him to use his powers of music and dance to bring beauty and happiness to the evil Witch Queen, played by Anjelica Huston.

EO's crew of misfits magically transform themselves into musical instruments giving EO the power to break free from the clutches of the Witch Queen's troops who surround him and attack him with whips. Genuine whips were used, so exact timing was crucial in filming the scene to avoid any injuries. While filming the scene, Michael was accidently struck in the face with one of the whips. Fortunately, it was not too serious and he was able to continue filming. Later, Michael sprained his right thumb when a set fell against his hand. He reinjured the same hand later during a dance routine.

Finally, EO is able to present the Queen with a gift, a gift that she "can not only see, but hear". EO and a group of back up dancers perform "We Are Here to Change the World", written by Michael Jackson with John Barnes. The dance routines are especially impressive when seen in 3-D. At one point, Michael goes into a moonwalk and glides out of the screen.

After the transformation of the evil Witch Queen into a beautiful woman, EO and crew perform "Another Part of Me":

> *We're sendin' out a major love*
> *And this is our message to you*
> *The planets are linin' up*
> *We're bringin' brighter days*

Despite his crew's comedic ineptness, Captain EO is successful in his mission and saves the Dark Planet from the evil Witch Queen. With their mission completed, they say goodbye.

Disney's new Captain EO movie premiered at Walt Disney World's Epcot Center in Florida on September 12, 1986. It premiered at Disneyland in California the next day. The premiere at Disney World was celebrated by a TV special hosted by Patrick Duffy and Justine Bateman which featured sneak peeks at the movie and showed the arrival of many of the celebrities who attended the premiere. The traditional ribbon cutting ceremony to the theater entrance was held with George Lucas, Francis Ford Coppola, and Anjelica Huston. Conspicuously absent from the festivities was the film's star. Michael did not attend the film's premiere. Or did he? It was later reported that perhaps Michael did attend, but was in disguise. Frank Dileo claimed he didn't even know for sure. Michael could have been disguised as an old lady, a nurse, an usher, or maybe even one of the parks animated characters.

A second TV special aired in the summer of 1988, *Captain EO Backstage,* hosted by Whoopi Goldberg. It featured backstage looks at the making of the movie, including creation of the special effects, makeup, and dance rehearsal. Incredible amounts of ingenuity and hard work went into making the film seem effortless. To make it appear EO was flying, a transparent platform, cables, and a harness were used to lift EO into the air. To make the harness undetectable, Michael's body was covered with plaster to form a perfectly contoured cast of his body used as a mold for the transparent harness.

Michael choreographed the dance routines with Jeffrey Hornaday. Hornaday was impressed with Michael's dancing abilities, "Working with Michael has for me been a unique experience in that usually a choreographer will devise sequences of dance and then give it to the dancers to do and tell them to perform this. Where as Michael's talent and approach is so unique that you're limiting yourself by just giving him what you do."

Rusty Lemorande, who lent to the production of *Captain EO,* also commented on Michael's talent: "As an entertainer and showman, Michael is one of the most passionate, dedicated and clever people I have ever met. His effect is almost spectral."

Six years after *Captain EO* opened at Disneyland and Disney World, Euro Disney was opened in France, in the spring of 1992. One of the biggest attractions at the new park was reported to be *Le Captain EO.*

Besides his work on the *Captain EO* movie, Michael rarely appeared in public during this period. In Early 1986, he did appear on *60 Minutes*, in an interview as part of a story on Quincy Jones. He spoke only of his association with Jones, nothing about himself. He spoke only for five minutes, and from behind dark sunglasses. Another rare venture out for Michael during this time was when he accompanied friend Liza Minnelli to the funeral of her father, Vincent Minnelli.

In the spring of 1986, the British Virgin Islands announced plans to release postage stamps featuring Michael Jackson. Shortly before their release, in fact after a few hundred sets were already printed, the production of the stamps were cancelled due to regulations stating that stamps bearing the likeness of living persons must be members of the Royal Family, not the Jackson family. Stamps with Michael's picture were subsequently issued, however, by a Caribbean Island, St. Vincent. The stamps, and accompanying collector sheets, features pictures of Michael from the Victory tour.

St. Vincent later issued a set of stamps in 1992 featuring eight entertainers. Included in the set was Madonna, Elvis Presley, David Bowie, Prince, Frank Sinatra, George Michael, Mick Jagger, and of course, Michael Jackson. Michael's stamp had a close up shot of him smiling with a background full length shot of him with a ball and chain around his ankle, from the video for "Leave Me Alone". Grenada also issued a set of eight stamps featuring entertainers in their Gold Record Award set. Featured in the collection, in addition to Michael Jackson, were stamps with Cher, Elvis Presley, Dolly Parton, Johnny Mathis, Madonna, Nat King Cole, and Janis Joplin. This stamp had a close up animated picture of Michael in a shirt and tie.

Michael Jackson has also been featured on stamps issued from the Republic of Guinea and Tanzania. The series of stamps issued from the Republic of Guinea features a close up shot of Michael smiling big, and a full length shot of him dancing from the video for "Billie Jean". Tanzania issued a Michael Jackson stamp as part of a series honoring Famous Black Entertainers. That stamp features a close up picture of Michael.

Magic Beat Perfume, endorsed by Michael Jackson, was introduced in 1986. There were three different scents, Unwind, Heartbeat, and Wildfire. This line of perfume, planned to coincide with the release of Michael's new album, failed to reach the expected level of success, for there was no new Michael Jackson album. A line of Michael Jackson clothes also failed due to the lack of a new Michael Jackson album to promote it. The follow up album to *Thriller* was being delayed.

A line of stuffed toys based on Michael's private zoo was also marketed. Bob Michaelson helped develop the line of toys with Michael Jackson. Michaelson told one publication, "He's (Jackson) very instrumental in the designing of the toys. And he's very instrumental in how it should be programmed. He might not always be right, but he's right 90% of the time. That's pretty good for a 29 year old. He's got tremendous intuition." Michaelson went on to describe Michael as "a hard working, tremendously talented kid."

There are ten Michael's Pets in all. One of which, Cool Bear, is based on Michael himself. Cool Bear is dressed in a black suit, red shirt and black tie. He's also wearing a fedora and sunglasses. Other Pets are based on Michael's real life pets, Jabbar, a giraffe wearing high top tennis shoes, Louie the llama, Muscles the snake, and the most popular of the collection, Bubbles the chimp. A frog is named Uncle Tookie, Michael's nickname for Frank Dileo. Spanky is a white dog wearing a red military jacket. Another dog, Mr. Bill, (named for Bill Bray?) wears a trenchcoat and hat. Suzy, a rabbit, and Jeannine, an ostrich, complete the line of Michael's Pets.

In 1987, singer Kenny Rogers published a book of a collection of photographs he had taken of some of his famous friends, entitled, *Your Friends and Mine.* In the introduction to the book, Rogers relates the story of how the idea for the book came about, and the first person he photographed for it:

The first person I shot for the book was Michael Jackson. In 1986, I hosted the Grammy Awards telecast in Los Angeles. That night, my son Christopher met Michael backstage. Christopher had always loved Michael. He would even dress like him at home- probably because he doesn't have silver hair and a beard, so he could look like me. As it happened, Marianne [Rogers' wife] sent me some flowers with a little plastic Grammy attached. Unbeknownst to me or anyone else, Christopher took the plastic Grammy, walked into Michael Jackson's press conference, and handed it to him.

The next day, Michael called to tell Christopher how much he appreciated it. He also invited him out to his house to see his animals, so Marianne and Christopher went out to Encino. Michael knew I was a photographer, he mentioned that he'd like it if I took a picture of him and Christopher together. I called Michael the next day to set up an appointment, and he agreed to come down to my studio.

I told Michael during our first session that I was thinking about doing a book of portraits and calling it Your Friends and Mine. I had heard about his chimpanzee, Bubbles, and we did a shot with the chimp. Later on Michael and I did another session alone, at his request. That was the start. Michael Jackson's agreeing to be part of the book was, in fact, the jumping off point for the whole project.

The photo of Michael holding Bubbles on his hip that was included in Rogers' book is still one of the best photos ever taken of Michael. Michael and Bubbles were photographed in black and white. Michael is dressed very casually. No fedora, no glove, no sunglasses. He's dressed in worn jeans and a simple shirt. According to the credits in the book, his hair and makeup were done by Karen Faye. Bubbles is also dressed casually in a long sleeved shirt and overalls. The relaxed and casual feeling of the photo may not be only due to their attire, as Rogers tells in the brief description that appears next to the photograph in the book:

Michael Jackson is unique, both as an individual and as a performer. Yet while I'd been around him many times, I never honestly felt I knew him until we spent a day together in the photography studio.

As I explained earlier, Michael had invited Christopher, my youngest son, to his home to see his zoo. They had such a good time that Michael, who heard I was a photographer, suggested I take a picture of him and Christopher in my studio. I told him of my ideas for this book and asked him to bring his chimp, Bubbles.

There were maybe twenty-five people in the studio that day, and the chimp was the center of attention. That meant the focus was off Michael, and I think the relative anonymity gave him a chance to relax. And Bubbles was so human it was almost frightening. He would take Christopher by the hand, walk over to the refrigerator, open it, take out a banana, and hand it to him. Christopher was amazed- we all were.

The session was the first time I'd had a chance to be one on one with Michael. It means a lot to me to be able to say that not only do I love his music, but I also like him very much as a person and consider him a friend.

Rogers' other photos of Michael, most notably a black and white shot of Michael sitting on the floor holding a fedora up to his face, just below his eyes, are also among the best photos of Michael ever published. The one noted above has been published in magazines and was used on Bad tour sweatshirts.

Janet Jackson was also included in Rogers' book of photographs. Hers is dramatically different from Michael's, printed in color with a bright multicolored backdrop.

In June, 1987, Michael was in the news and again stories arose concerning him becoming increasingly eccentric. Michael had supposedly offered the London Hospital Medical College $1/2 million for the remains of John Merrick, the elephant man. Merrick, who died in 1900, suffered from neurofibromatosis, a disfiguring disease. The hospital refused Michael's offer, saying the remains were not for sale. Michael, as the story went, doubled his offer but was still refused.

A barrage of jokes and criticisms ensued. Assuming the story had any merit at all, one of the most nervy criticisms attacked Michael for wanting to spend such an enormous amount of money on a dead man's bones. Even discounting Michael's financial gifts and contributions of his time and talent to countless charities and organizations many of which aren't publicized, it seems ludicrous that he should have to justify to the public any expenditures of his own money. To accuse him of being weird or eccentric is a subjective observation, but to attack him for spending his own money is mindless.

Michael's interest in the elephant man's remains becomes perhaps a little easier to understand when considered from Michael's perspective. He has spent virtually his entire life in the public eye, being scrutinized by critics, and even fans, for essentially every move. Being under such constant scrutiny and being very sensitive to it, is comparable to how John Merrick must have lived. Michael identifies with him. Michael and Janet have watched the movie, *The Elephant Man* several times, and Michael always cries. He also reads everything available about Merrick. Frank Dileo defended Michael's motive, "Michael was fascinated by the movie and really wanted the skeleton. Michael regarded the elephant man's remains for his private collection of memorabilia as a privilege and honor."

Another subject of great criticism surrounding Michael was his purchase of an hyperbaric chamber. Michael reportedly felt that by sleeping in the chamber, with purified air pumped in, it would be healthy for him and possibly prolong his life. According to the story, Frank Dileo and Michael's doctor advised him against purchasing it, but Michael insisted and purchased it anyway. Almost immediately, a photo of Michael lying in the chamber hit the cover of the *National Enquirer*.

It has since been suggested who sent the photo to the magazine: Michael Jackson. Actually he saw the contraption, which is used to treat burn victims, while visiting patients in a hospital. He then supposedly made up the story and posed for the picture which was "leaked" to the *National Enquirer*. Michael and/or Frank Dileo have since been exposed as the possible source of the elephant man story too.

Michael realizes the value of publicity. Good or bad, it is important to remain in the public's mind. He learned the value of publicity from his early days at Motown, and has since become a master at the game. All of the talk, jokes, and controversy that surrounded his efforts to buy the elephant man's bones and his wishes to prolong his life by sleeping in the oxygen chamber helped to increase the mystique around him.

Rumors about Michael's weirdness included stories about him having extensive plastic surgery. Some said he wanted to look like Diana Ross, others said he wanted to look like his sister, Janet, and still others said he wanted to look like LaToya. Some charged he underwent the surgeries to look less like his father, that he wanted to erase any resemblance of himself to his father. "Experts" in plastic surgery told various publications they estimate Michael has had nine or more alterations done to his face. What's amazing is that these "experts" were able to come to these conclusions by simply comparing photographs of Michael taken in his teens, or younger, to ones taken when he was thirty. They never met him to do any sort of actual examination, yet they could tell he had alterations done to his eyes, nose, chin, lips, cheekbones, and jaw. (Of course that's only six, but they never seem to be able to identify all nine surgeries they are sure he has had.)

Other stories told of a shrine Michael had built to Elizabeth Taylor in his home, in which her movies played twenty four hours a day. Michael had also reportedly proposed marriage to Taylor. If these eccentricities weren't enough, some others declared Michael to be weird simply because one of his companions often times is his chimp Bubbles.

Before the release of *Thriller's* follow up album, Michael was spotted in public wearing a surgical mask over his face. This started reports that Michael had become a second Howard Hughes, afraid of any germs. The stories even went so far as to say that he was going to perform behind a plexi-glass shield while on tour to protect himself from germs. Michael tells in *Moonwalk* that the mask was given to him by his dentist to keep out germs when he had his wisdom teeth removed. Michael grew to like the bit of privacy the mask offered in addition to his sunglasses and he continued to wear it.

Perhaps the most absurd stories circulating about Michael Jackson concerned him undergoing a variety of very painful and extreme treatments in an effort to lighten his dark skin. Some said he had undergone a skin peel (whatever that is), others claimed he had had acid applied to his skin! Still others claimed Michael had done some form of skin bleaching to make his skin appear white. Some assumed this indicated Michael was ashamed to be a black American, and was denying his race.

The rumors claiming that Michael is gay died out. Perhaps partially due to his statement that he would pursue legal action if such lies were printed about him. It may also have been due in part to Michael's new, tougher look. The sequined military jackets were replaced with jackets with rows of buckles. Rumors speculating as to Michael's sexual preference have always bothered his mother. Marlon said in a *People Magazine* TV special interview, "I'll tell you right now that I know he's not gay because, ...I know!"

All of these ridiculous rumors were eventually answered by Frank Dileo, Quincy Jones, and Michael himself. Dileo denied many of the rumors in the September 14, 1987 issue of *People Magazine*. Michael's photo was on the cover with the caption, "Is This Guy Weird or What?" Dileo told the magazine that Michael had no shrine to Liz Taylor in his home, and that he never proposed to her. Dileo also told *People* that Michael definitely never took hormones to keep his voice high. Michael is the only Jackson singled out as taking hormones to artificially maintain his high voice, even though all of the Jacksons, male and female, have very soft, high voices.

The article continued with Dileo denying Michael had any cosmetic surgery on his eyes or cheekbones. He admitted that

Mike did have his nose reshaped and he did have a cleft put in his chin. "Why?" "He wanted one." Dileo called the claim that Michael had his skin lightened by chemical or surgical means, "preposterous." Dileo admitted that Michael did purchase the hyperbaric chamber, but said he didn't know for sure if he actually slept in it. He did make it clear that he was definitely against Michael purchasing chamber.

Quincy Jones responded to these ridiculous claims in an interview with *USA Today:*

The public perception of what Michael is as a human being has been highly exaggerated. Those articles are hard for me to relate to. For instance, Bubbles is more fun than a lot of people I know. I saw Bubbles at a wedding in a tux. He has great table manners.

Jones went on to say:

The bottom line, after all the rhetoric, all the talk about plastic surgery, is that Michael is still one of the best entertainers America has ever seen. He's not accessible and doesn't do interviews, so people tend to fill in the blanks.

Jones also spoke to *US Magazine* about Michael's so-called strange behavior:

When you start in this business as young as he did, at age five, it's hard to get a realistic point of view on life. Considering his background, and what happened to him in recent years, he's surprisingly sane. I've seen dudes with one record go absolutely nuts. You've got to have a strong center to handle it, and I think Michael has that.

In commenting on Michael's private zoo, Jones replied:

That's not so bizarre. It could be cocaine. But I'm not crazy about it when Michael brings the python to the studio. The reason Michael loves animals and children is he likes the idea of the truth involved with them. He trusts children more than adults.

Jones told *Rolling Stone* magazine:

I'd rather have a kid who's talking about the Elephant man's bones than with a pound of cocaine. Anyday. Send me the bones. Oxygen tank too. I wish he were my little brother.

Michael himself even responded to a story claiming he had had several cosmetic surgeries done on his face. The news magazine program, *20/20* did a story on plastic surgery, calling Michael Jackson a "plastic surgery addict". Unsatisfied and angry with the story, Michael later phoned one of the programs hosts, Barbara Walters. He told her of his change in diet over the last several years, that he had became a vegetarian and this change in diet contributed to the change in his appearance. Michael now only eats healthy foods, primarily fruits and vegetables. Snacks are natural foods such as raisins and nuts, or popcorn, one of his favorites. This diet has produced a pronounced changed in his build and facial appearance. He told Walters he had his nose and chin cosmetically altered and *nothing* else. He also explained many of the conclusions that he has had several alterations to his face are based on comparisons of photos of him when he was very young to photos of him now.

He actually eats very little, leaving his mother to wonder at times what keeps him alive. He is just under six feet tall, approximately 5'10", and weighs approximately 125 pounds. It was reported that by the end of the Bad tour he had dropped ten pounds. (Frank Dileo, who obviously deals with the pressures of the road in quite a different manner, gained forty pounds.) The food he eats, while simple, is prepared for him very decoratively, with different colors and shapes. On Sundays, he eats even less than usual, fasting the entire day, taking in only water and fruit juices. And he dances. He dances until exhaustion.

David Robert Cellitti, a sculptor, created a wax figure of Michael for the Movieland Wax Museum in Buena Park, California. Cellitti, who took several photographs and measurements of Michael for the creation of the wax likeness, commented on his so-called extensive plastic surgery, "They make it sound like it's a total Frankenstein rework sometimes, but it really has been minor surgery comparatively, very well done and very effective, too."

Cosmetic alterations to Michael's face, for some reason, have always received a lot of attention. Michael's chin and nose jobs are unexplainably very interesting, or considered very weird, while the nose jobs of other celebrities, and even other Jacksons have gone relatively unnoticed.

Michael's so-called eccentricities were becoming the subject of an increasing number of press reports and rumors. However, his talent always prevailed over whatever wild story was currently circulating about him. In a not so flattering cover story on Michael Jackson focusing primarily on his eccentricities, *Rolling Stone* conceded, "Whatever can be said about him, Michael Jackson sings with a shimmery soulful voice and dances like a swirling comet, as an entertainer he has no peer."

Many of these wild stories spread about Michael were based only on a fragment of truth. In some cases the initial seed may have been planted by Michael himself, as with the hyperbaric chamber and possibly the shrine to Elizabeth Taylor in his home. While the stories of the sleeping chamber and the elephant man's bones may have gotten out of control, Michael realizes the value of such publicity and has become a master at creating and maintaining the public's interest and curiosity.

Some of the other stories, and lies, were simply made up to sell more newspapers. Michael generally refuses to talk to the press, so stories are made up and rumors are exaggerated to help increase circulation. Michael's decision to rarely, if ever, talk with the press seems to based on several factors. After having numerous lies and half-truths printed about him throughout most of his life, Michael grew to greatly distrust the press. He hates to be misquoted, or have his words taken out of context, distorting his comments.

He also wishes to maintain a level of privacy in his life. He has rarely discussed anything of his personal life with interviewers. Interviews he has consented to have focused on his career and future plans and goals.

Michael's extreme shyness makes it almost unbearable for him to talk with reporters. Around people he knows and is comfortable with, Michael relaxes and is somewhat of a prankster. In large crowds, especially with people he doesn't know well, he is painfully shy and uncomfortable, an almost different person from the Michael Jackson seen in videos or in concert performances. When Silvya Chase interviewed Michael in 1980 for the TV news program *20/20,* Michael talked about his intense shyness. "Being around everyday people and stuff, I feel strange, I do. That's something I work on. A lot of my family's like that." Silvya Chase asked Michael, "There are some people who feel that having always been on stage, you've never had to deal with the real world." "Yeah, that's true in one way. That's true in *one* way. But it's hard to in my position. I try to sometimes, but people won't deal with me in that way because they see me differently. They won't talk to me like they will a next door neighbor. So, it becomes difficult."

Before pasting a "weird" or "eccentric" label on Michael Jackson, consideration must be given to the circumstances under which he grew up. Michael has been a performer for nearly his entire life. He cannot remember a time when he wasn't performing. His brothers were a little older when the Jackson 5 first became successful. They can remember, with the possible exception of Marlon who is barely a year older than Michael, the quieter, more "normal" periods of their lives. Michael cannot. He grew up being constantly sought after by fans and the press to a much greater degree than his brothers experienced. In one of his last interviews, in 1983, Michael told *Rolling Stone's* Geri Hershey, "Being mobbed *hurts.* You feel like you're spaghetti among thousands of hands. They're just ripping and pulling your hair. And you feel that any moment you're just gonna break." Michael's early memories aren't of classroom buddies and schoolyard playgrounds, but of private tutoring sessions between concert dates, late-night rehearsals and recording sessions.

Actually, considering how much of his life has been spent in the music business, being forced to grow up much too quickly, Michael is astonishingly sane and normal. He missed out on nearly all of the childhood activities others take for granted. So, when he later indulges himself with his own zoo, video arcade, or whatever he wants, others are much too quick to single him out as being weird.

Probably the strongest center in Michael's life isn't being caught up in being the world's greatest entertainer, but his belief in God. Michael believes his talent truly comes from God and that he is merely a carrier bringing the music to earth. Michael's mother, Katherine, is a devout Jehovah's Witness. Only two of the Jackson children were baptized as Jehovah Witness', Rebbie and Michael. Michael would even participate in selling the Witness' religious magazine, the *Watchtower,* door to door. While he was on top of the music charts with *Thriller*, some were slamming doors in his face, failing to recognize him. While the Jackson 5, and later Michael on his own, became worldwide superstars, Michael maintained his strong belief in God.

Michael's religious convictions have helped him to maintain a strong moral character throughout his life and career. He has continually avoided the typical pop star lifestyle. He has never experimented with drugs; holding a strong dislike for all drugs, both prescription and illicit drugs. He rarely drinks alcohol and has a similar distaste for alcohol abuse.

The Jehovah Witness faith dictates an objection to premarital sex, which reportedly Michael also follows. His love life is probably the area of Michael's personal life about which the least is known. Besides Diana Ross, with whom Michael shares a unique and at one time very close relationship, his first love was admittedly Tatum O'Neal. The only other romance that is widely known is that with Brooke Shields. In *Moonwalk*, Michael allows only that he and Brooke were romantically "serious" for a while. How serious "serious" is is anybody's guess. Which is probably exactly the way Michael wanted it. However, Brooke has stated since that she is still a virgin.

Later, reports appeared linking Michael romantically with Karen Faye, a makeup artist he met while working on *Captain EO*. While these reports have never been confirmed or denied, she was on the set of the "Bad" video, and her name appears among the credits of the *Bad* album, the Bad tour, and for *Moonwalker*.

In mid 1987, Michael left the Jehovah Witnesses. It was a shocking and unexpected departure. But Michael did chose to leave the church, he wasn't asked to leave as many papers reported. William Van De Wall, a spokesman of the Brooklyn headquarters of Jehovah Witnesses, told *Ebony* magazine, "He took the initiative. We didn't take any action. We were informed his wishes." Also, there is no truth to the stories that followed, that Michael's mother, who remained with the church, could no longer speak to her son because of his choice to leave the church. In guarding his privacy, Michael has never expressed his reasons for leaving the Witnesses. It does seem reasonable to assume, however, that disagreements with the elders over the "Thriller" video and similar disagreements over his career contributed to the split.

Although he no longer officially belongs to the Jehovah Witnesses, Michael still holds onto his strong personal convictions. He maintains his strong moral standards, his greatest loves off stage being children and animals. He has become friends with both of his co-stars from each of his Pepsi commercials, Alfonso Rieberto and Jimmy Safechuck. Other friends of Michael's are child stars, such as Emmanuel Lewis and Sean Lennon, the son of

John Lennon. Michael also grew fond of Ryan White, a young student who was driven from his school when it was learned he had AIDS, contracted from a blood transfusion. During one phone conversation with Michael, Ryan mentioned one of his favorite cars was a Mustang. So, it was no mystery later as to who had anonymously purchased a bright shiny red Mustang for Ryan. Especially when Ryan's mother received a call from one of Michael's representatives asking, "What kind of car did Ryan tell Michael he liked?" Ryan and his mother had also been invited to spend weekends at Michael's ranch.

Many of Michael's other friends are fellow performers. His closest friends seem to be entertainers who, like Michael, have been in the entertainment industry for many years and who have also grown up in the spotlight. They are also predominately female. Michael shares close friendships with Elizabeth Taylor, Liza Minnelli, Jane Fonda, and Sophia Loren.

As well as working with Michael, Frank Dileo and Quincy Jones had both formed close relationships with Michael. Jones' nickname for Michael is "Smelly". Different explanations have been given as to how he got the nickname. Michael doesn't use profanity and supposedly doesn't even use the word "funky", preferring instead to use "smelly", even though he included the word "funky" in the lyrics of "Beat It". ("Show them how smelly and strong is your fight" must not have sounded quite right.) Somehow, the nickname stuck. The other version of how he inherited the nickname is in what Quincy Jones refers to as Michael's ability to smell out a hit song.

The December 9, 1989, issue of *Billboard* commemorated Quincy Jones' forty years in the music business. Included in the magazine's special section devoted solely to Jones was an extended interview with Jones and several congratulatory ads placed by his many friends and contemporaries. The first congratulations were from Michael Jackson. A black and white drawing of Michael with a fedora and glove was accompanied by the words, "Q, Congratulations - Michael Jackson".

Other of Michael's friends are performers he has admired for most of his life and strived to match their level of talent and showmanship. The performers Michael watched when he was growing up and who inspired him include James Brown, Jackie Wilson, Fred Astaire, Sammy Davis Jr., Smokey Robinson, and of course, Diana Ross. While Michael sees these entertainers as the best, they are in turn impressed with Michael's talents and strive to match his accomplishments.

A long time favorite movie star and dance idol of Michael's is Fred Astaire. Sarah Giles put together a collection of remembrances about Fred Astaire from his friends in a book entitled, *Fred Astaire: His Friends Talk*. Michael was one of the many people contributing his thoughts and feelings about Fred Astaire:

I could only repeat what has been said and written about Fred Astaire's perfectionism and enormous, one-of-a-kind artistry. What I can reflect on is the inspiration he afforded me personally, being privileged as I was to see him work his magic. Nobody could duplicate Mr. Astaire's ability, but what I never stop trying to emulate is his total discipline, his absolute dedication to every aspect of his art. He rehearsed, rehearsed, and rehearsed some more, until he got it just the way he wanted it. It was Fred Astaire's work ethic that few people ever discussed and even fewer could ever hope to equal.

Michael, it seems is one of the few who can equal Astaire's dedication and enormous talent and ability. Many have compared Michael Jackson's dancing talent to that of Fred Astaire's and consider Michael today's Fred Astaire, a compliment that must have pleased and flattered them both. Sandy Duncan expressed her thoughts in the special Michael dedicated *People Extra:*

Fred Astaire was to that era and that music, the way the music moved through him in the '30's, what Michael Jackson is to this era. You could put him behind a scrim and see his silhouette and you'd know who he was. It's like he's got a direct connection to God, because those moves just come from within him and through the music.

Terrence Trent D'Arby admired the Jackson Five when he was a child, and still today considers "I Want You Back" the greatest debut record ever. He too compared Michael Jackson to Fred Astaire: "In my opinion, Michael Jackson is my generation's Fred Astaire, and if Fred Astaire wasn't a genius, I don't know what word you would apply to him."

Another admirer of Michael's dancing style was Fred Astaire himself. Astaire told *People Extra:* "My Lord, he's a wonderful mover. He makes these moves up himself and it's just great to watch. Michael is a dedicated artist. He dreams and thinks of it all the time."

There was mutual admiration between Michael and Sammy Davis Jr. as well. Davis told *People Extra:*

He takes a step that you've been doing and then by the time he switches it around, you don't even recognize it. There is nothing new about thrusting your hips out, but when he does that with quick moves, the high kick out and that slow back-up step he does, people say, 'Jeez, what is he doing?' And he never lays on a move long enough for you to figure it out. I'm sure if he worked with Nureyev or Baryshnikov, he would come close to that level. Can he tap dance? I don't know. But then again I'd hate to leave my dancing shoes in his vicinity.

In Sammy Davis Jr.'s autobiography, *Why Me?*, Michael Jackson's and Sammy Davis Jr.'s respect for each other's talent is further evident. Among several quotes from various entertainers about Davis is one admiring him for his perfectionism: "Sammy Davis exemplifies the ultimate in showmanship. He personifies perfection and has he influenced my performances from the very

inception of my career. - Michael Jackson." Included in the book
is a picture of Davis and Jackson. Under the picture Davis wrote:

> *Michael used to come by my house-'Can I borrow some of*
> *your tapes, Mr. D.?' And he'd go to my library and take what he*
> *wanted of the shows I'd done. Visiting me in Monte Carlo in July*
> *of '88, he said, 'Y'know, I stole some moves from you, the*
> *attitudes. 'I'd known that. It's terribly flattering for the young to*
> *feel that way about you. Especially Michael, who I think is the*
> *ultimate professional. A lot of young performers have become*
> *multimillionaires on ten big records, but they don't know how to*
> *bow and get themselves off a stage. Everything Michael does on*
> *a stage, though, is exactly right.*

Smokey Robinson was an idol of Michael's before the
Jackson Five signed with Motown. Michael recalls in *Moonwalk*
the first time he met Smokey Robinson. He describes vividly how
it felt to meet one of his idols and shake his hand. Robinson is
also impressed with Michael's career. In his autobiography, *Inside
My Life,* Smokey Robinson stated, "I could ego-trip about my big
concert dates, but all I have to do is look over at Michael
Jackson's tour to put myself back in line."

The person who had the most profound influence on
Michael and his career is probably Diana Ross. But she too
longed to match some of the tremendous accomplishments Michael
had enjoyed throughout his career. In 1989, while working on
Workin' Overtime, her first album for Motown after returning to
the label, she questioned any influence she has had on Michael's
career and stated she wanted to take after him and sell records like
Michael Jackson. Her "Workin' Overtime" tour opened to the
strains of Michael's "Dirty Diana".

Another person keeping careful tract of Michael's accomplishments is Sir Georg Solti, the Chicago Symphony Conductor
who holds the world record for winning the most Grammys ever.
Solti told *People Extra:* "I am a vain creature. Tremendously

vain. My Grammys mean a lot to me. I have all 23 in my studio. There are so many now that it looks like some sort of contemporary sculpture collection. And I don't like [my record] being threatened by this Mr. Michael Jackson!"

Michael's other great passion is animals. He loves virtually all kinds of animals and has quite a large private zoo. Prince and Princess are two of his deer. Michael aided in the delivery of their son, Valentino, born on Valentines Day in 1985. Michael had the birth videotaped. Louie is a llama purchased from a circus, who can do tricks like walking on his knees. Thriller is a stallion, and Mr. Tibbs is a sheep who often times is mistaken for a ram. There are two swans, a white one and a black one, and several exotic birds including macaws, cockatoos, and a giant rhea.

Michael's love of animals even extends to snakes. He feels they are very misunderstood, and that they are actually very sweet. Evidently, not everyone in the Jackson household feels the same way. When one of his pythons got loose in the house, they all left for a day until it could be found. Nobody would sleep in the house even with a lovable twenty foot python missing. Although he has kept several snakes, the best known is his boa constrictor, Muscles, the inspiration for the single Michael wrote and produced for Diana Ross. During an interview for *Rolling Stone*, Michael told Gerri Hershey that Muscles was trained to eat interviewers! Muscles died in June, 1986. Mike's new buddy is an eighteen foot, three hundred pound python, named appropriately enough, Crusher. Another snake was returned to the pet store when it attacked and ate one of his birds.

Michael also keeps lovable, sweet, misunderstood tarantulas. And he loves to know if someone is afraid of them. If he knows someone is afraid of the spiders or snakes, he'll make sure they are around. Poor Frank Dileo has been the subject of many of Michael's pranks. Knowing Frank is terrified of spiders and snakes, Michael would hold his hand out to Frank saying, "Here hold this," and put a tarantula in his hand! Michael loved to torment LaToya too, putting fake rats and insects around her room, then watching for her reaction. LaToya would get even by putting buckets of water over the doorway of Michael's room, soaking him the instant he stepped in the room.

One pet that caused problems for Michael with his Encino neighbors was his giraffe, Jabbar. The neighbors complained of the smell from the giraffe's pen. Michael had had the giraffe shipped to California from a Missouri breeder, and he applied for a state permit from the Fish and Game Commission to keep the giraffe. Jabbar has since become a movie star, appearing in Pee Wee Herman's *Big Top Pee Wee*. Michael gave Herman permission to use any of his animals he wanted to in his film after agreeing to follow all instructions for their caring. Jabbar got a playmate in June, 1989, named Mahali. Michael purchased the second giraffe from the Sedgwick County Zoo in Wichita, Kansas, for $15,000.

The most popular of Michael's zoo is of course his chimp, Bubbles. In 1985, Michael saved Bubbles from a cancer research center in Texas. Since, Bubbles seems to be one of Michael's favorite companions. Bubbles accompanied Michael on his solo tour in Japan, has been featured in magazine articles (although I don't think he gives interviews either), and he has appeared on TV talk shows. With the help of trainer Bob Dunn, with whom Bubbles sometimes lived, Bubbles has been taught several tricks. Besides going to the toilet and flushing it himself, he kisses pictures of himself, plays dead, blows bubbles, moves his lips like he's talking, and will hold his finger up to someone else's just like E.T., one of his dad's favorite movies. Bubbles joins in pillow fights, sticks his tongue out, gives the high five, rides a horse, and rollerskates. His most impressive trick of all has to be his own special version of his dad's famous moonwalk. Like Jabbar, Bubbles is also a movie star, appearing briefly in Rodney Dangerfield's *Back to School*. Michael has even gotten Bubbles his own agent to help with his budding acting career.

Besides being Michael's most famous pet, he is probably the most pampered as well. Some stories reported that Bubbles has his own room in Michael's house, others report he sleeps in a crib in Michael's room. The best guess is that Bubbles probably sleeps where ever he wants to. Mike and Bubbles did not bunk together while in Japan, however. Bubbles had his own hotel room, which Michael asked to have re-wallpapered because Bubbles is sensitive to cigarette smoke. Bubbles has an entire wardrobe of his own, including designer clothes.

In January, 1990, the rumor mills began reporting that Michael's beloved chimp had died. In response to all of the inquiries as to the well being of the chimp, Michael's publicist, Lee Solters, made a public statement that Bubbles was indeed alive and well.

Another pet Michael had a hand in rescuing was Ivan, a gorilla. Ivan spent twenty five of his twenty eight years in a cage at Tacoma, Washington's B&I shopping mall. A television documentary stirred the public's awareness of the apes situation, after which several zoos offered to house the gorilla. The offer given the most consideration was for the ape to live on Michael's Neverland Valley ranch.

A later addition to the Jackson zoo was a baby lion, who first went to a trainer before joining his fellow zoo mates. Most of Michael's animals are harmless, having been declawed and no longer having any venom.

Besides children and animals Michael loves movies, and cartoons. Among his favorite movies are *E.T.: The Extra Terrestrial,* and *The Elephant Man.* Disney classics and Bugs Bunny are among his favorite cartoons, making up most of his extensive cartoon collection. Other favorites of Michael's are the Three Stooges and Charlie Chaplin.

In 1985, Joan Howard Maurer, daughter of Stooge Moe Howard, wrote a biography of her uncle, *Curly.* She asked one of Curly's, and the Stooges', biggest fans to write the book's forward, Michael Jackson:

My memories of the Three Stooges, and especially Curly, are still with me to this day. In my childhood, around our house in Indiana, it was a daily ritual for me to watch the Three Stooges on television. All my brothers loved them then and even more so now. Chaplin and the Stooges are the greatest to me - their humor survives each generation. Even my mother loved to see us have fun watching them. Rehearsing as a team and watching the Stooges were the only times we got together as a whole family.

The Stooges' craziness helped me to relax and to escape life's burdens. They influenced me so much that I even wrote a song about them.

Curly was definitely my favorite Stooge. He was unquestionably a comic genius who understood ad-libbing better than anyone. I loved the Stooges' slapstick action and especially Curly's funny noises and his silly, child-like mannerisms and attitudes. He should be honored much more than what has been done for him in the past, for everyone loves him.

As a kid, I imitated Curly all the time, and I enjoyed feeling superior to and smarter than those three silly grownups. I owe so much to them that I feel they belong to me. That's why I had to write the Foreword for this book.

Joan, the author, asked me whether I thought that Curly had suffered when he had to shave off his wavy head of hair in order to become a Stooge. My answer was that I was sure he did, that underneath the smile may have been a tear - after all, he was a clown. But it is our duty as entertainers to satisfy the people - to give of our souls even if it hurts.

Curly had a magic. He was God-gifted - a natural. Even when he didn't intend to be funny he was magic.

Today, thirty-three years after his death, Curly still has legions of fans because he was a natural. Such people appeal to the masses young and old - like the color blue.

I love everything about Curly and I would give anything to really know what he was like.

*Thanks to the author, this book will clear up much of the
mystery of Curly for me and his millions of devoted fans.*
- Michael Jackson

This one page foreword appears in the book opposite full
page photo of Michael's dressing table from the Victory tour that
appeared in the *People Extra*. Among the carefully arranged items
on the table is a snapshot of the Three Stooges.

Michael paid tribute to his other comic hero, Charlie
Chaplin, on the comedian's birthday in 1983. Several photos of
Michael and Samir Kamoun have been published with them each
dressed as Charlie Chaplin.

In addition to collecting cartoons and watching old Three
Stooges reruns, Michael's other hobbies include reading and art.
Michael is an avid reader. He has read virtually everything
available on John Merrick and Walt Disney. His favorite book,
however, is *Peter Pan*. It has been reported repeatedly that
Michael would play the little boy who refused to grow up in a
movie of Peter Pan, but as of yet, nothing has come of it.

While growing up, Michael gained an appreciation of art,
thanks in part to Diana Ross. Michael is quite a talented artist in
his own right and has enjoyed drawing since he was very young.
He has said that he still wishes to complete a painting that he is
happy with.

Of course Michael's main love is his music and performing. And nobody has greater expectations or sets higher goals for
him than Michael himself. Before *Thriller* was released, Michael
told LaToya that it would become the biggest selling album of all
time. While working on *Bad*, Michael's goal was to sell 100
million copies. It was reported that he had a note to himself on
his bathroom mirror reading simply, "100,000,000", to remind
him of his goal. While in Japan for the start of the Bad tour,
Michael was seen wearing a diamond pin also reading,
"100,000,000".

Michael is a perfectionist in everything he does, especially in his work. He will practice a small dance step until it becomes second nature. He refuses to settle for less than perfection in his dancing as well as his recording. He's very interested in taking an idea as far as possible and creating something new and different, being a leader in his field rather than a follower. This goal has been achieved and surpassed many times over throughout his career. In a 1979 interview Michael revealed, "I'm interested in making a path instead of following a trail and that's what I want to do in life - in everything I do." Michael has also said, "I love to create magic, to put something together that's so unusual, so unexpected that it blows peoples heads off. Something ahead of what people are thinking. So people can see it and say, 'Whoa! I wasn't expecting that.'"

His greatest joy comes from performing and bringing happiness to his fans. Michael told *Ebony* magazine, "My main love for what I do is the fans. I love the fans. When I'm out there doing a show and I see the fans there dancing and screaming, excited, and we're bringing that joy to them, that's what I love the most. And it's the greatest feeling in the world."

Michael was about to bring that kind of joy to his fans once again as he released an arsenal of songs, videos, and performances to continue to show his fans who's bad.

CHAPTER TEN

WHO'S BAD

The follow up album to *Thriller* was originally scheduled for release in the spring of 1986. There were delays and this date was pushed back to the middle of summer. Then fall. Then it was announced the album would be out before Christmas or early 1987. Christmas and the new year came and went with no new Michael Jackson album. May 1, 1987 was the next date given, one year later than the original date announced. It wasn't out then either.

There were a variety of reasons given for the delays. Some sources speculated Michael was waiting for his sister Janet's *Control* album to peak before releasing his own album, so as not to hinder her success. Others suggested a much more selfish motive, that Michael wanted to be the only Jackson on the charts. Still others focused on the insurmountable pressure they imagined Michael was facing to top *Thriller*. They suggested that Michael didn't want to release its follow up album, demanding that songs be re-recorded several times with the final cut being no different than earlier takes.

More realistic reasons for the delays, besides Michael's unrelenting perfectionism, is the amount of time that Michael had to take off from recording to complete other projects. In November, 1986, Michael took time out from recording to film the album's first video, "Bad". He took another break in February to shoot the video for "Smooth Criminal".

Whatever the actual reasons were for the delays, it certainly wasn't due to a lack of material. Michael had written over sixty songs from which to choose the ones to finally make it on the album. He recorded dozens of songs in his home studio, including a cover of the Beatles' "Come Together", one of his favorite Beatle songs. More of Michael's own compositions were included on the new album than were included on either of his earlier solo albums. Three songs on *Off The Wall* were written by Michael and four of *Thriller's* nine songs were penned by Michael. Having his own compositions become the biggest hits from these earlier albums seemed to increase his confidence in his own songwriting talents. Eight of the ten songs on the new album would be written by Michael. He most often writes on electric drum, though he also plays guitar and keyboards.

While recording Michael turned out the lights in the studio and almost always danced. A wooden stage was built into Studio D of Westlake Audio Studios in Los Angeles where Michael was recording the album. He would also dance during classes with his vocal coach, Seth Riggs. He would try to convince Michael not to use so much energy, but Michael insisted on dancing during vocal exercises.

Those Michael worked with in the studio commented on his incredible talent in recording. Keyboardist Steve Porcaro, who plays on the album, said, "Michael has strong melodic ideas and can come up with things I'd never think up in a million years." Quincy Jones added, "He has, even more important than playing an instrument, a concept of the colors of music, of rhythmic, percussive sounds and secondary melodic instruments. He hears it in his head and hums the line."

In July, 1987, the first single was finally released. "I Just Can't Stop Loving You", a duet with Siedah Garrett, was the public's first taste of what was to come with the new album. A New York radio station jumped the single's release date, playing the song two days early, prompting legal action against the station. Without a video to promote it, the single went to number one on both the pop and black singles charts. The week of September 19, 1987, "I Just Can't Stop Loving You" knocked one of the Summer's biggest hits, "La Bamba" by Los Lobos, out of the number one spot on *Billboard's* Hot 100. It held the top spot for one week.

A special edition twelve inch single of "I Just Can't Stop Loving You" was released in Spanish with the translation by Ruben Blades. The B-side was the English version of the song. Because there was only a limited number of the singles made, they are now a much sought after prize of Michael Jackson fans.

"I Just Can't Stop Loving You" was chosen as the album's first single from its very inception. Originally, however, it was intended as a duet with Michael and an established female singer. Barbra Streisand was asked and she refused. She didn't like the song. Whitney Houston was also asked. She had to turn the project down because of scheduling conflicts.

Meanwhile, Quincy Jones had come up with another song for the album, "Man in the Mirror", written by Glen Ballard and Siedah Garrett. Siedah Garrett met Michael in the studio when she was adding background vocals to "Man in the Mirror". He was impressed with her voice and decided to do the duet with her. In fact, their voices blend together so well it is sometimes difficult to distinguish between their voices. When Siedah sings her lines, it is difficult to tell which of them it is, when Michael joins in, there is no doubt.

There is a spoken introduction to the song by Michael. It appears on the album and the CD but was not included on the cassette tape, and most often was not played with the song on the radio. Michael wrote the introduction with Quincy Jones, and speaks it in a very soft voice:

> *I just want to lay next to you for a while*
> *you look so beautiful tonight*
> *Your eyes are so lovely*
> *Your mouth is so sweet*
> *A lot of people misunderstand me*
> *That's because they don't know me at all*
> *I just want to touch you*
> *And hold you*
> *God I need you*
> *I love you so much*

During recording sessions, Siedah told one interviewer, Michael would get playful. While Siedah was trying to be very serious and put a lot of emotion into her lines, Michael would make faces and throw raisins and peanuts at her to make her laugh.

Siedah next recorded a solo album, *Kiss of Life,* with Quincy Jones as executive producer. Rod Temperton also worked on the album, writing several of the songs. Garrett later contributed to *Back on the Block,* Quincy Jones' first album in several years.

Twenty five CBS executives and representatives from the largest record chains in the country were guests at a dinner party held at Michael's Encino home on July 13. They were treated to a preview of the album and the "Bad" video. Michael, dressed as he is on the album's cover, was accompanied by LaToya and Bubbles. Michael and LaToya sat with Frank Dileo, John Branca, CBS Records Group president Walter Yetnikoff and CBS Records president, Al Teller. Dinner was prepared by celebrity chef Wolfgang Puck and included grilled salmon, veal chops, and ended with Crystal champagne. After dinner Michael posed for pictures with his guests.

Michael, at this time, had a close relationship with Yetnikoff. The CBS Records CEO's New York office was once described by *Rolling Stone:*

Pictures of CBS artists like Mick Jagger and Barbra Streisand decorate the wall over an immense stereo system. The wall behind his desk is practically a shrine to the label's biggest-selling artist, Michael Jackson: there are platinum records for **Thriller,** *a letter from Jackson thanking Yetnikoff for his help and an assortment of photographs of the singer.*

The much anticipated album finally hit record stores on August 31, 1987, and it was *Bad.* A television special aired on CBS that same evening, *Michael Jackson: The Magic Returns.* The thirty minute special began with clips of Michael from throughout his career. Footage from home movies of the Jacksons taken in 1963 performing at home in Gary and their audition tape made in 1968 for Motown were both included. Also showcased on the special was footage of the Jackson 5 performing on the *Ed*

Sullivan Show, and on the Victory tour. Seldom before seen clips of his videos for "Don't Stop 'Til You Get Enough" and "Rock With You" were shown with the videos everybody has seen for "Billie Jean", "Beat It", "Thriller", and his performance from *Motown 25.* Scenes from the Jackson Pepsi commercials, Grammy award shows, Michael's visit to the White House, and the "We Are The World" video concluded the short retrospective of his career. The special concluded with the premiere of the seventeen minute extended video for "Bad". A very short teaser ad was shown at the conclusion of the special for Michael's new solo Pepsi commercials with the ending line, "The Magic Continues..." And it did.

Thirty percent of the approximately 85 million TV households in the U.S. tuned in to see Michael Jackson's latest video effort, making it the sixth highest rated show for the week. The executive producers of the special were Michael Jackson and Frank Dileo.

The "Bad" video was filmed in Brooklyn, New York, at the Hoyt Schermerhorn subway station, and took six weeks to make. The New York Metropolitan Transit Authority was paid $100,000 as stations had to be closed for filming. Michael's insistence that scenes be re-shot until they were perfect helped drive up the cost of the video, but it definitely paid off.

The story for the video, written by Richard Price, was based on an actual incident. Edmund Perry was a student at a private school. He was a good student and planned on attending college. During winter break he returned home, to Harlem, where he was shot to death by his old friends he had left behind.

In the video, Michael plays Daryl, a kid from the ghetto, who attends a private school, away from his friends. The school shown in the video is Masters School, an all girl school in Dobbs Ferry. Daryl returns home on break and finds he doesn't fit in with his old friends anymore. His friends test his loyalty to the gang by having Daryl help mug an old man. Daryl doesn't go through with it and helps the man get away. Daryl's friends realize he has changed and kick him out of the gang, "You ain't down with us no more, you ain't down, you ain't bad!" Daryl yells back, "You ain't bad, you ain't nothin'. You ain't NOTHIN'!" Suddenly the scene changes to color, the action up to now being in black and white, and instead of worn jeans and a sweatshirt, Michael is now dressed entirely in black, with buckles lining his boots, pant leg, sleeves and fingerless gloves. Michael's character is not killed, instead, with a snap of his fingers, Daryl and his magically appearing backup dancers sing and dance eventually uniting the two opposing sides. Through his performance, Michael/Daryl convinces his friends that he is indeed bad, really, really bad:

> *Well they say the sky's the limit*
> *And to me that's really true*
> *But my friend you have seen nothin'*
> *Just wait 'til I get through...*

The black buckled outfit worn in the "Bad" video became a hot item. A greeting card was marketed with Garfield the cat costumed in a "Bad" outfit. A picture of Mickey Mouse in the same outfit, drawn by Michael, was contributed to a Mickey Mouse picture book. The actual outfit Michael wore was auctioned off for $30,000.

"Bad" was choreographed by Gregg Burge, Jeffrey Daniel, and Michael Jackson. Martin Scorcese was chosen to direct the video. Scorcese was suggested by Frank Dileo, and was eventually chosen over Michael's first choice, Steven Speilberg. It is Scorcese's photo on the WANTED poster that is ripped from the subway station wall. The executive producers of the "Bad" video were Michael Jackson, Frank Dileo, and Harry Ufland. Quincy Jones produced the video with Barbara DeFina, wife of Scorcese. Daryl's mother, whose voice is heard reading a note Daryl finds when he returns home, is Roberta Flack.

With the new album came a new look for Michael. He no longer wore the sequined military jackets and the single glove. Now he was seen in tough guy duds, all in black with rows and rows of buckles, forty six in all, and his hair was much longer. There was one other recent change, Michael had added a cleft to his chin.

The photo that appeared on the *Bad* album cover was the second choice. The original photograph was a close up shot of Michael's face with black lace superimposed over it. A very quick glimpse of this photo was shown in the TV special *Michael Jackson: The Magic Returns*. The photo is also included in a book of celebrity photographs by Greg Gorman and in Michael's second book, *Dancing the Dream*. Walter Yetnikoff objected to the picture being used as the album's cover. A photo by Sam Emerson, Michael's personal photographer, taken during a break in the filming of the "Bad" video was used in its place.

On the inside album sleeve is a picture, also by Sam Emerson, of Michael and Frank Dileo, with their silhouettes facing each other. Michael is tall and lean, wearing a hat with his hair pulled back in a ponytail. Frank cuts a shorter, rounder figure and has the ever present cigar in his mouth. The caption under the photo reads, "Another Great Team. Frank M. Dileo Management."

With the release of the new album came more Michael Jackson merchandise. There were new posters, buttons, keychains, picture discs, calendars, puzzles, cooler cups, and even wrapping paper and clothes hangers. The most unique, and most expensive, Michael Jackson collectable was a giant ceramic figurine by artist Jeff Koons. The sculpture is a larger than life size figure of Michael and Bubbles reclining in a field of flowers. Equally large was its price tag, $250,000.

Michael Jackson was among the celebrity puppets in the cast of *D.C. Follies,* a comedy show that poked fun at celebrities and politicians. Another puppet of Michael was among the puppet singers appearing in a video for Genesis' "Land of Confusion".

Michael Jackson impersonators also began to surface again. The most notable is a young man from Los Angeles, E. Casanova. Casanova has made himself look startling similar to Michael Jackson. He has duplicated Michael's costumes, hair and makeup, but even more impressive is Casanova's skill in duplicating Michael's moves. Casanova performs in full Jackson attire at a Las Vegas nightclub. He claims his likeness to Michael Jackson is the work of Mother Nature and not a plastic surgeon, unlike Valentino Johnson, another Michael Jackson impersonator, who has spent $40,000 on plastic surgery to look like Michael Jackson.

The *Bad* album was an instant smash. *Rolling Stone* gave the album a glowing review, declaring that Michael "proves that he can out funk anybody anytime." Another reviewer concluded, "The Bad news is, Michael J. has never sounded better." Immediately after the album's release, record dealers said that its first few days of sales surpassed all of their greatest expectations. By its third day out, Epic reorders of *Bad* had reached one half million copies. The preorders for *Bad,* at 2.25 million, were the largest ever in CBS Records history.

Bad entered *Billboard's* pop album charts in the number one spot and stayed there for six weeks. *Bad* debuted on the black album charts at number three, and on the British album charts at number one. Coincidentally, *Bad* kept Def Leppard's *Hysteria* album out of the number one spot, just as *Thriller* had done to Def Leppard's *Pyromania* album. Bad spent its first thirty eight weeks of release in *Billboard's* top five, breaking the record of twenty six weeks set by the Eagles with *Hotel California.*

Michael became only the fifth artist ever to debut at number one on the pop album charts. In the mid 70's, two artists accomplished this feat. Elton John debuted at number one with *Captain Fantasic and the Brown Dirt Cowboy,* and its follow up *Rock of the Westies* both in 1975. Stevie Wonder's *Songs in the Key of Life* debuted at number one in October, 1976. Bruce Springsteen's five album package *Bruce Springsteen and the E Street Band Live/1975-1985* debuted at number one in 1985.

Whitney Houston's *Whitney* debuted at number one just three months before the "Bad" one did in September, 1987.

Bad went quintuple platinum in Canada in just a few weeks. In the year end issue of *Billboard, Bad* was called the most eagerly anticipated album of the year. This instant success of *Bad* must have been a great gift for Michael, having been released just two days after his twenty ninth birthday. Even though he doesn't celebrate his birthday, it doesn't prevent him from accepting gifts. Quincy Jones gave him some sterling silver and a compact disc player.

The second single released off of the *Bad* album was the title track. It became the album's second number one single the week of October 24, 1987. "Bad" stayed at the top of the Hot 100 for two weeks. "Bad" also went to number one on the black singles chart. The extended version of the "Bad" video aired on MTV for weeks with the air times announced each day. Later, an edited version of the video was aired.

Colors, a movie dealing with gangs and gang violence, was in theaters around the same time Michael was riding high on the music charts with *Bad.* Many feared the movies' real life depiction of gang life in Los Angeles would promote violence and gangs. Rap artist, and former LA gang member, Ice T became the target of criticism for his performance of the movie's title song. Ice T responded to the criticisms launched at him by saying that Michael Jackson started it all first by showing that gangs are cool and macho in his videos for "Beat It" and "Bad", and that Jackson had a much larger influence. Ice T obviously doesn't understand what "Beat It" and "Bad" are about. They are both actually statements against gangs and violence. Bob Giraldi, director of the "Beat It" video, told *Record* magazine:

The whole beauty of "Beat It" is how it shows that the macho-trip is bullshit. I had peace come through in this magical creature named Michael Jackson. Obviously, if anybody ever analyzes it properly they will see that it's anti-violence, not pro-violence.

Following the release of *Bad,* Michael did his first interview in almost five years. He chose to do a televised interview on a syndicated program, *Ebony/Jet Showcase.* Michael appeared on the program wearing a red shirt and black leather jacket, and surprisingly, no sunglasses. He talked with one of the program's hosts, Darryl Dennard. After a brief review of Michael's career and the *Bad* album, Dennard asked:

"How does Michael feel now that this amazing album is finally out?"

"I feel rejuvenated kind of. Because after working on it so long, it's so much work. A lot of people, they're used to just seeing the outcome of work."

"How long did it take to come up with that creative process?"

"I don't remember. I totally don't remember. I don't even count the hours or anything. Every song is different. Sometimes it happens quickly, sometimes it happens slowly. No one can quite say what the creative process is. I have nothing to do with it almost. It's created in space, it's God's work, not mine."

"Through Michael's creative process may have a spiritual touch, the idea for the 'Bad' video was definitely man made."

"There's a true story that we had taken from Time or Newsweek magazine. This kid who went to school upstate, in the country, whatever, who is from the ghetto and he tried to make something of his life, and he would leave his old friends behind. And when he came back on spring break, or whatever, Thanksgiving break,

his friends became so envious, jealous of him, that they killed him. But in the film, I don't die of course."

"Michael's number one hit 'I Just Can't Stop Loving You' shot up the charts before the album was formally released. The song's romantic lyrics are highlighted by a sexy rap intro."

[Michael giggling] "I was in a bed when I was doing that, I was lying in bed, with a cover and everything, when I did that whole rap, in the dark."

"And the lyrics go, 'People really don't understand me.'"

"I say, 'A lot of people misunderstand me, that's because they don't really know me.' I guess that's true. People believe a lot of crazy stories they read, some is true, some is not."

"Does it hurt when you see those crazy stories?"

"Sometimes. But it's part of the work."

"Do you ever want to lash out in any type of way and say, 'Hey, that's not true'?"

"Yeah, a lot of times, but why bring more attention it, you know?"

*"The **Bad** album is Michael's most artistically ambitious work to date. He tried several different music styles with his personal favorite being a fast paced tune with a heavy metal/rock and roll beat."*

"I love 'Dirty Diana'. That's one of my favorites because it's the life story of a groupie. I hate to say the word 'groupie', but that's what it is. And it's something that I've experienced and a lot of

people who grew up on the road, like me, I don't remember not performing."

"Do you feel as though you've missed out on a lot by not remembering not performing?"

"Of course, but I've gained a lot too. A lot of people never get out of their home town and get to see other wonderful places. A lot of kids read about things that I get to see in person, all over the world. I'm so happy about that, I mean, you never can have everything."

"How does it feel when you go in to do a concert somewhere and literally there are tens of thousands of people rushing over to you just to get a glimpse?"

"That's a wonderful feeling, especially when you see them smiling. I love the fans. I think it's very sweet. I feel thankful, is how I feel. I really do. I don't take any of it for granted."

The interview concluded with:

"Of all the songs on the album, I think the one I enjoy the most is 'Man in the Mirror'".

"It's my philosophy too, if you want to make the world a better place, take a look at yourself and then make a change. I'm never totally satisfied. I always wish the world could be a better place. Hopefully, that's what I do with my music, bring happiness to people."

The next single from *Bad* was "The Way You Make Me Feel". It became the album's third consecutive number one single, replacing George Harrison's "Got My Mind Set On You" at the top of the pop singles chart the week of January 23, 1988, where it stayed for one week. The single spent four weeks at the top of the black singles chart. "The Way You Make Me Feel" became Michael's seventh number one solo single of the eighties. This broke a three way tie between himself, Madonna and Whitney Houston for the most number one hits in the eighties. Michael Jackson was now the most successful solo artist of the decade.

The video for "The Way You Make Me Feel" premiered on MTV on October 31, 1987. In it, Michael chases after a girl who continually runs away from him. He finally gets the girl at the end and they hug, to the great disappointment of the fans who wanted them to kiss. The hug was enough for Michael, however, who wanted to leave the rest to the viewer's imagination. When this last scene was shot, Michael asked that anyone not absolutely necessary for the filming to leave the set.

The video was directed by Joe Pytka and choreographed by Michael Jackson and Vince Patterson. LaToya makes her second cameo appearance in one of Michael's videos in "The Way You Make Me Feel".

Michael is dressed in short black pants and a blue shirt with a white t-shirt underneath. A white sash is tied around his waist. It was said that the sash was in honor of Fred Astaire who had worn a necktie around his waist in a film.

Michael's co-star for the video was Tatiana Thumbtzen. When she was first told of the role, she was told only that it was a video for a "mysterious artist", someone of Michael Jackson's or Prince's status. When she arrived for the audition "Beat It" was playing, only then did she know it was a video for Michael Jackson. The initial audition had several hundred girls, only four of which were later called back. Tatiana met Michael at this second call. As a guest on *Hour Magazine,* she recalled filming the video and getting her foot caught in the car's upholstery:

The moment where we broke the ice was when my foot got stuck in the car upholstery. Michael put his hand on my leg to try and help me and I thought I'd die. I thought 'Oh my God, he's

*actually touching me.' I got so excited and the director, Joe
Pytka, was screaming, 'Keep going, keep going', so I pulled away
and landed outside the car on my butt. My face was beet red,
Michael was cracking up and I gave in and started laughing too,
because it was quite funny. And as I got up he was wiping me off.
It was great!*

Host Gary Collins asked what it was about Michael that
turned her to jelly like that and she replied, "I don't know, it's
magic. It really is. Michael has a power that you just *feel* when
he's in a room". When Collins asked if Michael was "spacey",
Tatiana replied emphatically and without hesitation, "NO!, not at
all. He's very normal. He's the most beautiful person I've ever
met and I wish there were more like him, I really do". Asked if
she and Michael were dating, she gave a shy smile, lowered her
eyes and answered, "We're friends".

Tatiana has since been seen in magazine ads for Impulse
cologne and a television wine commercial. She also appeared in
the opening credits of TV's *A Different World.*

Another acquaintance of Michael's was also making
television talk show appearances. Comedian Kin Shriner had a
very special guest on one of his shows, Bubbles was his guest
host. Bubbles' trainer, Bob Dunn, appeared with Bubbles and
helped him perform some of his tricks, including the moonwalk.
Bubbles was dressed in red pants and a t-shirt with a picture of his
likeness from the Michael's Pets toy line.

Bad ended 1987 as the year's biggest selling album, even
though it was only out for three months of the eligible period.
Bad reached number one on the album charts in a record setting
twenty five countries throughout the world. It reached the top of
the charts in Argentina, Australia, Belguim, Brazil, Canada,
Denmark, England, France, Germany, Greece, Holland, Hong
Kong, Israel, Italy, Japan, New Zealand, Norway, Spain, Sweden,
Switzerland, and the United States.

Michael started off 1988 with some more good news. A judge had dropped a $150 million paternity suit that had been filed against him by Lavon Powlis, who calls herself Billie Jean Jackson. Powlis claims that Michael fathered her three children. At least one of these children was supposedly conceived outside Michael's home in a blue Rolls Royce after he invited her to Los Angeles and they had a date in his car. Powlis claims this date was in May, 1975, making Michael sixteen years old at the time. Even though the paternity suit was dropped, she continued to harass Michael. A restraining order was placed against her, forcing her to stay 100 yards from his Encino home. She violated the order, was convicted, and in January, 1989, she was sentenced to two and one half years in jail. Michael Jackson is not the only celebrity she has claimed to be the father of her children.

Michael is not the only Jackson to be the target of stalkers. In June, 1992, a man was arrested outside the family's Encino estate for stalking Janet. He claimed he was Janet's husband. It was later discovered he had written Janet over forty letters threatening her, her boyfriend, Michael, and President Bush. At this time the earlier charges of trespassing and stalking were dropped when federal prosecutors took over the case.

Also with the close of 1987 came more awards and honors. Michael was honored at the British Phonographic Industry Awards as the Best International solo artist of 1987. The "Brits" are Britain's equivalent to the Grammys. Michael accepted his award via satelite from Los Angeles. He was dressed in the same costume he wore in the "Bad" video with taped fingertips and sunglasses. He said only, "I love you all. Thank you very much."

Sweden also honored Michael. In a poll conducted by one of Sweden's largest newspapers, *Aftonbladet,* Michael Jackson was voted as the Best Vocal Artist of 1987.

At the 1988 Winter Olympics, in Calgary, Canada, Michael Jackson's international appeal was once again illustrated. At the closing ceremonies, German gold medalist figure skater Katarina

Witt donned a black leather jacket and fingerless gloves and skated to "Bad". Her performance even included an ice skating version of the moonwalk.

In July, 1989, France celebrated their bicentennial. As part of the celebration, a parade was held which featured representations from several different countries. A snow machine was used to symbolize Russia's winters, and a rainmaker was used to represent Scotland. Representing the United States was a performance by the Florida A&M Marching Band imitating Michael Jackson.

In the U.S., *Billboard's* year end charts named Michael Jackson the ninth Top Hot Crossover Artist of 1987. The number eight position was held by Janet Jackson.

In January, 1988, MTV aired a Michael Jackson special, *From Motown To Your Town*. Film footage spanned Michael's career from the early days of the Jackson Five to Bad tour dates in Japan and Australia. Scenes of the Jackson Five performing "I Want You Back" at the very beginnings of their careers are blended into scenes of Michael performing the same song on his Bad tour. A peek backstage has the band, dancers, singers, Frank Dileo, and Michael gathered in Michael's dressing room for a prayer and group holler before hitting the stage.

Michael's travels around Japan, China, and Hong Kong are shown with visits with elementary school children, and of course, the many thousands of fans at each airport, hotel, and stadium.

Bubbles accompanied Michael to City Hall in Osaka, Japan, where Michael was presented with the key to the city. Bubbles was seated next to Michael, banging his hands on the table in front of them. Amid a sea of flash bulbs, Michael sipped from a small tea cup then held the cup for Bubbles to take a drink.

A short clip of Fred Astaire dancing in a black tuxedo and top hat is shown with a clip of Michael dressed in white tails and top hat performing a very similar dance segment from the Jackson's 1976 TV show. The special ended with Michael's performance of "Shake Your Body" in Japan and the narration,

"Michael Jackson, if it's never been done, he's the one who will do it."

This same month, the newest members were inducted into the Rock & Roll Hall of Fame. Among those being honored at this third annual induction ceremony was Motown founder Berry Gordy. In his acceptance speech, Gordy read a congratulatory telegram he had received earlier from a former Motowner: "Congratulations. You deserve it. You are the father of fine music. Love Always. Your son, Michael Jackson."

The fourth single off of *Bad* was one of two songs on the album not written by Michael. "Man in the Mirror", written by Siedah Garrett and Glen Ballard, is a song with a strong message about changing the world, and starting with yourself in making those changes:

> *I'm starting with the man in the mirror*
> *I'm asking him to change his ways*
> *And no message could get any clearer*
> *If you wanna make the world*
> *a better place*
> *Take a look at yourself and*
> *make a change*

The video for "Man in the Mirror" brings out the message of the song with a montage of film clips showing sad and unfortunate situations and those people who have made an effort to make a change and make the world a better place. Shots of starving children and homeless people are intermixed with shots of individuals who have made contributions toward helping them. Bob Geldoff, organizer of Band Aid and Live Aid for the relief of famine victims, and Willie Nelson, organizer of Farm Aid which benefitted farmers are included with shots of Ghandi, Sister Theresa, Dr. Martin Luther King, Bishop Tutu, and President Reagan with Soviet leader Mikhail Gorbachov. Sad events such as the assassinations of Martin Luther King, John F. Kennedy, and

John Lennon are all included with a more joyful occasion, the rescue of Jessica McClure from a well in Midland, Texas. There is only one brief shot of Michael in the video, standing among a crowd of people all wearing yellow hard hats. Michael is raising his arms giving the peace sign.

The "Man in the Mirror" video was Michael's concept. He told *Jet* magazine, "It was in Hong Kong that I called Frank and told him what I wanted to do. I wanted to show Martin Luther King, Mahatma Ghandi, Kennedy, opening with the starving child." Michael went on to say that his staff was "very helpful in compiling all this wonderful footage together, but they followed my vision on it. I wanted to touch people. [The video] makes you want to do something, which is the most important thing when you think of it."

A few critics had the nerve to criticize Michael for the "Man in the Mirror" video, charging that he was exploiting the unfortunate people that were shown in the video for his own purposes, to sell records and make money. The song has a very strong, positive message, the video only enhances that message and does exactly what Michael wanted it to do, it touches people. Michael accomplishes two objectives with the song and its video, he motivates others to make a change for the better, and he makes a real difference himself, with the donation of his royalties from the single to Camp Ronald McDonald for Good Times, a camp for children with cancer.

The week of March 26, 1988, the number one song on *Billboard's* Hot 100 was "Man in the Mirror", bringing the total of number one singles from the *Bad* album to four. It stayed at number one for two weeks. Michael became the first artist to ever have four number one singles from the same album. "Man in the Mirror" was also the album's fourth number one single on the black charts. These four solo hits and the Jackson Five's first four number one songs make Michael Jackson the only artist to ever have four consecutive number one singles as a solo artist as well as a member of a group.

With "Man in the Mirror" reaching the top of the charts, Michael also became the first artist to have four singles reach the top ten from three consecutive albums. Four singles from *Off The Wall* reached the top ten, seven singles from *Thriller* reached the top ten, and four singles thus far had reached the top of the charts from *Bad*.

To mark the special achievement of being the only artist to have four number one hits from one album, CBS Records congratulated Michael with an in *Billboard*. Appearing opposite the Hot 100 chart, the congratulatory ad featured a full page color photo of Michael and proclaimed:

> *IT'S NEVER BEEN*
> *THIS "BAD" BEFORE!*
> *UNTIL TODAY, NO ARTIST HAS EVER*
> *HAD FOUR NO. 1 SINGLES FROM THE*
> *SAME ALBUM.*
> *NOW MICHAEL JACKSON STANDS*
> *ALONE...AGAIN.*
> *"MAN IN THE MIRROR."*
> *THE FOURTH CONSECUTIVE NO. 1 HIT*
> *FROM "BAD."*
> *CONGRATULATIONS*
> *MICHAEL.*
> *FROM EVERYONE AT EPIC RECORDS*
> *AND THE CBS RECORDS SALES*
> *FORCE.*

In the same issue of *Billboard*, Michael was named the third most successful songwriter of the year. He had written three number one singles; "I Just Can't Stop Loving You", "Bad", and "The Way You Make Me Feel."

The video for the fifth single from *Bad* premiered on MTV on April 14, 1988. "Dirty Diana" was filmed in Long Beach, California, and is Michael's first performance video. Michael performs dressed in the black pants with buckles he wears in the "Bad" video, and a white shirt with long tails with a white t-shirt underneath. He has several black, studded, belts around his waist, and long the black fingerless gloves he also wears in the "Bad" video. White tape covers three fingertips on his right hand. Featured in the video is an appearance by Steve Stevens on guitar, who also plays on the record. Stevens is best known for his work with Billy Idol. The video opens with a shot of Stevens, dressed all in black, with long, spiked black hair.

While Michael performs, a pair of long legs in a very short skirt and high heels walk slowly from one car to another and gets inside. When Michael ends his performance of "Dirty Diana", about a girl who will "be your everything if you make me a star", he leaves the stage and heads for his waiting car. Opening the door, he finds that "Diana" is waiting for him in his car.

"Diana's" legs belong to model Lisa Dean. She was chosen over one hundred other girls, all of whom were auditioned and filmed. When Michael reviewed the film, he chose the first pair of legs that appeared on the screen, and Lisa Dean became "Dirty Diana". While Diana's legs belong to Lisa Dean, the brief shot of "Diana" at the end of the video looks very much like another cameo appearance by LaToya.

In June, 1988, U.S. sales of *Bad* exceeded six million copies. Of course this became another "first" for Michael. Michael Jackson became the only artist to have three consecutive albums with U.S. sales over six million copies each. To date, worldwide sales of *Off the Wall* are at eleven million, *Thriller* has sold at least 42 million copies, with some estimates as high as 50 million, and *Bad* has sales in excess of 28 million. *Bad* even sold well in China, were it is difficult to get albums released. In its first few weeks, *Bad* sold in excess of 250,000 copies, which is phenomenal considering the very limited market for records in China.

The number one pop song in America the week of July 2, 1988, was "Dirty Diana". Michael topped his own record set just a couple of months earlier with "Man in the Mirror", making him the first artist to ever have five number one singles from one album. Again, Epic congratulated Michael with a full page ad in *Billboard*. A full page color photo of Michael was accompanied with the words:

NO ONE'S EVER
BEEN THIS
BAD
Only one artist
has ever had five
No. 1 singles from
the same album.
CONGRATULATIONS
MICHAEL.

"Dirty Diana" spent one week at the top of the pop singles chart and peaked at number five on the black singles chart.

Michael also became the first artist to have five or more top ten hits from two consecutive albums. *Thriller* spawned seven top ten hits and "Dirty Diana" was the fifth top ten single from *Bad*.

"Dirty Diana" was Michael's ninth number one single of the 80's, and the fifteenth number one single of his career. Only six artists have had more, each one of the Fab Four, the King of Rock and Roll, and Diana Ross. Paul McCartney is the all time champ with twenty nine number one singles in his career, George Harrison has had twenty three number one hits, one more than John Lennon and Ringo Starr, each with twenty two. Elvis Presley and Diana Ross have each had eighteen number one hits.

Another single Michael had on *Billboard's* Hot 100 was "Get It", a duet with Stevie Wonder, that is included on Wonder's album, *Characters*. "Get It" received extremely little airplay on most pop radio stations and only went to number eighty on *Billboard's* pop singles chart. The single received much more airplay on black radio and peaked at number four on the black singles chart. The single's poor showing on the pop chart is not indicative of the song's quality. It is an uptempo tune with Michael and Stevie trading vocals on which one will eventually capture the heart of a girl they both have their sights set on. It is actually a better song than their duet, "Just Good Friends" from the *Bad* album. Each of their vocals were recorded separately. Stevie Wonder recorded his lines in the states, then had the tape sent to Michael, who was in Japan with the Bad tour, to record his vocals. Michael recorded another song with Stevie Wonder. "A Pretty Face" was not included on either of their albums, but may be released later.

On July 30, 1988, Michael had his own TV special. *Michael Jackson: Around the World* was a ninety minute special featuring concert footage of the Bad tour, with Michael, as usual, having final approval of the footage to be included. While the concert footage of the Bad tour was impressive, it still only gives a small taste of the excitement of seeing Michael Jackson perform live. Clips of Michael with his band, singers and dancers performing "Working Day and Night" gives only a small sense of the song's elaborate production. Footage is shown of Michael's concert performances of "I Just Can't Stop Loving You", "Human Nature", "Beat It", and the Jackson Five classics, "I Want You Back" and "The Love You Save".

Michael's band members speak of the excitement of playing London's Wembley Stadium. Frank Dileo adds, "Playing Wembley is one of the biggest honors any artist could have. It's a status symbol within artists themselves, whether or not they can sell out Wembley Stadium, and of course Michael set a new record. He sold it out seven times. You can't get any bigger than that."

The program also featured the premiere of Michael's latest video, for "Another Part of Me". Filmed at London's Wembley Stadium on July 15, 1988, the video is of an actual performance of the song from the Bad tour. Too frequent cuts, however, detract from Michael's fancy footwork performed during the song.

Michael Jackson: Around the World was the highest rated summer special ever in its time slot, it aired at 11:30 p.m. It earned a 8.7 rating, which is equal to twenty seven percent of the television audience. The program was later renamed *Michael Jackson: Fans Around the World* and rebroadcast on MTV several times. An edited, hour long, version was shown in April, 1989, on the Black Entertainment Television network. BET presented Michael with an award in recognition of the tour's success while he was winding up the tour in Los Angeles.

"Another Part of Me" peaked on *Billboard's* Hot 100 at number eleven. This broke a string of top ten hits for Michael seventeen songs long. The single, however, reached number one on the black singles chart, his fifth single from *Bad* to do so. This tied the record for the most singles from one album to reach number one on the black singles chart. He tied the record with Janet, her *Control* album also spawned five number one singles on the black chart.

"Another Part of Me" was Michael's ninth number one single on the black chart in his career, making him the artist with the most number one singles ever on the black chart. The number two spot is also held by a Jackson, but this one is not related to Michael. Freddie Jackson has had eight singles hit the number one spot on the black singles chart.

MTV premiered the video for Michael's seventh single off of *Bad* on October 13, 1988. The extended length, eight minute video for "Smooth Criminal" is one of Michael's most ambitious efforts to date, featuring one of his most impressive dance routines. It is taken from a mini-movie of "Smooth Criminal" to be found on his then upcoming movie, *Moonwalker*.

Michael is dressed in a white pinstripe suit, blue shirt, white tie and suspenders, spats, and a white fedora. He also wears a blue armband around his right arm and white tape on three fingertips of his right hand. These have been described as costume devices he uses to help get into his character. They give Michael that "on stage" feeling, very much like the single glove.

"Smooth Criminal" marks two interesting firsts for Michael. It's the first regular video, excluding the special live version of "Billie Jean" from the Victory tour, in which Michael performs his most recognizable step, the moonwalk. It's also the first time we see Michael actually dance with a partner, he had previously only danced around Ola Ray in "Thriller" and Tatiana Thumbtzen in "The Way You Make Me Feel". In "Smooth Criminal" Michael dances briefly with two of the ladies in the saloon. (It's also the first time we ever see Michael shoot anyone!)

In the video, Michael runs into a saloon the sight of which makes the others in the saloon prepare to draw their guns. Michael takes out a quarter and tosses it into the coin slot of a jukebox at the opposite side of the room. The music of "Smooth Criminal" begins and Michael dances, with some fighting techniques thrown in, and renders the criminals helpless. Michael then joins his dancers for one of the best displays ever of his incredible dancing ability. Gunmen surround the club, Michael magically acquires a machine gun, fires, and runs out of the club.

The choreography for "Smooth Criminal" was done by Michael Jackson and Vincent Paterson, who worked with Michael on the video for "The Way You Make Me Feel" and Jeffrey Daniel, who had worked on the "Bad" video.

"Smooth Criminal" became the sixth top ten single from *Bad,* peaking at number seven on the pop chart and at number two on the black chart. Only two albums had ever had six or more top ten singles, Bruce Springsteen's *Born in the USA* and Michael Jackson's *Thriller.* Since then, however, Janet has topped Michael and Bruce, with *Janet Jackson's Rhythm Nation 1814* becoming the first album to ever spawn seven top five hit singles.

In November, Michael was named as an honoree in the music category of the American Black Achievement Awards. *Ebony* magazine also named Michael Jackson as one of the twenty people to watch in 1989.

As the Bad tour finished up 1988 in Japan, several year end music charts were being compiled, with *Bad*, its singles and videos, and Michael himself doing very well on all of them. Those considered here are charts compiled by *Rolling Stone*, MTV's top 100 Videos of 1988, and *Billboard* magazine. On the year end chart ranking the years best albums, *Rolling Stone* named *Bad* the number seven album of the year.

Michael was the artist with the most videos making MTV's Top 100 Videos of 1988. All five videos he released during the year made the top 100. "Another Part of Me" placed lowest on the top 100. His current release, "Smooth Criminal" which had yet to peak on the network's weekly countdown, finished the year at number sixty. "The Way You Make Me Feel" was number thirty six for the year. Number nineteen belonged to Michael's second highest entry, "Dirty Diana". Michael's highest entry on the Top 100 was "Man in the Mirror", at number five. Another MTV year end special, *1988 All Stars,* included Michael Jackson's live performance video of "Another Part of Me".

Michael made the biggest impact on *Billboard's* year end charts, making twenty of their charts at least once:

Top Pop Artist- #4- Michael Jackson
Top Black Artist- #1- Michael Jackson
Top Pop Album- #5- Bad
Top Pop Album Artist- #3- Michael Jackson
Top Pop Singles- #21-"Man in the Mirror", #61- "Dirty Diana"
Top Pop Album Artist-Male- #2- Michael Jackson
Top Pop Singles Artist-Male- #2-Michael Jackson
Top Pop Singles Producer- #3- Quincy Jones
Top Hot Crossover Singles- #18-"Man in the Mirror", #20- "The Way You Make Me Feel"
Top Hot Crossover Artist- #2- Michael Jackson
Top Black Singles- #36-"Man in the Mirror", #58-"Another Part of Me", #77- "Get It", #98- "Dirty Diana"
Top Black Singles Artist- #1- Michael Jackson

Top Black Album- #2- Bad
Top Black Album Artist - #2- Michael Jackson
Top Dance Sales Artist- #8-Michael Jackson
Top Dance Club Play Singles- #19 "The Way You Make Me Feel"
Top Dance Club Play- Artist- #9- Michael Jackson
Top Adult Contemporary Artists- #19- Michael Jackson
Top Compact Disks: #9-Bad
Top Pop Singles Publishers- #24- MIJAC, BMI
Top Black Singles Publishers- #21- MIJAC, BMI

Michael wasn't only topping charts in the U.S. A Gallop Poll taken in England showed that the members of the Royal Family were the nation's most popular personalities. It was noted, however, that for those who responded to the poll under the age of twenty five, their number one choice was Michael Jackson.

Bad ended 1988, just as in 1987, as the year's biggest selling album. *Bad* was also the biggest selling album of 1988 in England.

At the beginning of 1989, as the 80's were coming to a close, a columnist for *Adweek* wondered who would be remembered as the superstar of the decade, "the defining figure of our age", Ronald Reagan or Michael Jackson?

Another list Michael was topping at the end of 1988 was *Forbes* magazine's list of the year's highest paid entertainers. Michael moonwalked past the previous year's highest paid entertainer, Bill Cosby, by $5 million and was ranked number one on the list with estimated earnings for 1987 and 1988 of $97 million. *Forbes* estimated that $37 million was earned in 1987, with the remaining $60 million being earned in 1988 from sales of *Bad* and its singles, proceeds from the Bad tour, sales of *Moonwalk*, his Pepsi commercials, and earnings from music publishing. The magazine estimated Michael's earnings from the Bad tour at $40 million. Estimates of his fee for the Pepsi endorsements were $15 million. Royalties from *Bad* sales, if assuming the same royalty rate he received from *Thriller* would be $32 million, since

Bad had sold 16 million copies by the end of the year. *Rolling Stone* estimated he would earn $5 million from ownership of ATV publishing, leaving $5 million from *Moonwalk* sales and other royalties, not bad!

On *Forbes* list the previous year, Michael was ranked at number nine with estimated earnings of $43 million. This isn't too bad for a singer who had no new albums, singles, or tours for almost the entire two year period. The *Bad* album was only out during the last four months of 1987, and the list is compiled in December.

CHAPTER ELEVEN

REALLY, REALLY BAD

Amidst the record breaking success of the *Bad* album and the Bad tour came award time. In January, 1988, Michael was nominated for two American Music Awards. He lost in his nomination for Best Pop/Rock Male Vocalist to Paul Simon. He won, however, with his second nomination, with "Bad" being chosen as the Best Soul/R&B Single. Janet was nominated in three categories. "When I Think Of You" was chosen as the Best Pop/Rock Video. She lost to Whitney Houston for Best Pop/Rock Female Vocalist, and she lost the race for Best Soul/R&B Female Vocalist to Anita Baker. Neither Michael or Janet attended the award presentation.

For the Grammys, Michael had earned four nominations and was scheduled to perform at the award presentation. *Bad* was nominated for Album of the Year, Michael Jackson and Quincy Jones were nominated for Producer of the Year, and Michael was nominated for Best Male Pop Vocal and Best Male R&B Vocal. Bruce Swedien was nominated for Best Engineered Recording for *Bad*.

Epic Records congratulated Michael on his Grammy nominations with another full page ad in *Billboard:*

ISN'T THIS JUST TOO BAD
ALBUM OF THE YEAR "BAD"
BEST POP VOCAL PERFORMANCE, MALE
"BAD" ALBUM
BEST R&B VOCAL PERFORMANCE, MALE
"BAD" (SINGLE)
PRODUCER OF THE YEAR
QUINCY JONES AND MICHAEL JACKSON
BEST ENGINEERED RECORDING
"BAD" (ALBUM)
BRUCE SWEDIEN, ENGINEER
5 GRAMMY NOMINATIONS...NOT BAD!
CONGRATULATIONS MICHAEL.
FROM EPIC RECORDS.

The ad featured a photo of Michael from the waist down. But the black loafers and white sequined socks showing below the short black pants, and the taped up fingertips, left no doubt whose legs they were!

Major newspapers, in reporting their Grammy picks, generally had Michael winning in three of the four categories. *The Los Angeles Times* and *USA Today* had Michael picking up the prizes for Best R&B Vocal Performance, Best Male Pop Vocal Performance, and sharing the Grammy with Quincy Jones for Producer of the Year. Both papers predicted U2's *The Joshua Tree* as the winner of Album of the Year, but by a very close margin. *The Los Angeles Times* even predicted a possible upset by Jackson's *Bad* album, and Michael possibly going home with all four Grammys for which he was nominated.

Michael's performance on the 30th Annual Grammy Awards was his first TV performance since the *Motown 25* special five years earlier. *TV Guide*, in its preview of the Grammys stated, "The Grammys are worth watching any year, but especially so this year: tonight's Grammy telecast from Radio City Music Hall is slated to include a live performance by Michael Jackson, his first live TV performance since 1983's 'Motown 25...Yesterday, Today, Forever' show." Grammy producer Pierre Cossette, when asked what the night's big moment would be, replied, "It would be very difficult to say anything other than Michael Jackson."

About half way through the Grammy telecast, host Billy Crystal read the rules impersonating Sylvester Stallone. He then introduced two representatives of the independent accounting firm which handles the Grammy ballots, Deloitte, Haskings and Sells. Suddenly, the lights dimmed and a silhouette appeared from behind a screen. The audience roared as they recognized the familiar figure. Michael stood, poised very still, with a hat perched on his head, down over his eyes. He slowly glided from one position to another as the screen slowly rose revealing Michael wearing short black pants, well above his ankles, and a blue shirt with a white t-shirt underneath it. He also had a white strip of fabric tied around his waist, and one around his wrist, looking he just stepped from the set of the video for "The Way You Make Me Feel".

He descended a small staircase and sang very slowly the opening lines of "The Way You Make Me Feel", putting out an imaginary cigarette on the floor. In a special cameo appearance, Tatiana crossed the stage in front of him. As the music assumed its usual uptempo beat, Michael tossed the hat, pulled his shirt tails out and was joined by four dancers. The dazzling choreography borrowed from the song's video, and showcased Michael's new variation on the moonwalk, gliding around in a circle.

After the performance of an abbreviated "The Way You Make Me Feel", the dancers left the stage to Michael. After a pause for applause, he began "Man in the Mirror". He was joined on stage by the New Hope Baptist Church Choir, all in blue gowns. Michael's other background singers included Siedah Garrett and Andre Crouch, who at one point went out to Michael to help him up from his knees and wipe his forehead, a gesture reminiscent of James Brown's performances. Michael gave an outstanding performance, falling to his knees at several points and giving full emotion to the song's moving lyrics.

Michael was given a standing ovation for his performance that evening, but no Grammys. In the biggest surprise, shock and disappointment of the evening, Michael was shut out in all four categories in which he was nominated. Immediately following his performance, the award for Album of the Year was presented by Herb Alpert and Diana Ross. For Jackson supporters, it seemed Michael couldn't lose, he was still backstage having just finished his performance and the award was being presented by Diana Ross, his friend and mentor. But he did lose, to U2's *The Joshua Tree*.

In the category of Best Producer, which many Grammy predictors said the team of Jackson and Jones were unbeatable, Narada Michael Walden won for Whitney Houston's album, *Whitney*. Sting was named Best Male Pop Vocal over Michael

Jackson and Bruce Springsteen. Another surprise came later when Smokey Robinson won as Best Male R&B Vocal over Michael Jackson and the seemingly most popular second choice, Stevie Wonder. The *Bad* album did win the Grammy for Best Engineered Recording, which went to *Bad* engineer, Bruce Swedien.

Following his performance, Michael sat out the remaining show seated next to Quincy Jones in the front row of Radio City Music Hall. He had changed into the black pants he wore in the "Bad" video, a khaki shirt with a black tie, and a red blazer with buckles at the shoulder.

A small amount of consolation came from the news coverage of the Grammy awards the following day. *USA Today* ran the headline, "U2 big winner, but Jackson steals show." The article went on to say, "Despite his shutout, Jackson won over the audience with a performance recalling his 1983 Motown special stunner." In its music news, MTV's reports on the Grammys spotlighted the winners, but they also gave a considerable nod to Michael Jackson:

*The evenings highest highs and lowest lows belonged to one man, Michael Jackson. His all stops out performance of 'Man in the Mirror', complete with full gospel choir was an eye-popping triumph. But by evening's end when the final tally was made, Jackson, who had been nominated for four Grammys, had won none. And his album, **Bad**, had garnered only a lonely engineering award. But Jackson's minimal showing in the statuette sweepstakes hardly diminished his uncontested talents.*

Other reviews said, "In a night when rock put on the dog, the evening's top cat of all, without a doubt, was Michael Jackson. Not only was his performance a show stopper, it stopped interviews in the press room. 'Let's watch Michael', said presenter Herbie Hancock, mid answer, 'you can talk to me later.'" *Jet* magazine wrote, "Even though he won no awards during the ceremony, Michael Jackson virtually stole the show with his performance. The singer, who had not appeared on television in 3 years, [sic] mesmerized the audience and television viewers on 'The Way You Make Me Feel', and poured out his heart in song with 'The Man in the Mirror'".

His performance did indeed win over the television viewers. This was reflected in the increase in album sales following the award telecast. Sales of Michael Jackson's *Bad* album rose higher than U2's *The Joshua Tree,* despite them winning the Grammy for Album of the Year.

Another highlight of the Grammy telecast was the network debut of Michael's new Pepsi commercials. For that story, lets go back to the beginning. In the spring of 1986, Roger Enrico, president of Pepsi, received a message. "It was from Frank Dileo and John Branca- Michael Jackson wanted to make more Pepsi commercials!" In *The Other Guy Blinked: How Pepsi Won the Cola Wars*, Enrico recalls flying to Michael's Encino home to discuss ideas for the commercials:

He sparks to it. It's an enormously difficult idea to pull off. It needs Michael Jackson, and an absolutely first rate director, to have a chance of succeeding. But no one has ever done anything like it before, and if we can make it happen, it will be gangbusters. Michael's reaction to the idea? 'Roger', he says, 'this time were going to set the world on fire!' He didn't, I assure you, mean that literally.

One of the commercials is made up of four parts. Part one, titled "The Chase", has Michael running from a horde of reporters. He runs to the roof of a building only to be whisked away at the last minute by a helicopter. He falls from the helicopter but luckily grabs onto a pulley on a rope and lands safely and unrumpled.

In part two, "The Chopper", Michael continues to elude the press by a variety of ways. He ski jumps, flies through the air and finally parachutes to the ground, driving off in a black Ferrari Testarossa.

Part three is titled "The Museum". Michael runs into a museum and escapes the reporters and photographers by becoming part of a painting of a diner. After successfully eluding the mob following him, he quietly walks away from the painting.

In part four, "The Finale", the reporters are still in pursuit of Michael. To escape, he runs inside a building, it's dark inside. Suddenly, spotlights hit him and he's on stage before a packed house. Feeling safe on stage, he begins to perform.

The second commercial features a young Michael Jackson fan who wanders into Michael's dressing room looking for him, calling, "Mr. Jackson?" The room is empty. He looks around, seeing Michael's jackets, a half full bottle of Pepsi and Michael's sunglasses lying on a table. Meanwhile, Michael is on stage performing "Bad" with new Pepsi lyrics. The young admirer tries on Michael's sunglasses. He dons one of Michael's sequined jackets and the fedora. He does a spin like his idol and pushes the hat down over eyes, as he does, he hears, "Looking for me?". He looks up very startled, at seeing Michael Jackson in the doorway, and he starts to giggle.

Michael's co-star for this commercial was Jimmy Safechuck. Jimmy is a big Michael Jackson fan and was very excited to be chosen to be in the commercial. However, when Jimmy showed up on the set for filming, he was told that Michael Jackson wouldn't be there. He would have to pretend that Michael was standing in the doorway. When Jimmy did the scene, wearing Michael's jacket and hat, he spun around, and heard "Looking for me?", Michael was really standing there. The surprised look on Jimmy's face in the commercial is genuine.

Michael and Jimmy have since become friends. Michael even accepted a dinner invitation from Jimmy's parents, arriving in a chauffeur driven limousine, and bringing his own food. Jimmy accompanied Michael to London with the Bad tour. Michael even had a look-a-like outfit made for Jimmy like the one

Michael wore in concert, black pants with a harness of sorts around one leg, and a "Bad" jacket filled with zippers and buckles, and a black fedora. Jimmy often joined Michael on stage with other children at the end of the concerts.

In these Pepsi commercials, Michael performed "Bad" with new "Pepsi" lyrics:

> *Gonna tell you right*
> *Gonna show your stuff*
> *Don't ever stop*
> *'Til you get enough*
> *The feelin's good*
> *Comin' off the day*
> *You're reachin' up*
> *The choice is made*
>
> *They say the sky's the limit*
> *There's nothin' stoppin' you*
> *You're a brand new generation*
> *And Pepsi's comin' through*
>
> *You know I'm bad*
> *I'm bad, come on*
> *And Pepsi's cool*
> *It's cool, you know it*
> *You know I'm bad, I'm bad*
> *You know it, you know*
> *And the whole world has to answer right now*
> *to tell you the Pepsi way*
> *It's cool*

Like just about everything else that Michael does, these commercials too drew criticism and stirred controversy. Paul McGuinness, manager of U2, criticized Michael for his endorsement of Pepsi. "What's the point of going to all the trouble of being

Michael Jackson and achieving so much musically and creatively if you are then prepared to place all that credibility at the disposal of a soft drinks manufacturer for a fee?"

Michael also came under fire from Neil Young. Young made a video, which MTV refused to show, that attacked rock stars for doing endorsements. "This Note's For You" is a tasteless attack on all pop/rock stars who make commercial endorsements, most notably Michael Jackson for Pepsi and Whitney Houston for Diet Coke:

> *Ain't singin' for Pepsi*
> *Ain't singin' for Coke*
> *I don't sing for nobody*
> *It makes me look like a joke*

The video used look-a-likes for Michael Jackson and Whitney Houston. Michael Jackson's hair catches fire and Whitney Houston puts it out with a Diet Coke.

It hardly seems rational to say that Michael placed his credibility as a musician at the hands of Pepsi. Michael, as in everything he does, oversaw the entire project, and made certain his high standards of excellence were upheld. As with the Jackson Pepsi ads, Michael had approval power over the lyrics of the song, editing and he was again not filmed drinking or holding a bottle of Pepsi.

When considering both Pepsi and Michael's objectives, the ads have to be considered successful, if not the most successful advertising campaign ever. For this second set of Pepsi commercials, Michael received the highest fee ever paid for a commercial endorsement. Reports vary as to the exact amount he received, but estimates place it between $10 and $15 million. At a press conference announcing the deal with Pepsi, Michael received an award recognizing the record breaking fee. Michael accepted the award, speaking a total of sixteen words: "This is a great honor.

Thank you Mr. Enrico, Pepsi associates, ladies and gentlemen. Thank you."

Whatever Pepsi's investment in Michael, it definitely paid off. When the Bad tour was in Japan, Pepsi sales rose two hundred percent. When Michael arrived in Australia for his performances there, Pepsi sales rose immediately sixty percent. During the U.S. leg of the Bad tour, Pepsi sales tripled.

Michael's Pepsi commercials then became the first American advertisements to be shown on Soviet television. A spokesman for Pepsi stated that the Soviet officials asked specifically for Michael Jackson's commercials. The endorsements were seen by approximately 150 million people in the Soviet Union.

Americans were also among those enjoying the ads. Studies on TV "zapping" showed that people don't run for the remote control during shows they especially enjoy. Two items singled out by the study as being "zap-proof" were the popular television series *LA Law* and Michael Jackson's Pepsi commercials.

Michael's solo Pepsi ads were the most eagerly anticipated and most popular since the Jackson Pepsi ads in 1984. Video Storyboard Tests, a New York Ad Research firm, conducts quarterly surveys to determine the top ten outstanding TV campaigns. For the third quarter of 1988, commercials for Pepsi and Diet Pepsi were rated number one. The commercials most often singled out by those surveyed were "Outfoxed", Diet Pepsi commercials with Michael J. Fox, and "The Chase", starring Michael J. Jackson.

As part of the deal, Pepsi sponsored Michael's Bad World Tour. Pepsi's logo was placed in the tour program. Even if Neil Young disapproved and didn't like the ads, a lot of other people did. They were the most popularly watched commercials, Pepsi sponsored the Bad tour, and Mike picked up a hefty paycheck. And last, but not least, the ads helped sell lots and lots of Pepsi. Some joke.

With these commercials, Michael seemed to have set precedents for other pop stars to follow. Again. Madonna was the next pop star signed to endorse Pepsi. Her new Pepsi ads were scheduled to coincide with the release of her new album, just as Michael's commercials were scheduled to do. Diet Coke countered in the cola wars by signing George Michael as their spokesman. George Michael's Diet Coke ads premiered during the American Music Awards. Coke also ran teasers of the ads with the tag line, "Diet Coke presents - January 30th..." Another less than original idea. One area in which they didn't compete with Michael was with their paychecks. Madonna came closest with a reported $9 million. George Michael was reported to have been paid $3 million by Coke. While these soda pop commercials continue to be very much opposed by some, to others it has become almost a status symbol to be asked to do Pepsi or Coke ads.

Later, Michael appeared in another TV ad, well, sort of. A new California Raisin commercial that first aired in theaters in July, 1989, and later on TV in September, featured a claymation Michael Jackson. The claymation Michael Jackson dreams of being Michael Raisin, who performs "Heard It Through The Grapevine". Michael's singing voice isn't used in the ad, but his speaking voice is. When clay Mike wakes up, he figures the strange dream he had must have been due to, "something I ate". Because of his exclusive contract with Pepsi, Michael's own singing voice could not be used in the ads.

He did contribute to the making of the ads, acting as a model for the claymation figure and contributing to the creation of six other backup raisins. A thirty minute film of Michael performing was made to serve as a model for the figure's movements. Michael received a $25,000 fee for his contribution to the ads, which he donated to charity.

The weekend following the Grammys and the debut of Michael's Pepsi commercials, was Michael Jackson Weekend on MTV. The video network devoted the entire weekend to Michael

Jackson videos, reports and specials. Special live performances from his concerts in Kansas City included "Heartbreak Hotel", "Rock With You", "Another Part of Me", and "Dirty Diana". *From Motown To Your Town* was rebroadcast with *The Making of Michael Jackson's Thriller.* Other special bits thrown in for Michael Jackson Weekend included the now rarely seen long version of the "Bad" video and "Thriller".

Interviews with Frank Dileo and members of the band, Jennifer Batten, Greg Phillinganes, dancer Dominic Lucero, and backup singer Sheryl Crow all gave insight into how very much in control Michael is over his career. Sheryl Crow told MTV, "I learned so much from him, just by watching him. He's a perfectionist. I like that. I like the fact that he's completely aware of what's going on as we're doing it." Greg Phillinganes, music director and keyboard player on the Bad tour, said, "He definitely knows what he's doing and what he wants and the elements that he would like to put together to give the best show that he can." Guitarist Jennifer Batten added, "He's very aware of everything, which is incredible because he's got seventeen people on stage including himself."

As well as admiration for his awareness of every detail of the show, the band members also had a great deal of praise for Michael's talent. Sheryl Crow told how she finds herself watching him, wondering, "How does he do that?" She added, "He has resonance that goes on forever. It's so bright and so clear sounding. The fact that he dances while he's singing, that to me is amazing." Greg Phillinganes also commented on Michael's singing voice, "He's a very strong singer and performer. He's got pipes of plutonium." The greatest praise came from Frank Dileo. Michael's manager described Michael as "extremely creative, he's probably the greatest entertainer of our day. I've been lucky to see the Beatles, and see Elvis, and been able to see Frank Sinatra and Sammy Davis, and by far this is probably the best entertainer of them all."

The second stop on the U.S. tour was New York. Michael performed at Madison Square Garden on March 3, 4, and 5th, with the first performance being a benefit concert for the United Negro College Fund (UNCF). On March 1, Michael appeared at a press conference held at 1018, a disco in Manhattan, to preview his new four part Pepsi commercial and to present a check to Christopher Edley, president of the United Negro College Fund, for $600,000, the proceeds from his first concert at Madison Square Garden. Michael, dressed in a red blazer with the familiar crest, spoke a total of eighteen words: "Thank you very much. I am very honored. I am very thankful. I love you all. Thank you." Three children joined Michael for pictures. They were the winners of a Be Against Drugs (BAD) anti-drug write-in contest. They read their winning letters, got to meet Michael, and won tickets to his concert.

Michael's benefit concert at Madison Square Garden, combined with his earlier donations, made him one of the UNCF's largest contributors. Michael's donations have been used to establish the Michael Jackson Scholarship Fund. Over ninety eight scholarships have been awarded from this fund.

In return for his very generous donation, Michael was honored by the UNCF on March 10, at their forty fourth anniversary dinner at the Sheraton Centre in New York. The UNCF presented Michael with their highest honor, The Frederick D. Patterson Award. Michael was also awarded with an honorary doctor of humane letters degree from Fisk University, a private liberal arts school in Nashville. The degree was presented by Henry Ponder, the president of Fisk University. It was presented at a dinner with approximately 2,000 people, many of whom were Michael's guests; Frank Dileo, John Branca, Walter Yetnikoff, Elizabeth Taylor, Liza Minnelli, Yoko Ono, Christy Brinkley, and Michael's parents. Whitney Houston performed at the award presentation, singing "Lift Ev'ry Voice and Sing" and "America the Beautiful". Diana Ross was invited but didn't attend. Long time friend and producer Quincy Jones did attend, and made a speech honoring his friend:

> *I would just like to say this tribute tonight is about growth as a human being, as a songwriter, as a singer, as a dancer, as a choreographer, as a mind, as a record producer, as a business magnate...and most important of all, as a humanitarian.*

Michael was also congratulated by President Ronald Reagan via a video taped message:

> *Michael, I'm sorry that Nancy and I could not be with you for this very special day, but I want to congratulate you for the honors you are receiving tonight from the United Negro College Fund and the honorary degree awarded you by Fisk University. Let me be the first to call you the new Dr. J.*

Michael made an uncharacteristically lengthy speech, well at least longer than the usual, "Thank you. I'm very honored. I love you all."

> *I can't believe I'm nervous, but I really am embarrassed. I appreciate everybody coming... First, I do want to thank God, who makes everything possible. Then my dear mother and father who are in the audience, thank you for all you have done for me. I really appreciate it from the bottom of my heart.*
> *I would like to say this about the United Negro College Fund. An education opens a person's mind to the entire world, and there is nothing more important than to make sure everyone has the opportunity for an education. To want to learn, to have the capacity to learn, and not to be able to, is a tragedy. I am honored to be associated with an evening that says this will never happen. Thank you. I love you all.*

Just after receiving these honors from the UNCF, the cable channel Showtime aired a special on Michael Jackson, *Motown on Showtime: Michael Jackson...The Legend Continues.* It first aired on March 12, 1988.   Motown's Suzanne dePasse served as executive producer on the special along with Michael Jackson. The program covered Michael's entire career, concentrating on his earlier years with Motown.   Motown sent collections of early Michael Jackson and Jackson Five film footage to Michael while he was on tour for him to preview and approve the footage to be finally included in the special.

The special was originally going to be hosted by Diana Ross.   She reportedly backed out of the project when Michael refused to attend the christening of her second son, Evan, with her new husband Arne Naess.   James Earl Jones was then asked to narrate the special.   The show opens with different shots of Michael and the words, "His name has become synonymous with superstardom.   He has redefined the term, 'professional entertainer.'   He is simply, Michael Jackson."

Three fans were included in the special.   They were winners of an "Ask Michael" contest sponsored by Showtime and MTV, in which fans sent in three questions they would most like to ask Michael Jackson.   Part of the prize was the opportunity to appear on this Showtime special, they also toured Michael's home, and met him following one of his concerts in Australia.

Clips of the Jackson Five's first appearance on the *Ed Sullivan Show,* when they performed "I Want You Back" and "Who's Lovin' You", was included along with many other TV appearances of the group from the beginning of their career.

Their performance of "The Love You Save" on *Diana!,* Diana Ross' 1971 TV special, their 1970 appearance on *American Bandstand* in which they performed "ABC", and their performance on *The Jim Nabors Hour,* also in 1970, in which they performed their fourth number one single, "I'll Be There" were all included.

The Jackson Five's performance of "Never Can Say Goodbye" on *The Flip Wilson Show,* is relived as is the Jackson

Five's own special, "Goin' Back To Indiana" with live concert footage of them performing the single, "Goin' Back To Indiana". Early Jackson Five rehearsals conducted by Suzanne depasse show the group learning dance routines while a very young Randy plays pattycake with baby sister Janet.

Michael is seen performing "Ben" on *American Bandstand* in 1972. The group performs "Dancing Machine" on *Cher* in 1976, during which Michael performs a dance step called the "robot" which later became a very popular dance craze. In a 1979 appearance on *American Bandstand* the Jacksons perform "Shake Your Body". Michael was now suddenly much taller and thinner than he was in "Blame It On The Boogie" just one year earlier. A later edition of *American Bandstand* featured the short film, "The Triumph", which Michael conceived and produced for the single, "Can You Feel It." Clips of Michael's later solo projects include the videos for "Rock With You" and "Don't Stop 'Til You Get Enough".

Some of the most enjoyable moments of the program show Michael having fun away from the stage; sliding down a water slide into a pool, playing with the children who appear in the "Smooth Criminal" video, riding a rollercoaster with some friends, including Bill Bray and John Landis, and riding in a hot air balloon with Emmanuel Lewis and Bill Bray. (Bill Bray gets to go everywhere!)

Michael's sweep of the 1984 Grammy Awards is highlighted with consecutive clips of award presenters announcing winners, "'Beat It', Michael Jackson", "Thriller, Michael Jackson", "Michael Jackson and Quincy Jones", and "Michael Jackson".

Almost his entire performance from *Motown 25* is shown with Martin Scorsese calling it, "One of the best performance things I've ever seen." Hermes Pan, a choreographer who worked with Fred Astaire, added that he was dying to know how he did that walk!

Marlon remembers standing backstage as a child with Michael watching other performers, especially The Godfather of

Soul, James Brown. Clips of a James Brown performance is shown with a portion of the Jackson Five's audition tape for Motown in 1968. Michael's ability to move like James Brown at such a young age, (he was nine years old), is truly remarkable.

The special concludes with several clips of Michael's Bad tour performances. Even the closing credits feature more irresistible footage of Michael. Michael with Quincy Jones, all smiles, holding an armload of Grammys; a shot of a very young Michael in the buff about to climb into the tub; a grown up Michael trading dance steps with Jimmy Safechuck; and Michael being called up on stage at a James Brown concert where he duplicates James Brown's steps then glides into a moonwalk. He also brushes up his martial arts, using Frank Dileo as his target. The final footage is of Michael performing "The Way You Make Me Feel" in concert.

Motown on Showtime, Michael Jackson: The Legend Continues and *From Motown to Your Town* were both nominated for ACE awards for Outstanding Musical Special. ACE awards are especially for shows and specials appearing on cable TV. The ACE for Outstanding Musical Special went to Billy Joel. *Michael Jackson: The Legend Continues* was awarded the ACE for Outstanding Editing in a Musical Special. Ted Levy and Glenn A. Morgan accepted the award.

In early 1988, Michael's lawyer, John Branca married Julie McArthur. Michael attended the ceremony at Branca's Beverly Hills home, with Bubbles. Michael was dressed in a dark blue suit with a lavender shirt, Bubbles wore a tux. Bubbles made a friend at the celebration in another guest, *Miami Vice* star Don Johnson. Michael and Bubbles' gift to the couple was his and her Patek Philippe watches.

Also in the spring of 1988, Michael finally moved out of his home in Encino which he had shared with his parents. Janet had moved out of the family home some time before and LaToya had just moved to New York. Michael had purchased a 2800 acre ranch in Santa Ynez, California, about 100 miles Northwest of Los

Angeles. The purchase price for his new home was reported as $28 million, though other sources said the price was closer to $17 million. To celebrate the purchase of his new home, Michael threw a spectacular house warming bash. He had several guests, his parents, however, were not among them. In fact, his father found out about his son's new home on the television news.

On the grounds of his ranch is a mansion, guest house, tennis courts, lakes, streams, thousands of oak trees, and plenty of room for his animals. Michael's new neighbors include Bo and John Derek, and Steven Segal and his wife Kelly LeBrock.

Shortly before Michael purchased his new home, his house in Encino was used as the grounds for an auction of artwork. The proceeds from this auction, over $2 million, went to the South African Council of Churches for housing, clothing, and medical supplies. The auction was hosted by Whoopi Goldberg. Michael was not at home at the time.

At another auction in June, several items belonging to music stars were auctioned off with the proceeds going to the T. J. Martell Foundation for Leukemia, Cancer and AIDS Research. Michael donated a black fedora to the auction, which brought in a winning bid of $4,125.

March ended with Michael picking up two Soul Train Music Awards, out of three nominations. *Bad* was chosen as Best Album, Male, and the single "Bad" won as Best Single, Male. "The Way You Make Me Feel" was nominated for Best Video, but was beaten by Janet's video for "Control". Neither Michael or Janet attended the award presentation.

The next month, "Weird Al" Yankovic released his second parody of a Michael Jackson hit. His follow up to "Eat It" was "Fat", a parody of "Bad". It is included on Yankovic's album, *Even Worse,* the cover of which almost exactly duplicates *Bad's* album cover. Yankovic is dressed all in black and buckles with "Even Worse" sprayed in red.

In order to parody an artist's song or video, permission by that artist must be granted. Michael has a great sense of humor and not only granted Yankovic permission to parody his song, he also helped the film crew gain access to the set for the "Fat" video. Michael enjoyed the "Fat" video so much he ordered twelve copies to give out to friends. Yankovic told one interviewer, "He doesn't have to let me do this kind of stuff. He doesn't need the additional royalties. The only reason he would let me is that he has a sense of humor. It is heartening to find somebody that popular, talented, and powerful who can really take a joke."

The single, "Fat" and its accompanying video are hilarious. "Weird Al's" reworking of Michael's lyrics went like this:

Your butt is wide...well mine is too
Just watch your mouth...or I'll sit on you
The word is out...better treat me right
'Cause I'm the king...of cellulite
Ham on, ham on, ham on whole wheat...all right.

In the video for "Fat", "Weird Al" is dressed in a costume very similar to what Michael wears in "Bad", only about forty two sizes bigger! "Weird Al" was padded to look enormous in the video. Al and his hefty dancers perform "Fat" in a setting very much like the subway station used in "Bad", and they clumsily execute the same move as in "Bad". "Fat" didn't match the chart success that "Eat It" did, but the "Fat" video did receive heavy airplay on MTV.

On April 20, 1988, after four years in the works, Michael Jackson's autobiography was finally finished and released. *Moonwalk* was published by Doubleday and was edited by Jacqueline Onassis. Bookstore displays, full size cut outs of Michael, featured a note in Michael's handwriting:

One of the reasons that I haven't given interviews over the years is because I've been saving what I have to say for my book. Love, Michael.

The day *Moonwalk* hit bookstores Michael was continuing the first leg of his U.S. tour in Chicago at the Rosemont Horizon where he was performing the second of three soldout shows.

Moonwalk is written in a very casual, relaxed style, giving the reader the sense that he wrote it just for one person, you. He discusses his childhood, and his start with the Jackson Five, winning talent contests in Gary and eventually signing with Motown. He describes how very happy and proud he felt when *Thriller* became the biggest selling album in history, and when he won a record breaking eight Grammy awards. He admits to having cosmetic surgery on his nose twice and having a cleft added to his chin. All other claims of his "extensive plastic surgery" he says, are untrue. He also denies the charges that he has had his skin lighted either by a skin peel, acid or whatever new means have been dreamed of. He makes no mention of the hyperbaric chamber, the elephant man's bones or his shrine to Elizabeth Taylor and his proposal to her. Michael describes himself as being one of the loneliest people in the world. He's unsure if he's happy being famous, he simply doesn't know any other way.

The most poignant portions of *Moonwalk* deal with his strained, cold relationship with his father. He describes being beaten after messing up at after school rehearsals. Even today, they rarely speak to each other.

In a special television edition of *People Magazine*, Joe Jackson attempted to answer the things Michael states about him in his book. He denied the beatings Michael said he received as a child, and refers to them as "little spankings". Marlon, who also appeared on the special, agreed with Michael, saying that they did get hit, and a lot. Marlon added, "My father is a person who loves to control your destiny. By him being your father, he feels he has the right to do that."

Even considering Michael's unequaled success, Joe Jackson still thinks Michael made a mistake going solo. He feels that if the family performed together, the shows would be stronger than with just one member of the family involved. He feels that his sons were trained to perform as a group, and that they should continue in that fashion.

Despite criticisms that *Moonwalk* actually revealed very little about Michael, the autobiography, in true Jackson form, entered the *Los Angeles Times* Best Seller List and the *London Times* Best Seller List at number one. *Moonwalk* debuted on the *New York Times* Best Seller List at number two, moving into the number one spot in its second week on the list. Within a few months, *Moonwalk* had sold over 450,000 copies in fourteen countries.

Following the release of *Moonwalk* MTV held a contest in which viewers could win autographed copies of the book. Each day for one week blocks of Michael Jackson videos were shown during which a phone number would appear. Selected callers could then win one of the autographed copies of *Moonwalk*.

There were doubts by many that Michael actually wrote the book himself, and didn't have a ghost writer complete the project for him. The first manuscript was put together by Robert Hillburn. His manuscript was refused by Doubleday because it was lacking in juicy details. Stephen Davis was next to be assigned to the project of helping Michael put the book together. Michael drastically edited Davis' manuscript, perhaps it was too juicy. Michael ended up writing *Moonwalk* himself with help from Shaye Ayreheart, although there were reports that she later quit when Michael threw a snake at her just to get her reaction.

Choreographer Jeffrey Daniels, who choreographed the "Bad" video with Michael, was reportedly disappointed that he wasn't mentioned in *Moonwalk*. Michael writes that he had been practicing the moonwalk for a long time before finally performing it for the first time in public on *Motown 25*. What he doesn't reveal is that Daniels is the one who originally showed him the step. Daniels has since worked on another Jackson video. He choreographed LaToya's "You're Gonna Get Rocked" video.

After the release of *Moonwalk* there were reports that Michael may write another book revealing more about his relationship with his father. It was said this second book would possibly be published after his father's death.

LaToya, feeling more of the real story should be told sooner, wrote her own book dealing with the Jackson clan, *LaToya: Growing Up in the Jackson Family*. There were press reports made by Jack Gordon, LaToya's manager, that Michael, and the other members of the family, did not want the book to be published. Gordon claims Michael offered LaToya $12 million to not publish the book. Failing that, he offered to buy the publishing company, Putnam's, for $84 million. Gordon stated further that Michael's lawyer, John Branca, threatened legal action against Putnam's if the book contained any statements that Michael was sexually molested as a child. In fact, her first manuscript was returned by the publisher because it lacked any juicy material. These attempts by Michael to prevent the book being published were never confirmed by Michael or John Branca. Other sources indicate the suggestion was made to Michael, possibly by Gordon himself, to pay LaToya off to prevent publication of her manuscript, he refused saying he would not be blackmailed by his own sister. This along with the fact that an advanced copy of the manuscript revealed no mention of Michael being sexually molested, makes Gordon's statements look like an effort to promote publicity and anticipation for the book. She then found a new publisher and the book was finally released in the fall of 1991.

The publication of LaToya's book coincided with her second photo layout for *Playboy*, appearing in the November, 1991, issue. Joe and Katherine scheduled, then cancelled, a press conference to answer the allegations in LaToya's book. It was reported they had decided not to dignify her book with a response.

LaToya upset the family further in February, 1990, when she announced her intentions to sell her 25% share ownership in Hayvenhurst, the family's Encino home she owns with Michael.

LaToya's decision to pose nude for *Playboy* and the charges made in her book, which the other members of the family claimed were false, alienated her from the rest of the family. She no longer had phone conversations with her mother like she always used to, Jermaine spoke out publicly against her, and it was reported that Michael changed his phone number and refused to take any calls from his sister.

After staying in New York for a short while, LaToya moved to London. From there she went to France where in the spring of 1992 she began performing eight shows a week at the Moulin Rouge in Paris. Having been a couple of years since he spoke to his sister, Jermaine attended one of her shows shortly after she opened saying, "Let's put the past behind us." It was rumored that Michael had bought out the one thousand seat theater so he too could attend one of LaToya's performances.

It was at this same time that LaToya, who converted from a Jehovah Witness to Judaism to marry her manager Jack Gordon, decided Catholicism was her true religious calling. To effect this change, she wrote to Pope John Paul II personally asking for an audience with the Pontiff.

Just after the publication of *Moonwalk* in April, 1988, Sean Lennon and Dave Winfield hosted a special edition of *Friday Night Videos*, a tribute to Michael Jackson. The program, never before dedicated solely to one artist, was made up entirely of Michael Jackson's videos. The rarely seen video for "Rock With You" and his latest, "Dirty Diana" were shown as was the fourteen minute long video for "Thriller". The rest of the show included now classic videos for "Billie Jean" and "Beat It", the first video ever shown on *Friday Night Videos,* and "Man in the Mirror". The show closed to "The Way You Make Me Feel".

In Grand Rapids, Michigan, an artist named Mark Heckman erected a billboard honoring, in his opinion, four "cool dudes". The four included the artist himself, then Presidential candidate George Bush, David Letterman, and Michael Jackson. These four were chosen by Heckman from an original list of twenty five names, for their ability to withstand and overcome criticism. "I really admire all these guys. They get a lot of criticism, but they're cool dudes because they can take it."

While Heckman was, in his own way, honoring Michael, others had quite different things in mind. Two men from Gary, Indiana, Reynaud Jones and Robert Smith, who knew Michael in his childhood, and a third man from Chicago, Clifford Rubin, filed a $400 million lawsuit against Michael Jackson, claiming that Michael Jackson and Lionel Richie had stolen "We Are the World" from them. They claimed further that Michael had stolen "Thriller" from them. Quincy Jones was named in the suit as well. They should have done some homework before filing the outrageous lawsuit. If they had, they would have found that Rod Temperton stole "Thriller" from them, not Michael Jackson.

MTV aired another Michael Jackson special on August 26, 1988, *Another Part of Me*. Patrick T. Kelly, Frank Dileo, and Michael Jackson served as executive producers of the program which included interviews with several people connected with the tour. Along with Frank Dileo, they spoke with the tour manager John Draper, electrician John Champion, production manager Bennie Collins, and lighting man Merle McClean, who explained that special lighting effects were manufactured especially for "Billie Jean". B.J., a truck driver, even runs down the number of trucks and other equipment necessary to run the shows. Band members Jennifer Batten and Greg Phillinganes and singer Sheryl Crow are also interviewed.

At a rehearsal in Rome, Michael practices his moves wearing a parka and sunglasses. Sheryl raises his glasses and says something to him. Michael slides the glasses down his nose, looking at Sheryl over the tops of them, and raises his eyebrows up and down quickly. The silliness lasts only a few seconds, then the sunglasses are back on and rehearsal resumes.

Another amusing scene at rehearsal has Michael sitting on the steps of the stage listening to an unseen voice, probably Greg Phillinganes, sing "She's Out of My Life" in a slowed down, Vegas style, "Sheeeeeeeeee's oooooooooout of my liiiiiiiiiife".

Michael smiles all thought it, and holding his mike between his knees, claps at the end and laughs.

Several excerpts from the concerts are shown, including pieces of "Working Day and Night", "Dirty Diana", "Man in the Mirror", "I Just Can't Stop Loving You", a rare glimpse of "The Way You Make Me Feel", "Heartbreak Hotel", and "Bad". Also, almost the entire Motown medley is shown. The special concludes with the video for "Another Part of Me".

On September 7, MTV held its music video awards. Michael had two nominations. Michael Jackson and Vincent Patterson were nominated for Best Choreography for "The Way You Make Me Feel" and Michael Jackson, Gregg Burge, and Jeffrey Daniel were nominated in the same category for their work on "Bad". The award went to Barry Lather for his work on Janet's video for "Pleasure Principle".

The MTV Video Vanguard Award is presented each year to an artist for career achievements in video. The 1987 recipient of the award, Peter Gabriel, presented the award to 1988's recipient, Michael Jackson. After a montage of clips from Michael's videos, the award was presented to Michael live via satellite from London, just before one of Michael's performances there. In presenting the award to Michael, Gabriel joked, "I sincerely hope this award will rescue this artist from obscurity and set him on the road to fame and fortune and it gives me great pleasure to give the Video Vanguard Award to Michael Jackson." In an extremely quiet voice, Michael accepted saying only, "Thank you. Thank you very much."

Following this lengthy acceptance speech, a special taped performance of "Bad" was shown. The performance featured Michael's new version of the moonwalk, gliding sideways instead of backwards. He also executed the original moonwalk, just as fascinating as ever, with another new just as impossible step in which he walks forward skidding his foot on the floor as he moves it forward, making his steps look rapid and choppy, like several animated pictures each slightly different than the one before, flipped through quickly making the figure appear to be moving. The review of Michael's career in video, his acceptance of the Vanguard Award and his performance were without a doubt the only highlights of the entire lackluster award show.

Seventeen years after the Jackson Five cartoon series first aired, Michael was a cartoon again. Michael lent his song, "Beat It" to be used in a Flintstone Kids cartoon special encouraging kids to say no to drugs. *The Flintstone Kids* aired in September, 1988. In it, little Fred, Barney, Wilma, and Betty work odd jobs to earn enough money for tickets to a Michael Jackstone concert. They finally make it to the concert and see Michael Jackstone singing new lyrics to "Beat It" about not needing drugs:

> *They told the girl*
> *Why don't you step over here*
> *You wanna be cool*
> *Take a look in here*
> *They wanna do drugs*
> *And they're words are really clear*
> *So beat it!*
> *You don't need it!*
> *(Say no!)*
> *You don't need friends*
> *Doing things that are wrong*
> *There's lots of kids like you*
> *Who are cool and strong*
> *It might be kinda tough*
> *But you can move along*
> *So beat it!*
> *And say it ain't fair*
>
> *Don't mean it!*
> *Don't need it!*
> *Just say no to drugs*
> *Defeat it!*

Have a life that's happy
A future that's bright
You make it happen
Drugs are wrong
And you're right
Just beat it!
Just beat it!
Say no
And defeat it!
Now Moms and Dads
You ought to listen to me
To be a kid today
It ain't easy
Just make your home and family
A loving place to be
So beat it!
Send it riding a wave!

In the cartoon, Stone Age Michael wears one glove and dons sunglasses. He moonwalks, and even grabs his crotch while dancing! LaToya also contributed to the special with "Just Say No" from her album, *LaToya*.

Michaelmania continued with MTV's Michael Jackson Marathon. On September 19, their entire prime time schedule consisted solely of Michael Jackson specials shown back to back. *From Motown To Your Town* was followed by *Another Part of Me*. The marathon was capped off with *Making Michael Jackson's Thriller*.

When you can't get Michael Jackson to appear on a talk show, you do the next best thing, invite Bubbles. Bubbles made another television appearance on *Dick Clark Presents-Live!* Bubbles came with a note from Michael typed on Moonwalker stationery and signed by Michael:

Dear Dick,

I'm giving Bubbles the night off so he can come play on your show.

Sincerely,
Michael Jackson

Bubble's trainer, Bob Dunn appeared with Bubbles and prompted him to perform his own moonwalk. Bubbles has made other public appearances too, including a fund raiser in New York for the prevention of child abuse.

The November 19, 1988, issue of *Billboard* celebrated the 101st anniversary of CBS Records. Several congratulatory ads to CBS Records comprised the special section of the issue devoted to the record company. One ad carried a congratulatory message from the record company's biggest selling artist. A full page photo of Michael Jackson accompanies Michael's words:

The joy of music...
to inspire the young
and the old...
To make the world
a better place.
- Michael Jackson
Congratulations

The portion of the extensive article on CBS Records' history pertaining to the Epic label begins with these words:

*...any overview of the EPA labels must begin with this universally popular performer. It seems safe to predict that **Thriller's** 33 million [sic] worldwide sales record will not be topped in this century; indeed it seems the only artist capable of such a feat would be Michael Jackson himself.*

Friday Night Videos concluded the year with a second special edition devoted entirely to Michael Jackson. Hosted by

Ahamd Rashad, this tribute to Michael Jackson included the new, shorter version of "Smooth Criminal", and a peek at "Leave Me Alone", both from his upcoming music video cassette, *Moonwalker.* The rest of the special was made up of Michael's videos for "Beat It", "Man in the Mirror", "Thriller", "Billie Jean", "Dirty Diana", and "Rock With You".

During 1988, Michael graced the covers of over one hundred magazines. With this second wave of Michaelmania came more releases of Jackson material from Motown. Motown released, through Silver Eagle Records, a three record set of Motown hits of Michael Jackson and the Jackson Five. Some never before released material was included with the biggest hits the Jackson Five enjoyed at Motown.

This record collection was only sold through television advertisements. Even though the album only contained early recordings by Michael and the Jackson Five while still with Motown, the commercials showed a grown up Michael singing and dancing to the old songs. Or at least that's what they tried to show. The person in the ads is obviously not Michael. The imposter is only shown for a few seconds at a time, and only in dark shadows. This person is quite a bit bigger than Michael and just doesn't look that much like him. Instead of using a photo of Michael from the Motown years the Michael Jackson impersonator is used as the album's cover too. The photo is dark and his head is tilted back, so you can't see his face, but it is still obvious it is not really Michael Jackson.

Within two weeks of the release of *Bad,* Michael hit the road with his first ever solo tour. If it didn't work out, he may of had an alternate career as a toy designer. Michael had presented an idea for a new toy to Matel, a transformer type toy that looked like an animal. Michael enjoyed his visit to the factory, and enjoyed meeting the company's toy designers, "He was intrigued to meet the designers and see how they worked. It was total role reversal, they were stars in his eyes." They rejected his idea however. Oh well, maybe this touring business would pay off after all.

CHAPTER TWELVE

THE FIRST
AND FINAL? SOLO
TOUR

Helping to push sales of the *Bad* album higher and higher throughout the world was Michael's first ever solo tour. The Bad world tour kicked off shortly after the album's release, on September 12, 1987, in Japan. Nine concerts scheduled for Tokyo, Osaka, and Yokohama soldout within hours. Due to the heavy demand, five more shows were added. With these fourteen shows, Michael played to a record breaking crowd of 450,000 fans. Ticket scalpers received up to $800 for tickets to see "Typhoon Michael".

With each stop on the Bad tour, Michael seemed to inherit a new nickname. In Japan, he was referred to as "Typhoon Michael". Australian fans dubbed him "Crocodile Jackson". In England, he became known as the "Earl of Whirl". The London press, in exploiting his so-called eccentricities, called him "Wacko Jacko". The Europeans renamed Michael "The Peter Pan of Pop".

One of the reasons given for starting the tour in Japan was that Michael wanted to work out any kinks in the performances before bringing his first solo tour to the States. Considering Michael's intense perfectionism, the detailed planning that went into every aspect of the show, and the continuous rehearsing, it seems unlikely there could be any kinks in the performances. Another reason given for kicking the tour off in Japan was that the Japanese fans hadn't had a chance to see the Victory concerts. A very real motivator for taking the tour to Japan, and his later return, would seem to be the financial opportunities. Ticket prices in Japan were set at $50 and Michael's unparalleled popularity allowed him to easily sell out Japan's 50,000 seat stadiums several times over.

Nippon TV, owner of Japan's largest television network, was a co-sponsor with Pepsi of the Japanese tour dates. This sponsorship deal with Nippon TV was arranged by Jimmy Osmond, the youngest member of the Osmond family.

The performances on this first leg of the Japanese tour closely resembled the Victory concerts with some songs from *Bad* added. Songs performed in the Victory tour, "Things I Do For You", "Shake Your Body", "Lovely One", and "Off The Wall" were performed with "I Just Can't Stop Loving You" and "Bad". "Thriller" was also performed in the shows in Japan.

While his first solo concerts in Japan broke attendance records, stories about Michael ran rampant in the press. Rumors of his extensive plastic surgery, his "weird" relationship with Bubbles, and lingering wisecracks about his offer to purchase the remains of the elephant man were only a few of the outrageous items appearing in newspapers and tabloids. Michael responded by sending a letter to the press. He wrote the note in his hotel room at the Tokyo Capital. It later appeared in *People* magazine in Michael's handwriting complete with misspellings:

like [sic] the old Indian proverb says do not judge a man until you've walked 2 moons in his Moccosins [sic]. Most people don't know me, that is why they write such things in wich [sic] most is not true I cry very often because it hurts and I wory [sic] about the children all my children all over the world, I live for them.

If a man could say nothing against a character but what he can prove, history could not be written. Animals strike, not from malice, but because they want to live, it is the same with those who criticize, they desire our blood, not our pain. But still I must achieve I must seek truth in all things. I must endure for the power I was sent forth, for the world for the children. But have mercy for I've been bleeding a long time now. M.J.

This was a shocking and unexpected move on Michael's part, for he rarely communicates with the media. On those isolated occasions when he has responded to the press, his statements are carefully prepared, planned and worded, unlike this one.

A special evening edition of ABC's *Good Morning America* was aired on the night the tour opened in Tokyo. Host Joan Lunden spoke live with Quincy Jones who was with Michael in Tokyo. Lunden asked Jones if Michael is really as strange as the press makes him out to be. Jones replied, "Absolutely not. He's just having a lot of fun, and I think he's more loose and having more fun with his life than ever now. I don't even recognize this person they talk about all the time."

Quincy was not the only one who travelled to Japan with Michael. Bubbles went too. He arrived on a separate flight from Michael's and was greeted by three hundred photographers. Bubbles later accompanied Michael to a formal tea ceremony at City Hall in Osaka, where he was presented with the key to the city, Michael that is, not Bubbles!

The hotel where Michael stayed in Japan, the Tokyo Capital, renamed the top floor of rooms The Michael Jackson Suite.

After completing the month long tour of Japan, Michael donated approximately thirty personal items to an auction the proceeds of which went toward educating children in third world countries. Among the items Michael donated were sunglasses, T-shirts, and a windbreaker. He also gave $20,000 to the family of a young Japanese boy who had been recently kidnapped and killed.

The second stop on the Bad tour was Australia. In Brisbane, Australia, "Crocodile Jackson" was joined on stage by Stevie Wonder, who was also touring Australia at the time. The Bad tour played to 120,000 Australian fans at five sold out shows. Concerts scheduled for two Australian cities, Perth and Adelaide, had to be cancelled. Some reports said the cancelations were due to poor ticket sales, others reported that the Cricket Association would not permit chairs to be placed on the grass playing fields in the stadiums. Concerts scheduled for New Zealand, the next stop following Australia, were also cancelled.

Following Australia, the Bad tour finally hit the United States. For the U.S. and European dates, a whole new show was created. In January, Michael attended a performance of Siegfried and Roy at the Frontier Hotel in Las Vegas. He met Siegfried and Roy after the show and spent the next day at their home. There they worked on illusions to be included in Michael's new performances.

In return, Michael wrote "The Might in the Magic", the theme song for Siegfried and Roy's performances at the Las Vegas Mirage Hotel. A tape of Michael performing the song opens each of their shows. Michael was said to also be contributing to the design of a multimillion dollar water park for the grounds of the Mirage Hotel and to the organization of the Jackson Attraction, which is to house Michael Jackson souvenirs and memorabilia. Michael created the attraction and even attended interviews held by the president of the Golden Nugget for reporters to see the 3100 room hotel. One reporter had to be convinced Michael was the real thing and not one of the many Las Vegas Michael Jackson impersonators.

The Bad tour required thirty five tons of equipment, including seventy two speakers, three thousand lights, and four video screens which was hauled in twelve semi-trailers. Technicians worked on developing special effects especially for Michael's tour. Michael was interested in patenting these newly developed techniques to limit their use by others.

Every detail of the show was Michael's concept. The staging, lighting, sound, costumes, illusions, choreography, everything was conceived by Michael. The technicians and crew worked to bring Michael's visions into reality. He personally chose the band, dancers, singers, and crew members, choosing "the best and the brightest and the most fun."

The new shows were rehearsed during February in Pensicola, Florida at the Pensicola Civic Center. Michael stayed in the Presidential Suite of the Pensicola Hilton and his chef prepared his meals in the hotel's kitchen. One dish he prepared for Michael had as one of its ingredients, flowers. It was never explained if these flowers were for decoration, or if Michael actually ate them.

While in Florida, Michael was invited to an antique bookstore where the owners offered him a first edition of *The*

Elephant Man and Other Stories by Sir Frederick Treves. Treves is the physician who befriended John Merrick.

Michael had wanted to begin the tour in Atlanta, Georgia, but Pepsi officials, the tour's sponsor, objected because Atlanta is the home base for Coca Cola. Instead, on February 23, 1988, Michael performed his first ever U.S. solo concert in Kansas City, Missouri's Kemper Arena. The newly revised shows included more songs from the *Bad* album than did the shows in Japan. For the first few shows, there were also surprise appearances by Tatiana Thumbtzen for the performance of "The Way You Make Me Feel". It was also a surprise for Tatiana, who was contacted by Michael's secretary only one week before the tour's opening. She was glad to be a part of the show, describing it as being like Christmas in February.

After the debut performance on the U.S. tour, a Kansas City Star arts and entertainment writer said Michael, "left the sold out house of about 17,000 spellbound with moves that weren't around until he invented them. When not dumbfounded the fans cheered and waved their arms in response to the Gifted One's world-class talent and showmanship."

To prepare for each concert, Michael spent time in his dressing room bending, stretching, and kicking. He breathed in herbs from a humidifier to prepare his pipes for two hours of singing. Just before hitting the stage, the band members, singers and dancers all gathered in Michael's dressing room. Frank Dileo, and probably Bill Bray, were also included. After a prayer the group would yell, "Whatever we play, it's got to be funky!" *Entertainment Tonight's* Mary Hart and a camera crew were present backstage on opening night to capture the special pre-show gathering.

The second stop on the U.S. tour was New York. The day following the Grammy's, where he also performed, Michael performed a benefit concert for the United Negro College Fund at Madison Square Garden. The reviews in New York echoed the sentiment in Kansas City. A New York Daily News critic's review read, "Michael's act has already gone well beyond a pop music concert. He uses music the way other performers from the Nicholas Brothers to Liza Minnelli have used it: his body is every bit as much an instrument as his voice." Another reviewer, from *Newsweek* magazine, declared, "...for sheer virtuosity as a contemporary songwriter and song and dance man, Michael has no peer. Even when he seems to have taken a bite from Bob Fosse or borrowed a gesture from Marcel Marceau, he makes it uniquely his own. The sight of him standing under a single spotlight, his fedora shoved down over his eyes as he slides into a moonwalk, has become as familiar an image in American popular culture as Charlie Chaplin's wobble. That's a rare kind of showmanship." The comparison of Michael to Charlie Chaplin must have genuinely touched Michael, as he has long admired Chaplin.

The next two concerts scheduled in St. Louis, Missouri, had to be cancelled. Michael had come down with a cold which then developed into laryngitis. He recovered in time to continue the tour in his old home state. On March 18, the Bad tour opened in Market Square Arena in Indianapolis, Indiana.

From Indiana, it was on to Denver, Colorado; Hartford, Connecticut; Houston, Texas; and Atlanta, Georgia. For the Atlanta concerts, one hundred tickets were given to the Children's Wish Foundation to be distributed to terminally ill children.

Chicago was the next city to host the Bad tour. Before one of the three performances there, Michael met backstage with Lola Falona. Falona, in her battle against multiple sclerosis, would play "Bad" during her vigorous workouts to help motivate and encourage her to continue. Michael also received the Key to the City from Chicago Mayor Eugene Sawyer. Chicago was one of several stops on the tour where "The Way You Make Me Feel" was not included in the show.

From Chicago, the tour moved back to Texas, this time to Dallas. Minneapolis, Minnesota followed the Dallas dates. Shows scheduled next for Cleveland, Ohio were cancelled and rescheduled for the fall. With these first U.S. dates, thirty in all, the Bad tour played to one half million fans.

After a couple weeks off, the tour moved on to Europe. The European tour kicked off on May 23 in Rome, Italy. While in Rome, Michael visited with his friend Sophia Loren. He was also the guest of honor at a party given by movie director Franco Zeffirelli at his Rome villa. Michael later passed out candy and autographed pictures to sick children at Rome's Bambin Gesie Hospital during a visit there.

When not out on one of these visits, Michael evidently spent long periods of time in his hotel room at the Hotel Lord Byron. He left the hotel a few mementos of his stay there. He drew pictures, in ink, on the linens. One picture on a sheet was a profile of himself.

Michael played three concerts in Italy, two in Rome and one in Turin. Together, these dates drew 123,000 fans. These dates in Italy are the sources of two bootleg live albums that were being found in record stores in the States. Epic officials were furious to learn there were two unauthorized tapings of Michael Jackson concerts in Italy. *Michael Jackson Live* purports to be a taping of a Bad concert in Italy on May 29, 1988. *My Way* is a taping of another concert on May 23, 1988.

The following European dates continued to sell out, often playing to record breaking crowds. The third stop on the European tour was Vienna, Austria, where 55,000 fans attended. The next three shows in Rotterdam, the Netherlands, attracted 150,000 fans. Two shows in Gothenburg, Sweden played to 110,000 fans. Bubbles had to stay home while his dad toured Europe; Sweden authorities denied Bubbles entry into the country without a six month quarantine.

A single show in Basel, Switzerland attracted 55,000 fans. During his stay in Switzerland, Michael had an opportunity to fulfill a childhood wish. He visited with Oona Chaplin, the widow of Charlie Chaplin.

West Germany hosted several concerts on the Bad tour. The tour played in Hamburg, Cologne, Munich, Mannheim, and West Berlin. Taking place prior to the reunification of Germany, the West Berlin concerts attracted several thousand people on the opposite side of the Berlin wall. East German officials used clubs and cattleprods in an attempt to dispel the crowd.

In Cologne, Michael, with Siegfried and Roy, his band, and entourage, visited Fantasialand, one of Germany's largest amusement parks. The park was closed for their visit.

Michael also wanted to visit the Berlin Zoo. However, plans for the zoo to close for his visit couldn't be arranged. So Michael visited the zoo during regular operating hours, in disguise. A British tabloid, *News of the World*, published photos of Michael in his disguise. He wore a false mustache, a wig with huge sideburns under a New York Yankees baseball cap, oversized sunglasses, and even false teeth that were crooked and uneven. This extensive disguise would have fooled almost anybody except the most ardent Jackson fan. While these articles did change his facial appearance, he still wore short black pants, white socks and black loafers. Fans also sometimes recognize his walk. If his clothes and mannerisms didn't give him away, having security chief Bill Bray accompanying him would have.

In France the tour played at the Parc des Princes. One performance in France was cancelled. Some reports said it was due to poor ticket sales. CBS said that more than sixty five percent of the tickets were sold when it was discovered by the local promoter that he couldn't stage the complex Bad tour production. With his extra time in Paris, Michael visited a toy store and toured the Louvre.

In Madrid, Spain, Michael was presented with a quadruple platinum award for *Bad*. The album had sales in that country of 400,000 copies.

The government of Malaysia denied Michael a concert there in December feeling that his intense popularity would cause too large of a commotion to control. The Welfare Ministry of

Malaysia wanted Michael Jackson to perform to raise money for the Welfare Fund which distributes money to orphanages and charities. The Ministry asked the cabinet, who gave the rejection, to reconsider their decision, but the rejection stood.

In Europe, the Bad tour played forty three concerts in twelve countries to over three million people, the largest audience ever for any European tour. The tour kept *Bad* at the top of the album charts in Europe and started a renewed surge of *Thriller* album sales. *Thriller* went back to the top ten albums in West Germany, six years after its release. While *Bad* was the number one album on *Billboard's* Pan European charts, *Thriller* wasn't far behind, ranking at number eleven.

By far the most successful of the European dates were those in London, England, at London's Wembley Stadium. Tickets for the July dates went on sale in January. Ticket demand exceeded 1.5 million, enough to fill Wembley's 72,000 seats twenty times! Michael ended up selling out seven nights at Wembley, shattering the previous record of the most sold out nights at Wembley. Madonna, Bruce Springsteen, and Genesis have each sold out four nights. More shows would have been added, but Wembley had reached their quota of live performance licenses. The enormous numbers of fans were not the only ones looking forward to the shows, so was Michael. He told the British press, "The British part of my world tour is going to be so exciting that I want to perform for as many people as I can while I'm with you. You British have always been fantastic for me." His enthusiasm may have dwindled slightly when Bubbles was again denied entry into the country to be with his master.

Taylor Dayne was the opening act for some of the European dates. For the British leg of the tour, Michael wanted one of Britain's newest, hottest groups, The Bros, to be his opening act. The group, who said they were big Michael Jackson fans, refused. They were planning to begin their own tour as a headliner and didn't feel they should accept any offer as an opening act. Kim Wilde was chosen next. Michael chose her himself, he had enjoyed her remake of the Supremes' "You Keep Me Hangin' On". Wilde opened for twelve concerts on the tour before ever meeting Michael.

The third concert at Wembley Stadium, on July 16, was attended by Prince Charles and Princess Diana. Michael met with the Prince and Princess before the show where he gave them Bad tour jackets for Prince William and Prince Harry. He also presented them with a framed set of cassettes and compact discs of *Off The Wall, Thriller,* and *Bad.* Michael Jackson is said to be Princess Diana's favorite pop star. Michael was equally happy to meet her. "I was so excited at meeting the royal couple. I'm very very happy that they came to watch me perform. I thought the Princess was just wonderful."

It had been reported earlier that Michael would not perform "Dirty Diana" that evening so as not to offend the Princess. Either these reports were wrong or Michael changed his mind, because "Dirty Diana" remained in the show as usual. Michael said later that he didn't want to disappoint his fans. It seems one big fan who would have been disappointed is Princess Diana herself. It was reported that she enjoyed the song and danced along.

With Pepsi, Michael made a $450,000 donation to the Princes' Trust, a charity for disadvantaged children. Michael also made a donation to the Wishing Well Fund, established to help finance the construction of a new building for London's Hospital for Sick Children. Michael toured the hospital and visited with some of the patients.

With each new stop on the tour, Michael continued to meet and visit with famous friends and fans. In London, Michael met with mime Marcel Marceau.

Michael couldn't resist shopping at Hamley's, the world's largest toy store. Shopping with Jimmy Safechuck, who had travelled to England with him, Michael purchased computer games, over twenty dolls and teddy bears, and six puppets; three Stevie Wonder puppets and three puppets of himself.

There was another toy Michael wanted but couldn't buy, a little something for the backyard of his new ranch, a carnival. He was originally interested in purchasing a merry-go-round, but ended up offering $2 million for an entire carnival. John Carter's Steam Fair features antique steam powered rides, including a 1895 Victorian merry-go-round. John Carter wasn't interested in selling and Michael's offer was refused.

As the tour continued playing in different cities around Great Britain, stories drifted back to the U.S. that Michael visited the famed Blarney Stone but refused to follow the custom of kissing it for fear of "catching AIDS, or something worse." Later it was reported that this story was false, not only did Michael not say this, he never visited the stone.

Given his many charitable donations, benefit concerts, and shopping sprees, it seemed Michael was spending money as fast as he could. His team of accountants were working to do just the opposite. They managed to save him $3 million in taxes from his concert proceeds earned in England, with tax form Revenue FEU 4. This form requires disclosure of expected revenue as well as the amount expected to be spent in the country. (It's not clear if the accountants considered the attempted purchase of a carnival.)

August was spent doing concerts in other cities throughout England. On his thirtieth birthday, Michael performed in Round-hay Park in Leeds. He told the crowd of 90,000 fans, "Thank you", after they sang "Happy Birthday" to him. The concert was a benefit performance for a British charity, Give for Life. Michael donated the proceeds of this concert, $130,000, toward the organization's goal of $1.9 million to help immunize 40,000 children against measles, diphtheria, polio, tuberculoses and other diseases.

During this performance in Leeds, an airplane swooped down less than two hundred feet above the crowd, a dangerous and illegal level. British authorities conducted an investigation to find the pilot, which wasn't expected to be too difficult since the plane flew low enough for the crowd to read the plane's registration number. Fortunately, there were no injuries.

CBS hosted a lavish celebration for Michael at London's historic Guildhall building. The party, held at the time of his birthday, was also to celebrate the *Bad* album and tour's tremendous success to date. Before the British concerts, *Bad* had sold nearly two million copies and was expected to return to the number one spot on the album charts. There were further predictions that *Bad* would possibly exceed *Thriller's* British sales of three million copies. This would be quite a feat since *Thriller* had returned to the British album charts and was selling like hot cakes itself.

The final concert of the European tour took place in the hometown of the Beatles, in Liverpool, at the Aintree Racetrack. The site of this last concert held a special meaning for Michael, "I have always considered Liverpool the home of contemporary pop music by virtue of it being the birthplace of the incomparable Beatles. I intend my Liverpool performance to be a tribute to rock's four greatest songwriters." His concert attracted the largest audience ever by a single artist at the Aintree Racetrack. It was also the site of another unfortunate incident, this one much more serious than the incident in Leeds. Over 125,000 fans crammed into the raceway for the show. At the start of the performance the massive crowd pushed forward crushing fans against the stage. Over 3,400 people were injured, forty of which needed to be hospitalized.

The Bad tour played to over 800,000 people in England and grossed L13 million, making it the biggest tour ever in England. A special ad was placed in *Billboard* magazine by U.K. concert promoter Barry Clayman Concerts, Ltd. congratulating Michael on setting a world record on U.K. admission figures:

The most sold out shows at London's Wembley
Stadium, total attendance of 504,00.
One soldout show at Cardiff Arma Park, 55,000.

One soldout show at Roundhay Park, Leeds, 90,000.
One soldout show of 60,000 at Milton Keynes Bowl
and one soldout show of 125,000 at Aintree Liverpool.

The Bad tour is also the biggest European tour ever.

Readers of *Blues & Soul* magazine, in the publication's annual readers poll, named Michael Jackson as the 1988 Outstanding Artist of the Year. Michael was also given honors for Best Live Show for 1988.

Just before returning to the U.S., Frank Dileo held a press conference to announce that this was Michael Jackson's final tour. (This makes his third "last" tour.) Dileo announced Michael would continue to record, but wanted to make films rather than tour.

This announcement was met with a great deal of skepticism by the press, fans, and even Michael's family and friends. The press doubted Michael would retire from the stage permanently, pointing out that if he wants to match his earlier record sales figures, he will need to tour with new albums. Even Michael's family questioned his decision. Marlon, who certainly knows how very much Michael loves to perform, thought his brother would someday return to the stage. LaToya, during an appearance on *Donahue*, commented on the announcement that Michael was giving up touring. "I don't think so. It's a part of him. It's in his blood, he could never quit that. When you've grown up with that all your life, you can't quit like that. No, I don't think so. Then again, I don't speak for Michael. But, I bet he hasn't."

If Michael actually did retire from touring, it would indeed be an enormous loss. To have the world's greatest entertainer stop performing live would leave an unfillable void.

The second leg of the U.S. tour kicked off in Frank Dileo's hometown, Pittsburg, Pennsylvania. Pittsburg honored Dileo by declaring September 22 as "Frank Dileo Day". Michael performed three concerts in Pittsburg, September 26 through the 28th.

Tickets for the second set of U.S. dates went on sale in June, four to six months in advance of any of the scheduled dates. As the first announced dates sold out in each city, more shows were added, having three concerts scheduled in most cities.

Ticket sales for many acts touring in the summer of 1988 were lower than expected. The unusual heatwave and drought being experienced in the U.S. was partially blamed for low ticket sales for acts playing outdoor venues. Another factor contributing to the disappointing concert crowds were the early sales of tickets by concert heavyweights Elton John and Michael Jackson. Music fans spent their concert budget on these early sales of tickets then couldn't afford to attend many, if any, other concerts. Luckily, they made excellent choices of who to see in concert. (Elton John's tour in support of *Reg Strikes Back* was among his best ever, but I'll leave that for another book!)

The return of the Bad tour to the U.S. included only eight cities. After Pittsburgh, it was on to East Rutherford, New Jersey, October 3-5. On October 10 and 11 dates were made up in Cleveland, Ohio. The Bad tour played in Largo, Maryland on October 13, and 17-19.

At the end of October, the Bad tour moved into Motown-Detroit, Michigan. Michael was scheduled to perform at the Palace of Auburn Hills on October 24-26. The first of the three night stand in Detroit was a benefit concert for Detroit's Motown Museum. The two story house, Hitsville USA, where Berry Gordy originally started Motown, had been declared a historical landmark earlier in the spring. Since Motown relocated to Los Angeles, the building has been turned into a museum, organized by Berry Gordy's sister, Esther Edwards.

When Berry Gordy was preparing to sell Motown Records to MCA and Boston Ventures, Michael was touring Europe. He wanted to do something for Berry and for Motown. Gordy suggested he do something for the Motown Museum. Michael did. He called Esther Edwards in Detroit from Hong Kong. The result was that Michael donated all of his proceeds from his first concert in Auburn Hills to the Motown Museum Historical Foundation. Michael has been a very strong supporter of the development of the museum since its inception. He told Edwards that he "would love to make the museum known all over the world."

On October 23, 1988, Michael Jackson presented a check for $125,000 to Esther Edwards and Berry Gordy in a ceremony held in front of Hitsville USA, the Motown Museum. Several blocks of West Grand Boulevard were closed to all traffic with mounted police lining the street. In spite of low temperatures, thousands of fans stood behind the barricades set up across the street from the museum and next door to catch a glimpse of Michael Jackson. Even though he wasn't scheduled to arrive until late afternoon, fans started gathering outside early in the morning. They waited. And they waited. Then it started to rain and it got colder.

Huge speakers placed outside played Motown hits continuously for the crowd, classics from Smokey Robinson, Stevie Wonder, and the Supremes. Conspicuously absent were any hits of Michael Jackson and the Jackson Five. Until 3:30 that is. At Michael's planned arrival time, Jackson Five and Michael Jackson solo hits with Motown were played back to back. The excitement continued to build as limos appeared and dropped off guests. Finally, over an hour late, a police escort made its way down West Grand Boulevard, going the wrong way down the one way street, leading two black limousines. Berry Gordy, Michael Jackson, and his bodyguards, including Bill Bray, stepped out. Michael was barely visible to the crowd as he made his way up the steps surrounded by guards, one of whom held an umbrella over him. Michael was dressed in black pants, a red shirt and a black military jacket with red trim, and sunglasses.

Detroit Mayor Coleman Young started off the presentation singing the praises of Berry Gordy and Michael Jackson. He then introduced Berry Gordy who spoke next, and who really knew how to bring the excitement of the Detroit crowd to an even higher level. With each mention of Michael's name, a thunderous cheer rose from the crowd:

Michael Jackson knows that success in life is not merely confined to fame and fortune and material gains, but it's also found in a continual awareness our roots. These are Michael Jackson's roots, right here. You are the first people that bought Michael Jackson's records and he loves you, and he loves you for it.

Gordy went on, calling Michael, "not only the biggest star to come out of Motown, but the biggest star to come out of any town!" He then introduced Michael. "I give you my pupil, my protege, my son, even my big brother at times, and my friend all of the time, and I love him ...MICHAEL JACKSON !!!!!!"

Michael, who had been standing next to Berry, stepped to the podium, his first words were practically impossible to decipher due to the cheering of the fans:

I just want to briefly say I'm honored to be here, to give back to the soil from which I came. And Berry Gordy is the man who made it all possible for me. I'd like to say thank you Berry, and I love you.

Michael then leaned over and hugged Berry. A large color photo of Michael Jackson hugging Berry Gordy was featured on the front page of the next morning's edition of *The Detroit News*.

In addition to the check for $125,000, Michael also donated to the museum a black fedora, a white beaded glove and the costume he wore in 1972 on *American Bandstand* when he performed "Ben". Michael's donation of money and memorabilia make up the largest contribution ever by one person to the museum.

Following the brief presentation, Michael, Berry, Esther and crew toured the museum. Michael and Berry, reminiscing about the early days, spent most of the time standing and talking in the small gift shop and posing for pictures with the staff and museum volunteers. Michael picked out one of everything the gift shop had to offer, having one of his bodyguards pay for it.

He was pleased with the museum's Michael Jackson room, the only room in the museum dedicated solely to one artist. A mirrored sign over the door reads, "Michael Jackson - Magic". The walls are filled with photos and posters of Michael tracing his entire career; photos with his brothers and Diana Ross when he was very young to a poster with Paul McCartney in the studio working on "Say Say Say" to a huge framed poster of his *Bad* album cover photo. There is also a poster of Michael from the video for "The Way You Make Me Feel" and several pictures taken from the 1985 Official Michael Jackson Calendar. Most of the posters are mounted on poster board and simply stuck to the wall, others are framed.

Two glass showcases hang side by side on one wall. One houses the costume Michael donated along with a platinum copy of the "Dancing Machine" single. The other houses a poster of Michael in a white shirt and yellow vest and a concert t-shirt from the Bad tour.

One corner of the room is enclosed behind a full length glass door. A sign on the door reads the same as the one over the doorway. Inside is Michael's sequined glove and black fedora. Originally, the highly treasured items were fastened to a bar with a thumb tack through them. Since then, the items have been rearranged, with the glove lying flat on a table and the hat resting on a pedestal just behind it. A tape player sits inconspicuously on a shelf inside with Michael Jackson and Jackson Five music playing continuously.

After about an hour and a half visit, Michael and Berry headed for a dinner held at Gordy's Detroit mansion. About twenty eight people attended, including museum staff and volunteers. Michael's chef also accompanied Michael to the museum and of course the dinner following it. His chef found out what was going to be served beforehand so he could plan and prepare Michael's meal to look as much like the others' as possible. Michael, sticking to his strict vegetarian diet, wouldn't allow himself to eat any of the goodies being served. His food was, as always, prepared very decoratively. He had corn, potatoes, cut into pieces exactly the same size, and an apple. The apple was cut into decorative diamond shapes. His meals are always prepared lavishly, with lots of color and interestingly shaped pieces. He drank bottled water, which must only be opened at his table in front of him. For dessert he had strawberry sherbert which was also beautifully decorated.

The next day Michael performed the first of three soldout shows at the Palace of Auburn Hills, in Auburn Hills, Michigan. The show was scheduled to start at 8:00 p.m. With no opening act for the U.S. shows, the crowd waited restlessly until Michael hit the stage at 9:00. When the lights went down the crowd forgot their wait and looked forward to seeing the most dazzling performance ever. And that's exactly what they got.

A huge billboard sized bank of lights flashes on and shows the image of Michael's legs as they walk slowly across the screen, moonwalk back, go into a spin and freeze up on his toes, bringing deafening cheers from the fans. Slowly the bank of lights rises above the stage, revealing the band, singers, dancers and Michael all on stage, frozen in their poses. Michael is dressed in short black pants up to his ankles, with a harness around his right leg, a silver shirt with straps and buckles lining each sleeve, a black jacket with silver badges along the front. His hair is pulled back in a ponytail and his first, third, and fourth fingertips of his right hand are wrapped with white tape.

With a flip of a wrist from Michael they begin "Wanna Be Startin' Somethin'". During this song Michael first excites the audience, grabbing his crotch as he dances. At the end of the song they all freeze in their places. After a few seconds of silence, they continue with some more of "Wanna Be Startin' Somethin'".

Before starting "Heartbreak Hotel" Michael removes his jacket. "Heartbreak Hotel" is highlighted with synchronized dance moves with Michael and his dancers, and a fire bomb Michael pretends to throw in front of guitarist Jennifer Batten. It ends with Michael being circled with green laser light beams. Then it's dark. Out of the darkness Michael calls out to the audience, "How ya doin'? I said, how ya doin'?" To the thunderous approval of the crowd, "Another Part of Me" is performed by Michael alone, without the dancers. The strong beats of the song are emphasized with green laser lights shot rapidly at the stage and ricocheting off in different directions.

"Human Nature" is also performed without the dancers. Michael invites the audience to sing along, "Everybody sing! If they say why, why tell them that it's human nature, why, why does he do me that way?" At the end of "Human Nature" Michael displays some of his most incredible moves. He walks slowly in place, sort of like moonwalking, only he doesn't move backward or forward. These steps are blended with very rapid mime movements like he's trapped in a box or behind a wall. His apparent mastery of mime amazes the audience, but even this is a small taste of the incredible moves yet to come, as the dancer return for the next song.

The stage is darkened and three white shades are lowered. Michael stands behind the center one, preparing for the next song. He pulls his hair back in a ponytail, most of it having come undone by now. Someone hands him a white blazer. He takes a few seconds to adjust the white fedora he's also just been handed. He gets into position. He's ready. One dancer stands behind each of the other two screens, also with blazers and hats. Spotlights hit the three shades and the dancers move slowly from one stance to another, very similar to the beginning of Michael's performance on the Grammys. A pink neon sign spelling "Hotel" is lit up and a taped, barely audible, story setting up the song is played. The three screens are raised and Michael runs to center stage for "Smooth Criminal". Much of the choreography is taken from the song's video, Michael even does the lean he performed in the video. At the end of "Smooth Criminal", Michael shoots his dancers with an air machine gun. The stage is dark except for a single spotlight on Michael. The four dancers, or criminals, fall to the ground to their death. Michael pushes his fedora down over his eyes and slowly walks across the stage and steps into a tiny white tent that just popped up on the corner of the stage.

He emerges a few seconds later having removed the jacket and hat. The stage is still dark, surrounded by tiny white lights resembling stars. Michael sings his first lines of "I Just Can't Stop Loving You" as a single spotlight hits him. A second spotlight hits Sheryl Crow as she steps forward on the opposite side of the stage to join Michael for the duet. Slowly they walk towards each other meeting in the middle of the stage. Michael draws wild cheers from the crowd as he reaches out and caresses Sheryl's thigh. They end the song abruptly with the line "And if I stop!" Sheryl leaves the stage to Michael. He rubs his eyes, weeping, and begins "She's Out Of My Life", bringing some of the night's loudest cheers as the song is recognized. He stops in the middle of one line and asks, "Can I come down there?" The crowd goes into hysterics thinking he'd actually go into the audience. A girl who had been selected earlier from the audience, is escorted to the stage. Michael comes down a couple of steps and hugs her. Taking her hand, he leads her up to the stage and hugs her again. She is escorted from the stage and Michael continues the song. He finishes the last line, "She's out of my...", hesitating before the last word, weeping again. When he finally sings the last word, "...life", it brings the house down. There's no doubt Michael Jackson is a well-studied showman who knows exactly how to get the biggest response from his audience.

For the first two performances in Auburn Hills, Michigan, Michael dedicated the next songs, "to a man who is in the audience tonight, Mr. Berry Gordy, who gave me my first big break in show business." The final show used the usual introduction, "Now we're gonna give you the old stuff the old fashioned way." Michael and his four dancers perform "I Want You Back" and the "Love You Save" with the same choreography the Jackson Five performed nearly twenty years earlier. It was great fun for those reliving the Jackson Five appearances on the *Ed Sullivan Show* and *American Bandstand* and for the younger fans seeing it for the first time. "I'll Be There" completed the Jackson Five medley, with one of the background singers singing Jermaine's lines. Michael had the entire crowd waving their arms in the air. At the end of "I'll Be There", Michael again pauses before singing the last word. In slow motion, he crouches down, putting his arm over his eyes. He raises up just as slowly and lets out the last word, "...there!" Again, it's a tremendous crowd pleaser, once again proving he can build excitement like no one else can.

"I THINK I WANNA ROCK!" starts "Rock With You". Michael displays even more of his fancy footwork while hitting each high note perfectly. After "Rock With You", he returns to the tiny tent which just appeared again. He emerges wearing a long white shirt, unbuttoned and untucked, white Bike knee pads and long black fingerless gloves with rows of buckles, and he literally lets his hair down, the ponytail is now gone. The familiar guitar sounds of "Dirty Diana" begin. Michael sings the song with deep emotion, spinning and landing on his knees, (thus the knee pads). He chases Jennifer Batten up a ramp at the side of the stage, across the back and down the other side, waving to the crowd at the sides and rear of the stage. The fans cheer wildly at Michael's acknowledgement of them. At the conclusion of "Dirty Diana", it's back to the tent. A light goes on inside this time, allowing the audience to see Michael's silhouette inside changing into his next costume.

After what seemed like an excessive amount of movement, Michael climbs out wearing a red and white varsity jacket and a werewolf mask covering his entire head. The eerie creaking sound of a coffin confirms "Thriller" next. This is especially thrilling because it is the first tour in which "Thriller" has ever been performed, having been left out of the Victory tour performances due to the wishes of the Jehovah Witnesses. He roams across the stage, becomes frightened, and runs back into the tent which explodes and immediately flattens. Instantly, Michael reappears on the opposite side of the stage and pulls off the mask. His dancers return to the stage, dressed in dirty, ragged costumes to join Michael in recreating the choreography from the "Thriller" video. Michael changes into a sequined version of the red jacket he wears in the video, the lights go out and the dancer's costumes and Michael's jacket light up.

The illusion at the beginning of the song works if you are seated far from the stage or aren't very observant. For those seated close to the stage and those who are ardent fans and notice every detail about him, it is obvious that it is not really Michael who initially steps from the tent wearing the mask. The tent apparently has a trap door beneath it. Michael went into the tent after "Dirty Diana" went through the trap door, beneath the stage and up on the other side, changing into another varsity jacket and mask. The person who comes out of the tent and then disappears as the tent explodes, is of slightly bigger build than Michael and moves differently. Nevertheless, "Thriller" in concert is exactly that, a thriller.

Michael, his singers and dancers leave the stage to the band for a short break. Each member of the band plays a solo. First, Greg Phillinganes shows his expertise on keyboards. Don Boyette takes center stage for an extended bass solo. Jon Clark does his guitar solo next followed by Ricky Lawson on drums. The rest of the band, dancers and singers then return to the stage with Michael for a grand production of "Working Day and Night". Michael has changed into a white jumpsuit with several black belts around his waist, the rest of the cast are all in black. Everybody takes part in the dancing, all lining up across the stage with Michael in the middle. There are several stops where the entire cast instantly stops and freezes for a few seconds before starting right up again. At one point, everybody on stage is frozen in their positions. Michael walks among them, waving his hands in their faces and snapping his fingers. They don't even blink. The finish of "Working Day and Night" features a second illusion that is much more mysterious as to how it was done than the illusion performed for "Thriller". Michael climbs a short set of stairs and stands on a small platform while a silver tube is lowered over him. The staircase is open underneath, leaving nowhere for Michael to go this time, either up or down. The tube is slowly raised and Michael is gone. BOOM!!! There's an explosion on the opposite side of the stage and Michael appears now wearing black pants, white t-shirt and a red sequined multi-zippered jacket. He of course had the pants and t-shirt on under the white jumpsuit, but how he got from one side of the stage to the other in two seconds remains a mystery.

Michael appears standing in the box of cherry picker. The huge crane slowly raises out of the floor of the stage and swings slowly out over the first few rows of the audience. Holding onto the railings on either side and hooking his toes on the bottom edge of the platform, he leans forward, out of the box, over the audience. Slowly the crane swings back to the stage. As Michael and his dancers perform "Beat It", the crowd goes wild, seeing live the choreography they had seen dozens of times from the song's video. Michael even breaks up a knife fight between two of the dancers.

After "Beat It" the stage goes dark. Michael moves about the stage in the darkness. He removes the red jacket and wipes his face with a towel. He walks slowly back and forth across the stage and suddenly tosses the towel into the crowd. A spotlight is shone on the audience where he threw the now treasured article.

Michael goes to the rear of the stage, where someone waits with another costume. He puts on a jacket. A black jacket. And a hat. A black hat. And one white glove. He positions himself in front of the microphone stand, knees bent, one foot out. One hand is on the hat, the other on his crotch. A spotlight hits Michael in this pose that only means one thing. "Billie Jean". Michael recreates his magical performance from the *Motown 25* special. He flawlessly brings that performance back to life, saving most of his moonwalking for this song. The performance of the song is extended to include even more awe-inspiring steps. The crowd is hysterical. Michael goes back to the microphone stand, retrieves his hat, and unleashes an incredible arsenal of moves. He sings the last line of the song, "Billie Jean is not my lover" and whips the fedora into the audience. A spotlight follows the hat into the audience and remains until it is grabbed up by an extremely grateful and happy fan. (One of the several semis used to carry the tour's equipment must be completely stocked with black fedoras!) Michael stands alone on stage watching with everyone else to see who gets the hat.

The stage is then darkened. The huge bank of lights is lowered again. Several seconds later it lights up, spelling out one letter at a time, B- A- D. Then it flashes alternately, "BAD" "WHO'S BAD". The excited crowd calls out each word as it appears, "BAD" "WHO'S BAD" "BAD" "WHO'S BAD". The sign is slowly raised and Michael is center stage, wearing a black jacket with several buckles, and black fingerless gloves, also with several buckles. The entire crowd seems to know every word as they sing along, "Your butt is mine, gonna tell you right, just show your face in broad daylight..." For "Bad" Michael unveils his latest step. He has taken the moonwalk one better. He performs the new sideways moonwalk just as he performed it on the MTV Music Video Awards, but for most of the crowd it is their first time seeing the new twist on the now familiar moonwalk. Michael ends the song with the words, "Who's Bad!" and in the exact stance as he started the song.

The stage is darkened while Michael walks up to the rear of the stage. Hidden fans send air up at him, blowing his jacket and hair. The lights come up and he resumes the song. He introduces each singer, dancer, and band member. He takes singer Sheryl Crow's hand and leads her to the front of the stage and they dance together. He leads her back and introduces the other singers, Kevin Dorsey, Dorian Holley, and Darryl Phinnessee. He introduces each band member, Chris Curell and Rory Kaplan on keyboards, pausing at keyboards and singing, "Greg ... Phillinganes". They perform synchronized moves and Michael rubs the top of Greg's head and Greg pokes Michael in the belly. Michael giggles and moves on to the drums. The friendly teasing between Greg and Michael seems to be the only nonscripted few seconds of the entire show, until he does the exact same thing the next night, and the night after that, and the night after that.... . Michael calls out "Rick, Rick, Rick" in between the beats of drummer Ricky Lawson. After introducing bass player Don Boyette he takes guitarist Jennifer Batten center stage for a brief solo and then guitarist Jon Clark. The dancers that accompanied Michael on the Bad tour are Randy Aelaire, Evaldo Garcia, Dominic Lucero, and LaVelle Smith. Smith would later appear in Janet's video, "Miss You Much" and accompany her on her Rhythm Nation tour. Garcia later became one of the Guys Next Door, Saturday morning TV's answer to The New Kids on the Block.

Michael then brings out several children on stage. These children are usually chosen at each stop from local hospitals or charitable organizations, such as the Make a Wish Foundation. The children dance and Michael joins in, dancing just like them. He leads them off stage, waves to the crowd, and tells the crowd, "Goodnight, I love you."

After several minutes of screams, whistles, and "We want Michael" chants, out of the darkness Michael calls out, "You knock me off of my feet now baby!" Sheryl Crow takes Tatiana's place for "The Way You Make Me Feel", as she walks across the stage in a similar very short and snug black dress. Michael, now dressed in black pants with white stripes down the sides, a blue shirt unbuttoned with a t-shirt underneath, and a white belt tied around his waist, chases Sheryl around the stage before joining his dancers. They recreate the steps seen in the song's video, bringing wild cheers from the crowd as they all hit the ground, lying flat on their stomachs and raising their butts off the ground.

The stage is then left to Michael for the second encore, "Man in the Mirror". Each performance is just as passionate as his performance on the Grammys, spinning around and landing on his knees. (This time he has knee pads on under his pant legs.) The crowd sings along and seem to know every word, just as with "Bad". Michael finishes with his arms held out and his head back, eyes closed. He seems to be exhausted, but also very emotional, perhaps shedding genuine tears.

He brings out all of the singers, dancers and band members to the front of the stage to take a bow. The band returns to their places and continues to play. Michael walks from side to side of the stage waving and saying goodnight. While the band still plays, he leaves the stage and exits the stadium, driving off before the house lights come on. Two hours have never flown by so quickly. Any fans already waiting outside stood a good chance of getting a big smile and wave from Michael as he left the stadium.

After each of his three performances in Auburn Hills, Detroit radio station Z95.5 played over one hour of back to back Michael Jackson and Jackson Five songs. It was a small consolation for those unable to attend the concerts, and a continuation of the excitement for those who did attend but were still trying to get out the parking lot!

Before one of his performances in Detroit Michael met backstage with Chrysler Chairman Lee Iacocca. Michael had read Iacocca's book *Straight Talking*, in which Iacocca defends his 1986 income of $20.5 million. "$20 million sounds more like Michael Jackson's income for a weekend than the annual pay of a guy who can't carry a tune in the shower."

The dates following Detroit, scheduled for Tacoma, Washington were cancelled. Michael's vocal cords had become swollen and on the advice of his doctors and Frank Dileo, all three dates were cancelled. The purchase price of the tickets were refunded and the dates were not re-scheduled. Later a class action suit was filed against Ticketmaster and Michael Jackson on behalf of the ticket buyers for the return of the service charge for each ticket, which had not been refunded. The lawyer filing the suit claimed Michael was not really sick when the shows were cancelled, and therefore he committed breach of contract. Nothing was said as to how he intended to prove Michael's illness was faked.

The tour's next stop was Irvine, California. The first show went on as planned but the remaining dates were cancelled due to Michael's continued illness. His first California performance was attended by several celebrities. Besides a slew of Jacksons, there was Lionel Richie, Quincy Jones, Barbra Streisand, Slyvester Stallone, Marlee Matlin, Magic Johnson, Danny DeVito and Rhea Pearlman. Los Angeles mayor Tom Bradley declared November to be "Michael Jackson Month". The following dates, scheduled for Los Angeles, were cancelled and re-scheduled for January. One of the concerts was a benefit concert for Childhelp USA, a charity for abused children. In return, plans were made to establish the Michael Jackson Institute for Abused Children.

After a few weeks of rest and recuperation, the tour headed back to Japan, where it all started over one year earlier. Nine concerts were scheduled between December 9 and 26 in the Tokyo Dome. All 405,000 seats soldout months in advance. Michael returned to Japan to end his tour because, "I appreciate the support that my Japanese friends and fans have shown me." The 405,000 fans who attended Michael's second set of concerts in Japan, combined with the 450,000 who saw his first set of shows there, makes Michael Jackson's 1987-1988 World Tour the largest tour ever in Japan. The total attendance of 855,000 fans is said to be four times greater than that of any other Japanese tour.

At one of these last concerts in Japan, Michael met backstage with two young fans and their parents. Nine year old Ayana Takada was the four millionth fan to attend the Bad tour. Michael met with her and her brother and presented her with a certificate to commemorate the now record breaking attendance figure. The Bad tour had played to the largest audience ever, four million people.

At these final concerts in Japan, farewell concert T-shirts and hats were sold. But it was not really his farewell concert, he still had dates to make up in Los Angeles. So, it was back to the U.S. again.

Backstage at one of the Los Angeles shows, at the Los Angeles Sports Arena, Michael met with Elizabeth Ashcroft. Elizabeth had won tickets to the concert and the opportunity to meet Michael in a contest. She gave Michael a t-shirt that read, "I've met Elizabeth Ashcroft"! Ten year old Andrew Wigglesworth also got to meet Michael at one of his Los Angeles concerts, and have one of his dreams come true. Andrew had lost a leg to a tumor. With the help of actor Martin Sheen, who met Andrew while working on a movie, Andrew's wish to meet Michael Jackson was fulfilled.

January 27, 1989, was Michael Jackson's final performance of the Bad World Tour. Los Angeles mayor Tom Bradley declared it "Michael Jackson Day" and presented Michael with the proclamation. Several celebrities showed up to wish him farewell. Among them were Raquel Welch, Michael Landon, Phil Collins, Dionne Warwick, Lola Falona, Tiffany, Diahann Carroll, Ava Gardner, and Sidney Poitier. Many of Michael's closest friends were also there; Suzanne dePasse, Sophia Loren, Jane Fonda, and Smokey Robinson. Rebbie, Jackie, Jermaine, Janet and his mother, Katherine, were all there for Michael's final concert performance. Elizabeth Taylor and Diana Ross also attended the last show. There were stories that they were upset when the other took too much of Michael's attention, and security purposely seated them at opposite sides of the stage to avoid any problems. One other very special friend visited Michael backstage that night, Bubbles.

For this performance, Berry Gordy was again in the audience. Michael dedicated the Motown medley to Gordy, and at the end of the show he told the audience, "Ladies and gentlemen, there is a man here tonight who helped my career. He is Berry Gordy. Stand up Berry!"

Among the children to join Michael on stage for this final performance was Jimmy Safechuck. Jimmy was dressed as Michael and performed the new sideways moonwalk right along side Michael.

Outside the Los Angeles Sports Arena that night was a camera crew and reporter from *The Pat Sajak Show*, trying to get in for an exclusive interview with Michael Jackson. The reporter tried several tricks to gain entry into the arena. He posed as a pizza deliveryman, pretended to have Michael's dry cleaning, and claimed to be Michael's choreographer. He never got in and never talked to Michael. It was all a gag to tease their viewers. Michael Jackson was among the guests on the show, though not the one viewers expected. Radio talk show host Michael Jackson was a guest on the show that evening. He told humorous stories of things that have happened to him as the result of sharing such a famous name. When he was awarded his star on the Hollywood Walk of Fame, his son told him he was very proud, but who would ever believe it was really his!

When the Bad tour finished in Los Angeles that night, after sixteen months, 123 performances in 15 countries, it had played to 4.4 million people and grossed $125 million. This made the Bad tour the largest grossing tour in history and also the tour to play to the most people ever. Michael Jackson had just earned himself two more places in the *Guiness Book of World Records*. The Bad tour was the sixth largest grossing tour of the year in the United States. Playing in only nineteen cities, the tour grossed $20.3 million.

Doubts still remained that this would actually be the end of live performances for Michael Jackson. These doubts seemed to be confirmed when Frank Dileo avoided stating that Michael would never perform live again, only that he wouldn't embark on a tour of such an enormous scale again. Although Michael has set new standards in video and has given two of the best television performances ever, on *Motown 25* and the 1988 Grammys, nothing can match the magic and excitement of seeing him perform live.

Only Michael's love of performing would bring him back. There are simply no other reasons for him to ever tour again; he hates most of the things that go along with touring, he certainly doesn't need the additional income, and there are no other records to top. He set out to put on the biggest, best tour ever, and he has done that.

CHAPTER THIRTEEN

MOONWALKER

The seventh video from *Bad* premiered on MTV on January 2, 1989. "Leave Me Alone", a unique blend of live action and animation, combines a small animated carnival setting with Michael cruising around in a small plane. With the use of special effects and humor, Michael confronts the press and the ridiculous stories that had been printed about him. Newspapers land on a doorstep all having outrageous headlines:

MICHAEL'S SPACE AGE DIET
BUBBLES THE CHIMP BARES ALL ABOUT MICHAEL
MICHAEL PROPOSES TO LIZ
MICHAEL TO MARRY BROOKE
MICHAEL'S COSMETIC NOSE SURGERY
MICHAEL AND DIANA SAME PERSON
JACKSON'S 3RD EYE STARTS SUNGLASS FAD
MICHAEL WEDS ALIEN

Michael sings from the photos of himself in newspapers with the headlines, "MICHAEL FROZEN FOR 50 YEARS", "MICHAEL CONFIDES TO PET CHIMP" and "MICHAEL SLEEPS IN HYPERBARIC CHAMBER". Michael delivers lyrics aimed at the media, "leave me alone, stop doggin' me around" while coasting by a proposed image of his "shrine" to Elizabeth Taylor, lying in his hyperbaric chamber, and dancing along side the skeleton of the elephant man. At the video's conclusion, Michael frees himself from ties binding his wrists and holding him down. He stands up, destroying a roller coaster, and towers over the now tiny carnival.

The "Leave Me Alone" video was successful on MTV and VH-1 and the song did receive some radio airplay, but it was never formally released as a single in the U.S. by Epic Records. It was released as a single in England. The song is not included on the *Bad* album or cassette, appearing as a bonus track on the CD format only.

The weekend following the debut of the "Leave Me Alone" video, Sunday, January 8, was Michael Jackson Sunday on MTV. All of his videos, concert clips, and behind the scenes footage of the Bad tour were featured for the entire day.

The "Leave Me Alone" video is taken from the music video cassette, *Moonwalker*. After the usual delays incurred before the release of any new Michael Jackson product, the video cassette was finally released in the United States on January 10. Gift certificates were issued in major record and video stores in mid December so Christmas sales wouldn't be lost. *Moonwalker* was released earlier in Europe, in theaters. It opened Christmas week in France and was the week's largest grossing film. It was released on cassette in Japan in early December and was sold at his last set of concerts there on the Bad tour.

In Japan, a music video is considered to be very successful if sales exceed 20,000 copies. *Moonwalker* was shipped out at 120,000 copies and sales were expected to reach 200,000. In the U.S., 300,000 copies were initially shipped, the largest first shipment ever for a home video. This made *Moonwalker* automatically the second most successful home video ever, behind *Making Michael Jackson's Thriller* which still held the number one spot. For now.

Moonwalker begins with one of Michael's Pepsi commercials, the concert version. Critics attacked Michael for including the ad on the cassette, saying it detracted from the rest of the features of the film. Actually, it doesn't detract from the rest of the video at all. Even though it is intended to sell Pepsi, it is also yet another great performance of Michael's worth watching over and over again. Seen from Michael's perspective, it's one of his performances that has been very successful, winning awards and international recognition, even setting a new world record. These factors no doubt played a key role in his decision to include the ad on the cassette.

For the presentation of "Man in the Mirror" at least two different live performances are blended with scenes from the song's video. Michael's energy filled and emotional delivery of the song's inspirational lyrics demonstrate how touching the song's message is to Michael. Like "She's Out Of My Life", "Man in the Mirror" seems to touch Michael every time he performs it.

The retrospective of Michael's career is one of the most interesting and revealing segments of the video. Scanning a tabletop filled with many years of memorabilia, it is interesting to note the items chosen to be included. It would be a safe bet to assume each item was personally chosen or approved by Michael. Included are numerous awards; several Grammy awards, an American Music Award and a MTV Music Video Award. A mug holding makeup brushes sits with sunglasses, and framed photographs of the Jackson Five, Michael with Diana Ross, Quincy Jones, George Lucas and Francis Ford Coppola. Three sequined gloves, a red one, a blue one, and a white one are arranged on top of the shoes he wears in the video for "Smooth Criminal". The white fedora he wears in "Smooth Criminal" and a black sequined fedora are both carefully arranged. There are tiny figurines of Louie the llama and Uncle Tookie from the line of Michael's Pets and larger statues of Mickey Mouse and Pinocchio. Behind the table hangs several of Michael's sequined military jackets and the sequined shirt he wears in the *Motown 25* special. The only items not connected directly with his career are the statuettes of Mickey Mouse and Pinochio, reflecting his personal interest in cartoons.

At the end of the table sits a TV monitor playing clips of early Jackson Five performances including a new claymation version of "ABC". Clips of the videos for "Beat It" and "Billie Jean" are shown with clips with his then latest videos for "The Way You Make Me Feel" and "Dirty Diana".

A short clip of "Bad" begins with the camera panning from Michael's buckled boots to his face. Only when the camera gets to his face, it's not Michael. Brandon Adams portrays a miniature Michael Jackson for "Badder", a humorous version of "Bad" with a cast of children. Adams lip syncs to Michael's voice and does an excellent job of recreating Michael's moves. Russell and Michael Higgins did the choreography for the remake of "Bad". One of the young dancers in "Badder" is Jermaine Jackson Jr. The WANTED poster ripped from the subway wall in "Badder" has Michael's picture on it reading, "Wanted For Questioning".

This undoubtedly makes Michael the first artist to spoof his own video.

The "Speed Demon" video has Michael on a studio lot being chased by a horde of fans. He escapes MJJ studios, which has Michael's Moonwalker logo on a water tower, on a bike, dressed in a rabbit costume. The scene changes to claymation as Spike the rabbit is chased by a claymation crowd of fans armed with cameras and autograph books. Michael's perception of fans and members of the press following and hounding him is perhaps illustrated when one claymation figure after Michael holds his movie camera like a gun and has a belt of film canisters around his shoulder and chest like an ammunition belt. Finally losing the crowd Michael sheds the rabbit costume which then magically comes to life and a dance challenge ensues between them. The competition is ended when Michael is issued a citation for performing a prohibited dance step.

Included in "Speed Demon" are some humorous references people close to Michael. Michael's guards who are literally flattened attempting to halt the stampeding crowd are claymation versions of Michael's real life bodyguards Bill Bray and Miko Brando. There are also child versions of Bray and Brando in "Badder". During his escape in "Speed Demon" Michael, dressed as the rabbit, rides through the drive thru window of a fast food restaurant, a Frank-in-the-Box. On top of the restaurant is a huge caricature of Frank Dileo, complete with his cigar. The director on a movie set Michael interrupts looks very much like a claymation charactiture of George Lucas.

The choreography for "Speed Demon" was done by Vincent Patterson, who had worked with Michael on the video for "The Way You Make Me Feel". The claymation was done by Wil Vinton, who first become known for his work with the dancing California Raisins.

Next is the video for "Leave Me Alone" in which Michael tells his critics just that, leave me alone. This is followed by the forty two minute version of "Smooth Criminal". It was directed by Colin Chilvers, who directed *Superman*, and produced by Jerry Kramer. Kramer worked with Michael before when he directed *Making Michael Jackson's Thriller*. In the mini movie Michael and his child friends accidently discover an evil plan to turn young children into drug users, to gain control of the world. This is the scheme of the diabolical Frankie Lideo, another reference to Frank Dileo. Michael teams with his friends; Zeke, played by Brandon Adams; Sean, played by Sean Lennon; and Katie, played by Kellie Parker; to foil Lideo's plan. Rick Baker, who transformed Michael into a werewolf in "Thriller" now transforms him into a robot for "Smooth Criminal". Michael destroys Lideo's, also known as Mr. Big, and saves the world.

The role of Mr. Big was played by Joe Pesci, but was originally written for a friend of Michael's, Marlon Brando. Pesci has since become known for his roles in *Lethal Weapon 2* and *Lethal Weapon 3* with Mel Gibson and Danny Glover and as a burglar in *Home Alone*. He later won an Oscar for Best Supporting Actor for his role in *Goodfellas*.

"Smooth Criminal" leads directly to Michael's performance of the Beatles' hit "Come Together". His band from the Bad tour join Michael on stage for one of his best performances since *Motown 25* and the 1988 Grammys. Michael wears shiny black pants, a huge ornate gold belt and yellow shirt with a white t-shirt underneath, and taped fingertips. During the performance, obviously made up of several takes, his t-shirt goes through various stages of being torn down the middle to his waist, and then back up again. He delivers the lyrics in a voice lower than usual, in a performance that is nothing less than dazzling, brilliant, sexy and all too short.

The ninety four minute video concludes with Ladysmith Black Mombazo performing "The Moon is Walking". The song was written especially for Michael after the group met him on the set of "Smooth Criminal". Michael enjoyed the song so much he included it on the *Moonwalker* video.

As the lengthy closing credits roll, too brief glimpses of rehearsals for "Smooth Criminal" are shown with Michael giving direction to other dancers and putting the white tape on his fingertips. The shorter version of the "Smooth Criminal" video is shown with the credits. At the conclusion of the long list of credits and acknowledgements is a special thank you to one man, Quincy Jones: "A special thank you to Quincy Jones for 10 years of collaboration and inspiration."

At least one feature Michael wanted to include on *Moonwalker* never made it. Michael was disappointed when he was refused permission to use footage of Fred Astaire from one of his movies. Michael had wanted to superimpose himself onto the film becoming Astaire's partner. It is unfortunate it couldn't have been done, it would have been a great tribute to Fred Astaire and a thrill for Michael. Astaire's widow would not grant Michael permission to use the footage.

The story for "Smooth Criminal" was Michael's creation. The screenplay was written by David Newman. Newman spoke about his experience working with Michael:

A lot of what it is with Michael, working with Michael, is just falling into the groove that he's in, and he does things with an incredible savvy and canny understanding of how they will ultimately affect the audience. They're not about Michael, they're about making the piece work.

Michael explained to his dancers what he wanted in the video:

... the two beats should be more internal, you've got more movement. It should be more like somethin' goin' on inside of ya. That's why we build it to a mountain and then bring it back down. We've got to have that emotion.

I want the music to represent the way we feel. It's got to dictate our emotions, our moves. We're expressing the way everybody feels. It's rebellion, you know what I mean? We're letting out what we've always wanted to say to the world. Passion, linger, fire!

After *Moonwalker's* first two weeks in release, it was announced that in this very short time it had outsold the now former number one best selling music video of all time, *The Making of Michael Jackson's Thriller.* Michael Jackson now has the number one and number two best selling music video cassettes of all time. *Moonwalker* has also been released on laserdisk and is expected to outsell all other releases on that format as well. *Moonwalker* continued to top video cassette sales even after it aired on Showtime on April 15, 1989.

Moonwalker debuted on *Billboard's* top music video cassette chart at, where else but, the number one position. It held the top spot for twenty two weeks before being knocked out by the only one who could- Michael Jackson himself, with his latest release, *Michael Jackson: The Legend Continues.*

On *Billboard's* top video cassette sales chart, *Moonwalker* took over the top spot in three weeks, outselling *ET: The Extra Terrestrial.* It was knocked out of number one by U2's *Rattle and Hum. Moonwalker* soon returned to number one on the sales chart and remained there until Michael again replaced himself on the list of best selling video cassettes. The week of June 17, 1989, *Moonwalker* slipped to number two on the chart, while the number one best selling video cassette in the U.S. was *Michael Jackson: The Legend Continues.*

In a special issue devoted to video cassettes, *Billboard* magazine named *Moonwalker* as the fifth best selling video cassette for the year ending July, 1989. *The Legend Continues* placed at number twenty four. These placements are significant when considering these charts reflected the sales of video cassettes of all categories, not just music videos, and that neither cassette was in release for the entire twelve month period being reviewed. *Moonwalker*, released in January, was only in release for approximately six of the twelve months being charted. *The Legend*

Continues was only in release for four of the twelve months being charted. *Moonwalker* was ranked as the fifth Top Music Video Cassette for the same period.

The Video Software Dealer Association named *Moonwalker* as the Favorite Musical Video. *Moonwalker* earned further honors with an award nomination from the National Association of Recording Merchandisers.

At the close of 1989, *Billboard* ranked *Moonwalker* as the fourth best selling video cassette of the year. Two of the year's top 10 music video cassettes belonged to Michael Jackson. *Moonwalker* was the third Top Music Video Cassette for the year, and *The Legend Continues* placed at number ten.

Doubleday published three accompaniments to *Moonwalker*. A Michael Jackson Moonwalker calendar had been published earlier in the fall featuring photos from *Moonwalker* and from the Bad tour. The other two items were geared toward children. A Moonwalker coloring book and a storybook told the story of "Smooth Criminal".

On September 13, 1989, a press conference was held in Los Angeles where LA Gear announced they had just singed a new multimillion dollar endorsement deal with Michael Jackson. Michael signed a two year deal to design and market a line of sportshoes and sportswear for the company. At the press confer- ence, Michael wore black pants and jacket with a purple shirt and sunglasses. He also wore, instead of the usual black loafers, a pair of black and silver LA Gear tennis shoes. As usual, Michael was very brief with his comments: "I am very happy to be part of the LA Gear magic and I hope we have a very rewarding, successful career. Thank you."

The deal was said to be for double what Pepsi had paid him, the highest corporate association ever. The company's stock responded strongly, rising four points in the three days following the announcement.

The line of shoes and sportswear was scheduled to be in stores in summer 1990. Teaser ads began running in the spring.

The ads used Michael's music, "Wanna Be Startin' Somethin'", but Michael did not appear in them. Ads with Michael began airing in movie theaters in July, 1990, and the next month on television. Michael dances down a dark, deserted street when a street lamp suddenly explodes. As Michael shields his head from the flying glass, he hears the sole applause of a little girl watching out a window. The young girl appearing in the ads is Brandi Jackson, Jackie's daughter. Brandi also appeared in the print ads for the shoes with Uncle Mike. The print ads had Michael standing among several young children all decked out in LA Gear fashions. Michael, in addition to his black and white MJ LA Gear high tops, sported quite a different look, wearing a black leather jacket and blue jeans with both knees torn out and the thighs worn to threads.

The MJ line of shoes featured Michael's Moonwalker logo on the tongues, soles, and on a tiny gold stud on the side. The deal with LA Gear allowed for Michael to design a line of shoes and sportswear and to appear in print ads and television commercials. Three commercials were scheduled to be completed by December, 1991. An added bonus for the shoe company was that Michael Jackson actually did wear the shoes in the ads, unlike the Pepsi ads where Michael would not drink or hold the soda.

The LA Gear shoes and sportswear were scheduled to hit stores the same time as the new album. When the new album didn't happen, sales of the shoes failed to meet expectations. Despite reports that the shoe line bombed, LA Gear officials allowed that profits from Japanese sales alone would recoup their investment in Jackson.

Three years after signing the deal, LA Gear filed a $10 million lawsuit against Michael Jackson charging him with fraud and breach of contract. LA Gear claimed that as part of the contract, Michael was to deliver to LA Gear, videos featuring him wearing the shoes. Failure to deliver any of these videos and failure to release an album to coincide with the newly available line of shoes were given as the grounds for the legal action. In

November, 1992, Michael filed a $44 million countersuit against L.A. Gear citing them with similar charges.

The announcement of this $20 million deal with LA Gear was made shortly before *Forbes* magazine compiled its annual list of the world's highest paid entertainers. Again Michael Jackson was ranked number one with a two year total income estimated at $125 million. The magazine estimated Michael Jackson's 1988 income to be $60 million with the remaining $65 million being earned in 1989. Bill Cosby placed at number two for the second consecutive year.

While Michael was enjoying phenomenal success with his album, tour, and new home videos, one of his most beloved mentors was going through some very difficult times. The Godfather of Soul, James Brown, had been arrested and sentenced to six years in prison on drug charges and eluding police. Michael Jackson was among the many entertainers and admirers to give Brown a phone call of support.

Another of Michael's idols, Sammy Davis Jr. was then battling throat cancer. In November, 1989, Michael joined with several other stars at the L. A. Shrine Auditorium in celebrating the 60th year in show business for Sammy Davis Jr. Jessie Jackson appeared on the program and spoke briefly about how Davis had helped to ease racial tensions and break down the walls separating the different races. This lead directly to Michael's performance. With no introduction, Michael stepped from the glare of several spotlights to perform, "You Were There", which he wrote with Buz Kohan especially for the occasion. Michael's was the only performance in the tribute which included Frank Sinatra, Bob Hope, and Ella Fitzgerald, not to have an announced introduction.

Dressed in black pants and red shirt with white strips tied at his waist and wrist, and white tape covering three fingertips, Michael's touching lyrics brought tears to Sammy Davis Jr.:

Thanks to you, there's no door we all can't

walk through
I'm here because you were there

It was certainly one of the more stationery performances Michael has ever given. With very few of his customary moves, Michael stood relatively still behind the microphone stand delivering the song only a few feet away from Davis. He finished the performance with one hand raised in the air, the other on his crotch. Afterwards, Michael walked over to Sammy and hugged him warmly.

Later in the show, Michael and host Eddie Murphy escorted Ella Fitzgerald to the stage. The program aired on ABC on February 4, 1990, with all proceeds, $250,000, being donated to the United Negro College Fund.

On May 16, 1990, Sammy Davis Jr. died of throat cancer. At the funeral services, Frank Sinatra, Dean Martin, Bill Cosby and Michael Jackson were named as honorary pallbearers. On Sunday, June 3, the special honoring Davis was rebroadcast. At the 1990 Emmy Awards, the special was awarded the Emmy for Outstanding Music Special.

Just a month before Davis died, Ryan White was near death in an Indiana hospital. Among the thousands of callers and well-wishers was Michael Jackson. When Michael called, a speaker phone was taken to Ryan's bedside. Michael told Ryan he loved him and that God was with him. "Hang in there buddy and get better."

Following his visit to Washington DC to accept the Entertainer of the Decade Award, Michael planned to visit Ryan in the hospital. Ryan died before he got there. On Sunday, April 8, 1990, Ryan White finally lost his five year battle with AIDS. Michael arrived at Ryan's house early the next morning with Donald Trump. Ryan's mother, Jeanne, met Michael at the door of her home and broke down sobbing, "He really wanted to see you." "I know", Michael replied. He stayed through Wednesday, the day of the funeral. Michael comforted Jeanne at the funeral which was attended by several other celebrities including Barbara Bush, Phil Donahue, Judith Light, who had portrayed Jeanne White in the TV movie, "The Ryan White Story", and Elton John, who had spent many hours at Ryan's bedside.

After the ceremony, Michael and Elton John joined Jeanne White in a final viewing of the body before the casket was closed. Ryan was buried in jeans and denim jacket with a watch Michael had given him.

The inscription on Ryan's six foot, eight inch headstone was written by Ryan's friends Elton John and Michael Jackson:

> *Turn me loose from your hands. Let me fly to*
> *distant lands. Fly away Sky Line Pigeon fly.*
> *From all things you left so very far behind.*
> *Love*
> *Elton John*

> *Gonna make a difference*
> *Gonna make it right*
> *Forever Friends*
> *Michael Jackson*

Later Michael paid $1,000 for a step inside a restored war monument, the Indiana Soldiers' and Sailors' Monument in Indianapolis to honor Ryan White. On the step is a bronze plaque inscribed with the words:

> *In honor of Ryan White,*
> *His spirit lives on in us all*
> *We miss you. Michael Jackson.*

Earlier in the year, Michael had two nominations for the 1989 American Music Awards, held on January 30. He was nominated for Favorite Pop/Rock Male Vocalist along with George Michael and Steve Winwood. His second nomination, for Favorite

Soul/R&B Male Vocalist, pitted him against former New Edition member Bobby Brown and again, George Michael. George Michael won in both categories. Surprise and criticism followed George Michael's win in the traditionally black category of R&B Male Vocalist. Many felt the award should go to a black entertainer. While many were steamed over the choice for Favorite R&B Male Vocalist, the first one to congratulate George Michael backstage at the award presentations, was Michael Jackson.

Michael Jackson did not go home empty handed however. He was honored for his ground breaking artistry and technology in video, and for the record breaking success of his *Bad* album and tour. *Cashbox* magazine awarded Michael the Video Pioneer Award in recognition of his excellence in video as captured in the *Triumph* video for "Can You Feel It", *Thriller*, and *Moonwalker*. The inscription on the Video Pioneer Award reads:

For his pioneering efforts in the field of music videos epitomized by 'The Triumph', a pre 1980's breakthrough in concept and special effects, and 'Thriller', an innovative combination of drama, music and dance. This Video Pioneer Award is given to Michael Jackson on the occasion of his new feature length film anthology, 'Moonwalker' becoming the largest selling music home video of all time.

A short tribute to Michael and his unprecedented success in video was shown that included pieces of the each of the videos mentioned. Short clips of *The Triumph* and *Thriller* were showcased with footage from *Moonwalker*.

The second special award Michael received was an American Music Award of Achievement. Its inscription reads:

Because his album, 'Bad', is the first ever to generate five number one singles, because it has been a number one best seller in a record breaking twenty five countries around the world, and because it has been the largest international seller in each of the last two years, the American Music Award of Achievement is presented to Michael Jackson on January 30, 1989.

Both of these special awards were presented to Michael by Eddie Murphy, at Michael's request. Even though Michael is the subject of many of Murphy's jokes, the two have become friends. Murphy's movies, *Trading Places, Beverly Hills Cop, Raw,* and his cameo appearance in *Best Defense* as well as several of his skits on *Saturday Night Live* all make mention of, or make fun of, Michael Jackson.

Before introducing Michael, Murphy narrated a fourteen minute tribute to Michael Jackson showcasing his international tour and recapping the *Bad* album's five number one hit singles. Walking shyly toward center stage to gather his awards, the audience greeted Michael with deafening applause and a standing ovation. Michael was dressed in black and red, buckles, and no sunglasses.

As the applause subsided and Michael began to speak, his soft voice could bearly be heard over the microphone, which was on a very low stand. He had to bend over and speak directly into the mike to be heard. Holding his awards, he asked Eddie to adjust the mike stand for him, "Could you lift that up please?" Eddie tried to adjust it but it wouldn't budge. "You do it" Eddie told Michael. Michael replied, "I can't, I need your help." It became a joke when Eddie told the audience what was happening. (Their conversation was bearly audible.) "He said, 'Pull it up Eddie', like I was working for him! And I do it! Yes Michael!" So, bent over, Michael spoke briefly as always:

I'd like to thank God, who makes all things possible. I'd like to thank my mother and father, Katherine and Joseph Jackson. I'd like to thank Berry Gordy, who gave me my first professional start in show business, the Epic family, Walter Yetnikoff, Larry Stessel, Glen Brundman, Frank Dileo, Quincy Jones, and Bruce Swedian. I love you. And the public. Thank you.

While he was very shy, Michael appeared to be enjoying himself and seemed to be genuinely honored with the awards, the tribute, and the overwhelming response from the audience.

Earlier in the month, an episode of the country's top rated TV program, *The Cosby Show*, centered on the Huxtable family attending a Michael Jackson concert. Even the grandparents went along, with Grandpa Huxtable saying, "Yeah, I'm going. I like Michael Jackson, he's Bad!" They returned home from the concert with several items of authentic Bad tour merchandise.

With the Bad tour just completed, Michaelmania was still in full force. Michael Jackson wasn't just on MTV, record charts and award shows; one of the floats at New Orleans' Mardi Gras parade was in the image of Michael Jackson.

The week of January 21, the cover of *TV Guide* featured photos of Elvis Presley, Bruce Springsteen, Madonna, and Michael Jackson. In the accompanying article, the authors searched for the greatest live television performances. They ruled out videos because they felt they don't show the true performer because they are able to reshoot and use special effects to make everything perfect:

Nothing validates that decision as much as the case of Michael Jackson, who has poured untold time and money into video. Jackson is responsible for the genre's most elaborate and expensive works -- mirco-epics like 'Thriller' and 'Bad'. His 'Moonwalker' cassette, released last week, is the most ambitious, grandiose use of music video to date.

Yet his most unforgettable moment on TV was only three minutes in the making and required no other props than a hat and a single glove. It was, of course, his performance of 'Billie Jean' on the 1983 NBC special 'Motown 25: Yesterday, Today, Forever.'

After singing a medley of old Jackson 5 hits with his brothers, Michael took the stage alone, donning a single gold-lame glove and an old fedora. As the pumping rhythm of 'Billie Jean' took hold, he unleashed the inimitably bold whiplash dance style that has since become his trademark. Jackson took the stage that night an aging child prodigy. He left it an emerging superstar.

That was probably the flashiest TV performance ever. The most spirited? It's Jackson again. At last year's Grammy Awards ceremonies, he worked his way through a gospel-influenced rendition of 'Man in the Mirror' like a man possessed. That performance, which drove the singer to his knees at several points, may have been the most passionate appearance ever televised.

In February, Michael was named Artist of the 80's at the World Music Awards, held in Monte Carlo. Michael did not attend the award presentation. His award was accepted for him by Barry White.

It was around this same time that the March issue of *Playboy* hit the news stands. The issue featured a pictorial of LaToya Jackson. Her decision to pose for the magazine shocked, disappointed, and angered her family.

Among the reasons LaToya gave for posing nude for the magazine was to assert her independence. She wanted to prove, especially to her parents, that she wasn't a child anymore and could make her own decisions. She posed for the photos shortly after becoming the latest Jackson to fire their father as their manager. She had also just left the family's Encino home and moved to New York. Money was certainly another motivator in her decision to pose nude. Although the exact amount she received wasn't disclosed, she did allow that she was *Playboy's* highest paid model.

It's interesting that LaToya gave declaring her independence as her reason for doing the pictorial. Unlike Janet, LaToya has never seemed to be able to break out of the shadow of her very famous brother. Even though she too wanted to become successful without help from her family, she has never seemed to do much without at least a hint of Michael. On the back cover of an early album, *Heart Don't Lie,* she is pictured wearing Michael's yellow vest and pins he wears in one of his most famous posters. "You Blew", from her *LaToya* album has the lines, "I'll teach you your ABC's, I'll be there, just like your brother used to say, I want you back." In her stage shows, Jackson Five material and Michael's "Wanna Be Startin' Somethin'" are part of her act. Even her *Playboy* pictorial has references to Michael. On the cover of the magazine it reads, "LATOYA JACKSON. MICHAEL'S SISTER IN A THRILLING PICTORIAL". Inside it reads, "Don't tell ... Michael" over her photos. In two of the photos she is wearing a single glove and a black fedora. Remind you of anybody? On the back of chair in one photo is a black military style jacket. In another photo, she poses with a snake, one of Michael's favorite pets. If these pictures did little to strengthen her individuality, they would certainly put an end to the stories that her and Michael are the same person!

While LaToya explained in one interview after another how her family reacted to her posing, some family members were telling quite a different story. In an interview with *USA Today*, LaToya told of her family's reactions, saying her parents were very upset and that they disapproved. Her brothers and sisters, however, according to LaToya, either didn't mind and felt she should do whatever she wanted, or they approved. LaToya claimed Michael, who had obtained advance copies of the photos, approved, and loved the photos:

I spoke to Michael for four hours before he said anything about it. We talked all around it. I just had to bring it up. I said, 'I'm sure you know about Playboy. He said, 'I didn't want to embarrass you. You scream when we see your back. But I saw the pictures and I loved them.'

A few days later in a TV interview, Tito and Jermaine said they were disappointed in LaToya's decision to pose nude and that Michael felt the same way. While these two very different stories circulated about how Michael felt about the pictorial, Michael himself, as usual, wasn't talking. It has been revealed since that while Michael did support her decision to pose nude for the sake of furthering her career, he in fact did not like the photos, and was upset that LaToya was telling interviewers that he did.

With the lengthy tour finished it would seem Michael would be content to stay at home on his new ranch venturing out only to pick up his latest award. But he did make a rare public appearance on February 7, 1989. He visited the Cleveland Elementary School in Stockton, California. A few weeks earlier, the school's playground was the scene of a massacre. A gunman shot and killed five children, and wounded several others before killing himself. Michael visited two children who were still hospitalized and met with the other children at a nearby church.

Fans gathered outside the hospital, church and school never saw Michael. He entered through back entrances accompanied by bodyguards. He wore black pants with multiple zippers and buckles, a black and red military jacket and no sunglasses. He handed out gifts to each child, an autographed photo, a Bad tour t-shirt, and a *Bad* cassette. Michael Jackson's visit to the school helped the children who were traumatized by the tragedy tremendously. Some said Michael Jackson's visit finally made them feel safe again.

Then it was on to pick up more awards. Michael was again named the Best International Male Artist at the 1989 British Phonographic Industry Awards. The category had been split this year into male and female categories. (It was either this or rename the award, The Michael Jackson Award!) Michael was chosen over Alexander O'Neal, Prince, Terence Trent D'Arby, and Luther Vandross. The award was presented by former fellow Motowners, The Four Tops.

Footage of the Bad tour was shown with scenes of Michael receiving the Excalibur Award in London at a very elaborate presentation. Michael stood on a small platform with Bill Bray, Frank Dileo and Jimmy Safechuck. A marching band played while a knight on a white horse pranced up to the platform and pulled a sword from a stone. He dismounted and presented the long golden sword to Michael. Michael saluted the knight and the band resumed playing, now switching songs. Michael, looking very serious up to this point, broke out in a big smile and laughed recognizing "Billie Jean".

Michael did not attend the "Brits", but he was shown live via satellite from California to accept the Best International Male Artist Award. He wore a red shirt and black tie, and no sunglasses. And as always, he spoke briefly, "Thank you very much to all the fans in the United Kingdom. I look forward to seeing you again in the near future. The tour was a wonderful experience. I love you all. Thank you."

Michael won another "Brit" with his second nomination for Best Video. "Smooth Criminal" was chosen as best video over Bananarama's "Nathan Jones", The Christains' "Harvest for the World", George Harrison's "Fab", and Wet Wet Wet's "Temptation". The award was accepted for Michael with thank yous given on behalf of Michael and Bubbles.

Just following these award presentations, on February 14, 1989,Michael's publicist, Lee Solters, made a shocking and unsuspected announcement on Michael's behalf. Michael Jackson and Frank Dileo were parting ways. Even though it was described as an amiable breakup, it took most people by total surprise. Frank Dileo and Michael Jackson had formed a close personal relationship as well as their professional relationship. Dileo was often described by the media and Jackson insiders as Michael's sole confidant, a second father. In the statement read by Solters, Michael said only, "I thank Frank for his contribution on my behalf during the past several years."

The media could only speculate as to the reasons for the abrupt split. Among the possible causes given was that Michael may have been disappointed that the sales of *Bad* didn't match *Thriller's,* not to mention his personal goal of 100 million copies. This hardly seems rational. *Bad* had sales of 20 million copies, making it the second best selling album of the eighties, behind *Thriller.* Sales of *Bad* later topped the 25 million mark, giving

Michael the top two best sellers of all time. That's hardly something to be disappointed with.

Dileo's high profile media image was given as another possible cause for the abrupt split. While Michael was well aware of Dileo's manner before hiring him, he had become angered recently that Dileo continued to feed stories to the media about him. After giving stories to the tabloids about Michael sleeping in the hyperbaric chamber and bidding on the elephant man's skeleton, Dileo reportedly continued to create new stories about Michael for the press, much to Michael's chagrin. These stories, instead of keeping Michael in the public's mind as intended, served more to foster the conception that Michael is weird.

Speculation on the firing of Dileo included the notion that Michael was unhappy with the handling of his *Moonwalker* video cassette. The release of the video in January undoubtedly cost valuable Christmas sales. Also, Michael had wanted *Moonwaker* to have a theatrical release in the U.S., as in Europe, before being released on video cassette. The blame for these blunders evidently feel on the shoulders of Frank Dileo.

Whatever the reason for the split, it was sad to see the long friendship end. At the time of the news, Frank Dileo was adding a room on to his new home in Ojai, California especially for Michael's visits. Their five year relationship was all ended with a cold phone call from Michael's lawyer. Frank threatened to sue Michael for breach of contract. They reached a settlement without going to court, the amount of which was estimated at $5 million.

Soon after firing Frank, Michael hired Mike Ovitz, the head of Creative Artists Agency whose clients include Robert Redford, Dustin Hoffman and Barbra Streisand, to look for a suitable movie script for him. No formal management agreement was entered into with Ovitz. Again, while between managers, Michael's day to day business affairs were handled by John Branca and Bill Bray.

Frank Dileo, however, was the first one to land a movie role. He signed to play a Mafia boss in *Goodfellas*. Having had worked with the film's director was undoubtedly an advantage in getting the role. The movie was directed by Martin Scorsese, who was Dileo's choice to direct the "Bad" video. Dileo's second film role was a bit part in *Wayne's World* portraying a record producer.

Dileo was later named co-president of Savage Records in New York while continuing to manage other musical acts, including Laura Branigan, Al B. Sure!, Richie Sambora and Cher.

For the thirty first annual Grammy Awards, "Man in the Mirror" was nominated for Record of the Year. The other nominees were "Fast Car" by Tracy Chapman, "Don't Worry, Be Happy" by Bobby McFerrin, "Roll With It" by Steve Winwood, and Anita Baker's "Giving You The Best That I Got." This was Michael's sole nomination. Given all of the hit singles he had released during the year it seemed Michael had been overlooked by the Grammys. However, because of the complicated rules of the Grammys, Record of the Year was the only category in which Michael was eligible.

The Grammy for Record of the Year goes to a record's producer and the performer. If chosen as Record of the Year, the Grammy for "Man in the Mirror" would go to Quincy Jones and Michael Jackson. Jones did attend the ceremony, Michael did not. Well, he did sort of. Michael watched the Grammy telecast on TV in his limo, parked behind the Los Angeles Shrine Auditorium. If "Man in the Mirror" won, Michael planned to go inside and accept the award.

Record of the Year went to Bobby McFerrin for "Don't Worry, Be Happy", so Michael never had to leave his car. The 1989 Grammy Awards were the most disappointing and weak Grammy telecasts of recent history. Nominations and winners were dominated by artists who had had only one hit single throughout the entire year. One bright spot was when the Grammy for Best Concept Recording went to "Weird Al" Yankovic for "Fat". And this was announced as one of the awards given out earlier in the evening, prior to the broadcast.

On February 23, the second annual Hope Award was presented to Elizabeth Taylor for her work in raising money for AIDS research and her other humanitarian efforts. The award was presented to Elizabeth Taylor by Bob Hope and the tribute was televised on March 9. There were reports beforehand that the tribute was to be hosted by Bob Hope and Michael Jackson. Other reports included Michael among those who would be performing at the tribute. As the date grew nearer, reports on Michael even attending the event grew more indefinite. *TV Guide's* ad for the special featured a large photo of Michael Jackson with a note that at press time it wasn't clear if Michael would be in attendance. He did not attend.

In mid March, The People's Choice Awards were presented. Michael was nominated for Favorite Male Musical Performer along with George Michael and country singer Randy Travis. Travis, surprisingly, won. "Smooth Criminal" was chosen as the people's Favorite Music Video. Michael did not attend the award presentation.

A newspaper for school children began publication in early 1989. The cover of the first nationally distributed *Young American* featured a review of *Moonwalker* and included a large photo of Spike the rabbit from the "Speed Demon" segment of the video and a small picture of Michael from the "Leave Me Alone" video.

The third annual Soul Train Music Awards were presented on April 12. As with the American Music Awards, Michael was again presented with two special honors. He was the third recipient of the Heritage Award for career achievement. The two earlier recipients are Gladys Knight and Stevie Wonder. Michael also received the first ever Sammy Davis Jr. Award for outstanding stage performance. The newly created award is to be presented each year to the artist whose live performances have had the greatest impact on audiences during the year. Davis didn't present the award in person but he did send a taped message to Michael:

You know, since my childhood I have heard every superlative used to describe my own personal ability on stage. But the standards we were able to set back in the old days have been somewhat redefined by a young man by the name of Michael Jackson. Wow! I am personally delighted over his selection as the first recipient of this award.

As you know, he has just finished doing probably the most exciting and the most successful concert tour in modern musical history. Michael Jackson to me is simply one the most amazing entertainers I have ever seen in my life. And in sixty years in show biz, I have seen quite a few. I'm one of his biggest fans and I love him dearly as a friend. And Michael, I personally would like to say something to you, I regret being unable to be with you on this occasion but as you know as I'm talking to you now on tape, at this very moment I'm in Oslo, Norway. But I'm honored to have you accept this award and I'll certainly have a big hug for you as soon as we get back together again. In my absence, however, we've invited a mutual friend and a brilliant young talent in his own right who will make the presentation of the first Sammy Davis Award. Ladies and gentlemen, Mr. Eddie Murphy.

Eddie Murphy walked on stage and was immediately joined by Elizabeth Taylor. She introduced a tribute to Michael consisting of video clips and concert footage, this time including some footage of "Thriller" rarely shown before. She then introduced Michael:

Thank you Eddie. I'd like to say a few words about a wonderful human being who's also one of my dearest friends. I would adore Michael Jackson whether he was the world's biggest greatest star or not. But it so happens he is the greatest and perhaps one of the most gifted music makers the world has ever known. What makes Michael even more unique may be the fact that all of his accomplishments, rewards, have not altered his sensitivity and concern for the welfare of others, or his intense caring and love for his family and friends and his fans. Especially all the children all the world over. Michael is indeed an international favorite for all ages. An incredible force of incredible energy. The art of music, a pacesetter for quality of production, a vanguard for high standards of entertainment. What is a genius? What is a living legend? What is a mega star? Michael Jackson. That's all. And just when you think you know him, he gives you more.

Ladies and gentlemen, the 1989 Heritage Award and Sammy Davis Jr. Award recipient, and in my estimation, the true King of Pop, Rock and Soul, Mr. Michael Jackson.

Finally, dressed in red, black, and buckles, Michael walked out on stage. He did not wear sunglasses, but he did have his latest two trademarks, taped fingertips and an armband. While he stood at the podium, waiting for the crowd to quiet before speaking, Eddie Murphy adjusted the microphone for him, recalling the trouble Michael had had with the mike stand at the American Music Awards. Murphy continued the joke, brushing off imaginary lint from Michael's shoulders and holding a hand up the audience to quiet them so Michael could speak. Host Amad Rashad had joked earlier he would personally adjust Michael's microphone for him. The crowd, and Michael, all found Murphy's antics very funny. Then Michael spoke, "Thank you. Thank you very much, Elizabeth Taylor." He leaned over and kissed her. "Thank you Eddie Murphy." Murphy quickly held his hand out to Michael to avoid being kissed, again breaking up the crowd as well as Michael. Michael then gave almost the exact same speech he had given at the American Music Awards, pausing to find Quincy Jones in the audience and leaving one person out of his list of people to thank, Frank Dileo:

First I'd like to thank God, who makes all things possible. I'd like to thank my mother and father, who I love very much, Joseph and Katherine Jackson. I thank Quincy Jones, whose in the audience. I don't see him, he's somewhere, he was right there. Thank you Quincy. I thank Bill Bray, John Branca, the Epic family, Walter Yetnikoff, Larry Stessel, Glen Brundman, I love you. Thank you very much.

Michael had three nominations in addition to these special honors. He fared much better here than with the American Music Awards or with the Grammys, coming away with two awards out of three nominations. After Michael was presented with the two special honors, the next award presented was for the Best R&B Urban Contemporary Single by a Male. "Man in the Mirror" was nominated along with "My Prerogative" by Bobby Brown, "Just Got Paid" by Johnny Kemp, and "Make It Last Forever" by Keith Sweat and Jacci McGhee. The Best R&B Single went to "Man in the Mirror". Michael was still backstage when he was announced as the winner. He was standing with a small group of people, one of whom was Bill Bray. Michael accepted the award saying, "Again, I say thank you. Thanks to God. Thank you Quincy Jones and Bruce Swedian and Siedah Garrett and everyone who worked on the project. I love you. Thank you."

The next award category was for Best R&B Urban Contemporary Song of the Year. Michael Jackson's "Man in the Mirror" was nominated with Anita Baker's "Giving You The Best That I Got", Bobby Brown's "Don't Be Cruel", and Keith Sweat's "I Want Her". Song of the Year went to Anita Baker.

Michael's third nomination was for Best R&B Urban Contemporary Music Video. The video for "Man in the Mirror" was nominated with the videos for "Parents Just Don't Understand" by D. J. Jazzy Jeff and The Fresh Prince, "Wild Wild West" by Kool Moe Dee, and Stevie Wonder's "Skeletons". "Man in the Mirror" was chosen as the year's best video. Quincy Jones presented the award with Anita Pointer. They announced Michael as the winner and stepped away from the podium for the winner to step up. But Michael wanted Quincy to join him at the podium, "Quincy, come up here", motioning for Quincy to join him, "I'm glad, I'm so happy to see Quincy again, I was looking for him earlier and he wasn't there." Michael looked genuinely pleased with picking up his fourth award of the evening and at seeing Quincy Jones again, as he recognized another familiar face in the audience, "Hi Rashida", saying hello to Quincy's daughter. Michael also remembered the children from the Cleveland School he had visited a few weeks earlier:

Thank you again. I want to thank the entire public. I want to thank everybody who worked on these wonderful projects. I'd like to thank all the children at the Cleveland School in Stockton, California. I love them very much. And the public, thank you very much. I love you.

Michael had one nomination for the first International Rock Awards. His 1988 World Tour was among the nominees for Tour of the Year, along with Amnesty International (made up of Bruce Springsteen, Sting, Peter Gabriel, and Tracy Chapman), George Michael, Pink Floyd, and Prince. Amnesty International was chosen as Tour of the Year. Michael did not attend the ceremony.

Michael was also being honored this same spring for his charitable and humanitarian efforts. In a ceremony held at the Universal Amphitheater in Universal City, California, Michael was presented with the Black Radio Exclusive Humanitarian Award. One of the presenters of the award was Tatiana Thumbtzen, his co-star from the "The Way You Make Me Feel" video.

Further honors were bestowed on Michael on behalf of the "Say Yes to a Youngsters Future" program. For his participation in the program, Michael received the National Urban Coalition Artist/Humanitarian of the Year Award. The program encourages kids to study math and science.

While 1989 started out with Michael winning more awards and setting more records, the *Rolling Stone* 1988 Readers Poll had very different and disappointing results. Evidently the twenty million people who bought *Bad* and the record four million people who attended his concerts and spent $125 million on tour merchandise, don't read *Rolling Stone*. They certainly didn't respond to the magazine's poll. The poll, which was based on the responses of only 24,289 readers, named Michael Jackson as the number one worst male singer, the most unwelcome comeback, and the worst dressed male singer. *Bad* placed fourth for both worst album and worst album cover. Two of Michael's videos made the worst video list, "Bad" placed at number three and "Smooth Criminal" placed at number five. Michael Jackson's tour was voted as the second worst tour of the year.

Us magazine's reader poll had similar disappointing results. Michael Jackson was voted as the most unwelcome comeback, *Bad* was voted as the worst album, and "Bad" was named the second worst single. These poll results, while disappointing, can hardly be considered very significant. They are based on the responses of relatively few people, as compared to the masses of people who bought Michael's records and flocked to his concerts.

The May 1989 issue of *Ebony* magazine featured the results of a readers poll also, "Who's Hot, Who's Not in 1989". While also based on relatively few responses, it did offer more favorable results for Michael. "Thriller" was voted by the magazine's readers as their favorite video of all time, with 37 percent of the vote. In second place, with 23 percent of the vote was Janet Jackson's video for "Control".

In the spring of 1989, MTV counted down the Top 50 Most Requested Videos of All Time. The artist with the most videos making it to the top fifty, with six, was Michael Jackson. "Bad", Michael's lowest ranking entry, placed near the bottom of the countdown. "Thriller" placed at number forty, "Dirty Diana" was number thirty three, "Smooth Criminal" was number twenty six, "Beat It" was number fifteen, and the sixth most requested video of all time was "Billie Jean".

In between collecting awards, Michael was settling into his new home. Even though he had purchased it a year earlier, he had spent relatively little time there because he was on tour. To help meet his new neighbors, Michael went to Circus Vargas in Santa Barbara taking with him two hundred disadvantaged children. The children were from St. Vincent's Home for Dysfunctional Children and from the Big Brothers and Big Sisters program.

On May 3, *Michael Jackson: The Legend Continues* was released on video cassette. *The Legend Continues* is the retrospective of Michael Jackson's career that was broadcast in March, 1988, on Showtime. The video cassette was released earlier in England, in June 1988, where it became the best selling video cassette ever in England. *The Legend Continues* sold over 400,000 copies in Great Britain and U.S. sales were expected to at least match its British sales, giving Michael Jackson the top three best selling music video cassettes worldwide.

In late April, Michael was at work in Los Angeles filming the eighth video from the *Bad* album. "Liberian Girl" features model Beverly Johnson as the Liberian Girl and cameo appearances by forty other celebrities, including Bubbles who makes his second video appearance with his master. For the first time, Michael tries his hand at directing, co-directing the video. The "Liberian Girl" single and accompanying video were only released in England, but has since been shown on MTV in the United States as part of special Michael Jackson weekends.

The same weekend Michael was in Los Angeles to make the video for "Liberian Girl", he was spotted shopping in a Simi Valley shopping center. Michael and Jimmy Safechuck visited a small gift store and a Zales jewelry store. Michael was in a disguise to keep from being recognized. He wore the same wig, false teeth, and mustache he wore to visit the zoo in Berlin. While he wasn't exactly recognized, he did attract attention to himself. The obviously fake mustache aroused the suspicions of the jewelry store employees and they called the police. The police officers questioned him as to why he was in disguise, and asked him for identification. One officer thought he was nuts claiming be Michael Jackson, until Michael lifted the wig and the officer recognized the strands of hair that normally hang down Michael's forehead.

BET, the Black Entertainment Television network, jumped on the Jackson bandwagon by playing lots and lots of Jackson videos. On June 1, their two hour Video Soul program was dedicated to the Jackson family. The program consisted entirely of videos by the Jacksons, and each of the Jacksons individually. Solo videos by Jackie, Jermaine, Marlon, and LaToya were all shown with a major portion of the program coming from videos by Michael and Janet.

A new Jackson album was released on June 23, 1989, titled *2300 Jackson St.*, their former address in Gary, Indiana. The new album features only four Jackson brothers, Jackie, Tito, Jermaine, and Randy. Marlon and especially Michael are conspicuously absent, except for the title song. "2300 Jackson St." reunites all of the Jackson brothers as well as Rebbie and Janet and several nieces and nephews. "2300 Jackson St." is a tribute to their parents and their roots, one of the best tracks on the album.

While the new "2300 Jackson St." single seemingly reunites the Jackson brothers for the first time in five years and marks the first time ever that their sisters joined the brothers on one of their records, actually most of their individual lines were recorded separately in several different studios. Janet recorded her few lines at Marlon's home studio and Michael recorded his portion at the Encino home studio.

If recording the single didn't really reunite the family, filming the video did. The video was filmed at "Family Day", a special day when the whole family makes a point to get together. Each one takes a turn hosting family day. This time it was Tito's turn. Joseph and Katherine appear briefly in the video along with several of their grandchildren. Each of the Jackson children were there except for LaToya who was in Moscow for a performance and Marlon, who was in New Orleans.

Included in the video are shots of the Jacksons tossing a football, and gathering around a pool table, with Michael evidently just winning some money off of Rebbie, and being quite proud of it. A group shot of the whole clan has Katherine and Joseph each holding a grandchild on their laps. Janet also has a little one, and Jackie's daughter, Brandi, sits on Uncle Mike's lap.

The *2300 Jackson St.* album is definitely a much stronger effort by the brothers than their previous album, *Victory*. Without their former lead singer, Jermaine takes over the lead on most of the songs, giving the album a much more consistent feel than *Victory*. The album's title song, "Nothin' (that Compares 2 U)" and "Maria" are among the best tracks on the album. In "Harley" there is an obvious reference to Michael. The song, describing a motorbike, includes the line, "She's bad, She's bad, bad" repeatedly.

A reunion tour was supposedly in the works to support the album, said to include *all* of the brothers plus Janet. This seemed doubtful at best. Janet had just released her follow up album to *Control, Janet Jackson's Rhythm Nation 1814,* and was at work planning her first solo tour. Michael had just come off of a tour that kept him on the road for sixteen months. He badly needed rest, his weight had reportedly dropped to 105 pounds. Also, considering the problems, frustration, and public embarrassment of the last Jackson tour, it is an easy bet that Michael won't be touring with his brothers again. Ever. They also wouldn't be recording together. With the completion of *2300 Jackson St.*, the Jackson's contract with Epic Records expired. It was not renewed.

A Jackson tour with the remaining brothers didn't seem probable either. Without Michael, public demand for tickets would be next to nothing and the brothers were also working on solo projects at the time, leaving little time to devout to any touring plans. Randy had recently formed his own band, Randy and the Gypsies with A&M Records, Janet's label. Their first single, "Love You Honey" was released in March, 1990. Jermaine had also just released a new solo album, *Don't Take It Personal*. Needless to say, the tour never did materialize.

Janet told *Rolling Stone* in an interview following the release of her *Rhythm Nation* album that her biggest inspiration for recording her first successful album, *Control,* was her brother Michael and his success with *Thriller.* She described Michael as her idol and model and said that they are the closet of all the Jackson children. Michael gave Janet, whose nickname is Dunk, a key on an earring, which has since become her trademark. The key Michael gave Janet belonged to some animal cages on their Encino estate. A key is also her logo for her company, JDJ Entertainment.

Janet also told *Rolling Stone* how she would love to break some of Michael's records. When she was questioned as to how Michael would feel about it, she responded that one side of him would be very happy for her, the other side of him would be saying, "I'm going to break that record."

On September 6, 1989, the MTV Music Video Awards were presented. Dominating the nominations, with nine, were videos by none other than Michael Jackson. "Leave Me Alone" was nominated for Best Video, Best Special Effects, Best Art Direction, Best Editing, Breakthrough Video and the Viewer's Choice Award. "Smooth Criminal" was nominated for Best Dance, Best Choreography, and Best Cinematography. The outcome was disappointing with the only award for Michael's videos going to Jim Blashfield for Best Special Effects for his work on "Leave Me Alone". Michael did not attend the award presentation.

Around this same time, as part of the World Music Video Awards, Michael received the Lifetime Achievement Award for Video. The award was presented to Michael at his home by Whitney Houston. After the presentation of the award, Michael gave Whitney Houston and the crew a horseback tour of his ranch.

On October 10, Michael paid a visit to his former elementary school, Gardner Elementary School, in Los Angeles where he attended sixth grade for a short time. The school's auditorium had been recently refurbished and was renamed the Michael Jackson

Auditorium. Michael's former sixth grade teacher, Mrs. Gerstin, and Mrs. Rose Fine, his tutor when he was on the road with the Jackson Five, both attended the dedication.

After several speeches by the school superintendent, PTA representatives, and teachers, Michael's former sixth grade teacher introduced Michael and presented him with a plaque: "It's an honor to present this plaque to you on behalf of the parents and faculty, past and present, of Gardner School as a token of our respect and our love for you not only as a performer, but as a fine human being." Dressed in black pants and a red shirt covered with buckles, and long black fingerless gloves, Michael accepted the honor and spoke briefly as always:

> *First of all I'd like to thank my teacher, Mrs. Gerstin, Mrs. Rose Fine, she's another one of my teachers, she's here also and I'd like to thank her. I am deeply touched and honored that the PTA, principal, faculty members, and students have been so kind as to dedicate the auditorium where I sat as a child, in my honor. We must all never forget that the children are our future and without them mankind would become extinct. I thank Mrs. Gerstin, I love you, and Mrs. Rose Fine, I love you, the Gardner Street School associates, and all the children. I love you. Thank you.*

Following the presentation of the plaque, a very happy student presented Michael with a key to the school. Michael then joined the student choir in singing "We Are The World." A small crowd then moved outside as Michael unveiled the new letters on the face of the building identifying it as the Michael Jackson Auditorium.

Following the unveiling, Michael was given a tour of his former school. He visited his old classroom and autographed the wall with a marker, "Michael Jackson Love the Children". Epic official Larry Stessel, Bob Jones and Bill Bray accompanied Michael.

While speculation continued as to whether Michael would join his brothers on tour, or if there would be a tour at all, Michael was at work on several new projects. A double album of greatest hits was scheduled for release in November, 1989, (of course it would be delayed), he was still searching for a movie role, and he was helping to design a new video game.

CHAPTER
FOURTEEN

DECADE

As 1989 came to a close it was time once again for numerous TV programs and seemingly every magazine publication to begin compiling a look back at not only the past year, but at the closing decade. Not surprisingly, Michael Jackson dominated the various countdowns and charts compiled to reflect both the past twelve months and the last ten years.

Michael's showing on *Billboard's* year end charts for 1989 didn't stand up to the previous year, but considering he had had no new album in release and had only one single, "Smooth Criminal", the results weren't too disappointing. "Smooth Criminal" placed at numbers ninety three and fifty eight on the year end pop and black singles charts respectively. Michael was ranked as the nineteenth Top Pop Male Singles Artist and as the eighty third Top Pop Singles Artist. The Jacksons placed at numbers forty nine and forty one on the Top Black Artist and Top Black Singles Artist charts respectively. *2300 Jackson St.* was ranked at number sixty on the Top Black Album Chart for the year.

Michael's videos earned four nominations, but no awards, in *Billboard's* 1989 Music Video Awards. "Leave Me Alone" was nominated in three categories, Best Video, Best Male Video, and Best Art Direction. "Smooth Criminal" had one nomination for Best Concept Video.

Even though "Leave Me Alone" was never formally released as a single in the U.S., the song's video did receive numerous recognitions. *USA Today's* music critics chose "Leave Me Alone" as the number one Best Video of 1989. Janet Jackson's "Miss You Much" was ranked as the year's fifth best video. "Leave Me Alone" was further honored with a Teddy, an international and Canadian music award. Jim Blashfield won a Golden Lion Award at the Cannes film festival for his work on the special effects in "Leave Me Alone". The Golden Lion is the highest honor given in the category of commercials, short films, and videos.

"Leave Me Alone" was ranked as the fifth best animated video by MTV's Animation Invasion, a countdown of the best animated videos.

The December 23, 1989 issue of *Billboard* recapped both the year and the decade passing. Reviews of the decade in general and of the decade's pop and black music all began by focusing on the artist making the biggest impact of the eighties. An overview of "The Decade in Charts" began with mentioning the biggest selling album of the decade:

Michael Jackson was both the hottest and most immediately influential artist of the 80's. The Gloved One was far and away the top artist of 1983 in pop, black, and dance music, and also had the top album in all three formats, Thriller.

Thriller was such a monster that it was also the no. 1 pop album of 1984. The Grammy winning collection was the first album to top the year-end chart two years running since the West Side Story soundtrack in the early 60's.

The scope of Jackson's crossover potential was first suggested in 1980 when he was rated the year's top singles artist in both pop and black music. He was also that year's top black album artist, but was nosed out by Pink Floyd on the tally of top pop album acts.

Jackson's success confirmed once and for all the sales potential of black music and opened the door for other black artists. And many follow his lead...

The recap of pop music in the 80's began:

Michael Jackson was the hottest pop artist of the 80's, though, Prince, Madonna, Whitney Houston, and George Michael gave him a run for his money in the second half of the decade...

Jackson was far and away the top pop artist of 1983 for both albums and singles. The only year-end pop title which eluded him in 1983 was the top single citation, which went to the Police's 'Every Breath You Take'.

The publication's review of black music in the 80's also focused on Michael Jackson:

> *In addition to his dominance on the pop charts, Michael Jackson was the top star in black music in the 80's. Jackson was the no. 1 black music act for combined albums\singles three times, in 1980, 1983, and 1988. No other artist took that title more than once...*
>
> *...Michael Jackson swept the 1980 recaps, emerging as the year's top black music artist in both albums and singles. His blockbuster Off the Wall was an easy winner for top black music album. Jackson yielded just one award, top black music single, and that was to his brother, Jermaine, for 'Let's Get Serious'.*
>
> *Jackson was a repeat winner in those same categories in 1983 with his mega hit, Thriller. Again he yielded just one award, top black music single, which went to Marvin Gaye for his landmark hit, 'Sexual Healing'.*
>
> *Jackson also registered strongly in 1988, when in addition to his overall title he was named top singles artist...*

Billboard polled its readers to find their favorite artists and recordings of the eighties, the results of which were published in the May 26, 1990, issue. Michael Jackson dominated the poll, placing eleven times in eight categories. Readers voted Michael Jackson as the number two pop artist of the decade, and as the number four dance artist of the decade. Michael Jackson was voted as their number one favorite black artist of the decade and *Thriller* was voted as both the decade's number one favorite pop and black album.

In the same poll, "We Are the World" placed just behind the Police's "Every Breath You Take" as the second favorite pop single of the decade. "Billie Jean" tied with Prince's "When Doves Cry" at number four on the same chart. "Billie Jean" was the reader's number one favorite black single of the decade and "Beat It" was their fifth favorite. "Billie Jean" was voted the second favorite dance single of the decade and "Beat It" was voted as the forth favorite.

Epic Records placed a full page ad in the same issue of *Billboard*, congratulating Michael on topping four of the Readers Poll categories. A black and white drawing of Michael in a pose from "Smooth Criminal" was accompanied by a listing of the categories in which he placed first, and the line "CONGRATULA-TIONS FROM YOUR EPIC FAMILY".

Rolling Stone likewise named *Thriller* the number one album of the 80's. The ranking of each album was determined by the number of weeks the album spent at number one on the album charts. Ties were broken by the number of weeks the album spent in the top forty.

The decade in review themed features continued to appear in one magazine after another well into 1990. *Rolling Stone* ranked the Top 100 Greatest Albums of the Decade, with *Thriller* placing at number seven. This list was evidently based on the opinion of the publication's editors or critics and not based on chart performance, where *Thriller* placed at number one.

The year-end issue of *Musician* magazine, dedicated to a review of the eighties, included a look at Michael Jackson's *Thriller* album, crediting *Thriller* for releasing "enough energy of one sort or another to create the rings around Triton". *People* magazine was not about to be left out in publishing an issue devoted to a look back on the decade. Their publication included Michael Jackson as one of the twenty people who helped define the decade.

Media stars of the decade were the focus of *Vanity Fair's* year end issue. Michael Jackson was chosen as the issue's cover photo. It was the first time Michael posed for a magazine since 1984. He was pictured perched up on his toes, in jeans and a white shirt, unbuttoned and untucked, his shirttails and long hair blowing back in an unseen wind. Tina Brown, then editor-in-chief of *Vanity Fair,* appeared on ABC's *Good Morning America* program to promote the issue and spoke with program host Charlie

Gibson. Gibson questioned Brown's choice for the cover, describing Michael Jackson as "a guy who made one big album and a Pepsi commercial." Brown defended her choice replying that Gibson's remark was "a very slim claim for the biggest entertainer all time. We chose Michael Jackson because he is the premier entertainer of our time. He's the biggest. He's also in a funny way emblematic of the whole era of synergy because he does ads, a book, an album, MTV, all these things seem to us systematic of the 80's and as such he really does stand for the media explosion." Gibson then questioned her judgment on naming Michael Jackson as the biggest entertainer, "You characterize him as the biggest entertainer of all time?" Brown again defended her point brilliantly, "I think he is. In terms of the money he's made and the audiences he has commanded, absolutely yes. Number one."

The photos of Michael and the other celebrities in the issue were shot by photographer Annie Leibovitz. Other photos of Michael by Leibovitz were later published in a book of her photographs.

In October, 1989, *Friday Night Videos* counted down their picks for the greatest artists of the decade. After showing videos by Prince, Whitney Houston, Madonna, Bruce Springsteen, George Michael, Phil Collins and Genesis, they announced their choice for the Number One Artist of the Decade: Michael Jackson. Clips of all of Michael's videos were shown.

Another *Friday Night Videos* special edition aired in January, 1990, featuring the viewers' choices of their favorite videos of the decade. "Thriller" was voted as one of the viewers' favorite videos of the decade.

Entertainment Tonight named Michael Jackson as the Most Important Entertainer of the Decade and presented a short tribute to him including a montage of video clips and concert footage.

On December 6, 1989, MTV aired a special, *Rate The 80's*, in which they revealed how viewers had voted in several phone in categories, including their choices for Best Movie, Video, and TV show of the 80's. Viewers phoned in their choices for one month. Michael Jackson had the most nominations with three. "Thriller" was nominated for the Greatest Video in the History of the World, *Thriller* was nominated for Really Big Album, and Michael was among the nominees for Mega Artist of the 80's. Michael placed fourth in the race for Mega Artist with 15% of the vote. *Thriller*, with 14% of the vote, placed third for Really Big Album. "Thriller" was chosen as the Greatest Video in the History of the World with 35% of the vote.

This award was presented to Michael when he made a surprise appearance on the *Arsenio Hall Show*. This was a dream come true for Hall who had earlier told an interviewer he hoped Michael Jackson would make an appearance on his show, even if it was a very brief appearance, just to say, "I don't do TV!" Hall's guest was Eddie Murphy. Murphy had been chosen by MTV viewers as the Humor God of the 80's. Michael made a special appearance on the show to surprise Murphy and present him with the award. Murphy then surprised Michael by presenting him with the video award.

After the audience's deafening applause to Michael's unannounced appearance subsided, Michael, dressed in red and black, spoke only briefly from behind his dark glasses: "Presented to the King of Comedy, of all time, the King." Michael handed the award to Eddie and hugged him. Eddie then presented Michael with his video award: "Viewers Award for Michael Jackson for the Greatest Video in the History of all Videos, 'Thriller'". With no mike, Michael smiled big and waved to the crowd before walking off the set.

American Top Forty with Casey Kassem counted down the Top 40 Dance Hits of the 80's as compiled by *Billboard* magazine. Michael dominated the countdown with four entries. "Wanna Be Startin' Somethin'" started the countdown, at number forty. Michael's remaining three entries were all in the top ten. "Bad" was ranked at number seven. The top three entries all belonged to Jacksons. "Beat It" placed at number three, just behind Janet's

"Miss You Much". Sitting on the top of the heap as the decade's top dance hit was "Billie Jean".

MTV was busy at year end compiling video countdowns for the year and for the decade of nearly every imaginable configuration. Countdowns reflecting the top 100 videos of the year, of the 80's, the most requested videos ever, classic videos, and top dance videos are only a few of the numerous special lists compiled by MTV to keep viewers glued to their sets. The video network's countdown of the 100 Best Videos of 1989 placed "Leave Me Alone" at number fifty six, and "Smooth Criminal" at forty five. The countdown of the Top 100 Videos of the 80's placed "Man in the Mirror" at number forty, "Billie Jean" at number twenty seven, and "Beat It" at number thirteen. The number one video of the 80's according to MTV was "Thriller". MTV's listing of the Most Requested Videos Ever had slightly different results. "Beat It" placed at number twenty four, and "Billie Jean" was number thirteen. "Thriller" was ranked as the third most requested video.

About six weeks after presenting the Most Requested Videos Ever, MTV was counting down the Top Dance Videos Ever. Four of Michael Jackson's videos were included, "Leave Me Alone" at number forty, "Beat It" at number twenty six, "Billie Jean" at number fourteen, and "Smooth Criminal" at number two, just behind Paula Abdul's "Opposites Attract".

Three of Michael's videos were included on MTV's Classic Video countdown. "Beat It" was ranked at number twenty nine, "Billie Jean" at number thirteen, and "Thriller" was ranked as the number one classic video.

In January, 1990, MTV announced its choice for MTV's Video Vanguard Artist of the Decade Award, Michael Jackson. The award was presented to Michael by VJ Adam Curry and MTV Network CEO, Tom Freston. Dressed in black pants and red shirt lined with the familiar rows of buckles, black gloves, and no sunglasses, Michael stood quietly while Adam Curry, then Tom Freston spoke:

Every year at the MTV Music Video Awards we honor those artists whose work has left a lasting mark on the world of video. We're here today to handout the big one, the MTV Video Vanguard Artist of the Decade Award. To call our recipient worthy is an understatement of Epic proportion, believe me this guy really deserves it. Every single time we think we see him at his best, he goes out and tops himself all over again. I'm talking about, of course, about the one and only Michael Jackson. Now I'd like to let the President, head honcho and Chief Executive Officer take it from here, Tom Freston.

Tom:

Michael, everyone knows you as a gifted singer, dancer, musician, choreographer, composer and performer. I hope I didn't leave anything out. But we're here today to highlight your accomplishments to the video arts. Throughout the 80's, your work has expanded the art form. You are not afraid to tell a story, take risks, to visually stimulate the audience and of course to give all of those dancers a paycheck. I remember the excitement in '82 when 'Billie Jean' broke. Then you followed that with 'Beat It'. People everywhere were glued to their sets, watching you on MTV. And with each passing video project, you've kept the excitement going. So, on the behalf of MTV, and our audience, I'm thrilled to present you, the biggest selling recording artist of all time, the award for MTV's Video Vanguard of the Decade. We can't wait to see what you have planned for us in the 90's. Congratulations.

Then Michael spoke, briefly as always:

It's very beautiful, Thank you very very much, MTV. It's wonderful. And to all the fans, thank you very much.

The award presentation was followed by an evening of Michael Jackson specials and videos. One hour of Michael Jackson videos followed the airing of *Making Michael Jackson's Thriller*.

One thousand Artist of the Decade awards were produced by Platinum Limited Editions declaring Michael Jackson as the artist of the decade. The award includes a platinum album, a listing of Michael's record breaking achievements and a small figure of Michael in a pose from "Smooth Criminal". Each is numbered and autographed by Michael.

On January 27, 1990, at the Beverly Hilton Hotel, The American Cinema Foundation awarded special honors to three entertainers. Elizabeth Taylor and Gregory Peck were honored for their career achievements in film. The Entertainer of the Decade honor was awarded to Michael Jackson.

Among Michael's guests at the award presentation were Janet, Tito, and Jermaine. The award ceremony was a little late getting started, as Michael showed up two hours late. When he finally showed up, dressed in a red shirt, and black military jacket, Sophia Loren presented Michael with his award, and he gave an incredible three minute speech. "I'm giving a long speech because I'm not on television." In fact, no cameras were allowed to film him. In his speech, Michael spoke of his deep affection for fellow honoree Elizabeth Taylor. Taylor had had similar praise for Michael in her own speech saying she was happy to be honored with "my beloved Michael, whom I would have loved and admired if I had never seen him dance or heard him sing."

The day before receiving this honor, Michael was again at the Beverly Hilton Hotel to help unveil a portrait that had been painted of himself. Brett Livingstone Strong painted the portrait, titled, "The Book", of Michael sitting in a chair holding a book on his lap. In the background is a statue of Peter Pan and another painting of Michael. The painting was sold to a Japanese business-man for $2.1 million, the largest sum ever paid for a portrait of a living person.

On February 20, Michael was honored at a breakfast press conference held at the Regent Beverly Wilshire Hotel by CBS Records. Michael received an award for being the label's biggest selling artist of the 80's, selling in excess of 110 million records.

CBS Records' Tommy Mattola presented Michael with the award, a figure of Michael in a pose from the "Smooth Criminal" video against a large disk reading "100 Million". Mattola read a list of Michael's accomplishments and stated, "If I stood here 10 years ago and told you any artist would accomplish what Michael Jackson accomplished, you would have probably laughed me off the stage."

Michael attended the press conference dressed in red and black, the same black sequined military jacket he had worn to the American Cinema Awards, black gloves, and sunglasses. As usual, his thank yous were brief:

Thank you Tommy, and thank you ladies and gentlemen. I'm sure it won't surprise you that I'm gonna make this one short again, but I have to say however, that no album sells itself. It's up to the people out there to buy it, and so I not only want to thank CBS Records and Epic Records, but I especially want to thank everyone everywhere who helped make this award what it is, first a possibility, and now a reality. Thank you Quincy Jones, thank you Dave Glew, thank you Bruce Swedian, John Branca, Mother and Joseph, Walter Yetnikoff and Hank Caldwell. And all of the children of the world. I love you. Goodbye.

Among those in attendance were Michael's parents, Berry Gordy, Little Richard, Elton John, Gladys Knight, and Siedah Garrett.

On April 5, Michael was presented with the Entertainer of the Decade Award on behalf of the Capital Children's Museum. The award was presented by President Bush at the White House. Michael was dressed in red and black, black gloves and sunglasses. Mrs. Bush, who complimented him on his silver tipped boots, gave him a tour of the White House. He spoke with Vice President Quayle, autographed some Easter eggs for the annual White House Easter egg roll, and presented President Bush with a collection his compact discs. That evening, Michael was guest of honor at a museum fund raising reception. There he had further thank yous: "I'd like to thank the Kays and Karen for their wonderful hospitality and little Lauren for showing me around today and being so kind. Thank you very much."

The day before receiving the award, Michael visited the Children's Museum. He played with many of the exhibits and was uncharacteristically comfortable with the crowd around him, primarily because most were children.

One year earlier, the Capital Children's Museum honored Michael with the Best of Washington Humanitarian Award for his fund raising efforts for the hands on educational museum.

Michael ended the 1980's with the number one and number two best selling albums of the decade. He is the artist with the most number one hit singles of the 80's, with nine, as well as the artist with the most top ten hits, with 17. His Bad tour set new records around the world, that will likely only be topped by Michael himself. But, he's not touring anymore. Or is he?

CHAPTER FIFTEEN

THE MAGIC CONTINUES...

During the eighties Michael focused primarily on music and videos. His projects lined up for the nineties look to be more diverse. He would, however, start the new decade collecting awards and honors one after another and releasing another record-setting album with more chart topping singles and videos. He even announced another world tour.

For the 1990 Grammy Awards, Michael had two nominations. "Leave Me Alone" won the Grammy for Best Short Form Video and *Janet Jackson's Rhythm Nation 1814* edged out *Moonwalker* for the Grammy for Best Long Form Video. Neither Janet or Michael attended the award ceremony.

The Hollywood Chamber of Commerce awarded a star on the Hollywood Walk of Fame to Janet Jackson on April 20. It was reported that Michael wanted to attend the presentation but didn't want to take any of the attention from Janet, so he planned to attend wearing one of his disguises. It was never confirmed by Michael or Janet whether or not he actually was there.

To celebrate their fiftieth anniversary BMI, Broadcast Music, Inc., an organization for songwriters, composers and music publishers, instituted a new award for career excellence, The BMI Michael Jackson Award. The award was presented to its first recipient on May 8, 1990, to appropriately enough, Michael Jackson. Michael accepted the award at the Regent Beverly Wilshire Hotel. Dressed in his customary red and black he, as usual, had very little to say: "It is a pleasure to be associated with such a fine organization and I only hope to be celebrating BMI's widespread accomplishments five decades from now." He added, "I'm honored and happy to be in the room with so many people I admire. I love you very much."

A congratulatory ad was placed in *Billboard* and other magazines to mark the special occasion. The two page gold and black ad featured a drawing of Michael and read:

Congratulations Michael!
Celebrated Songwriter and Composer
Artist of the Eighties

*Creative Innovator In Music, Dance, Video and Film Trendsetter
and Role Model For the Youth Of The World
Benefactor And Humanitarian
BMI
On the Occasions Of Its 50th Anniversary Is Proud To
Inaugurate the
BMI
Michael Jackson
Award
In Honor Of These Unique And
Ongoing Achievements
May 8, 1990*

Over three hundred artists, songwriters and industry executives attended the award presentation, including Jackie Jackson, Little Richard and Elton John, who ordinarily avoids such functions.

On June 3, despite not having felt well for the past few days, Michael was home in Encino doing his regular Sunday dance exercises; he began suffering pains in his chest. He called his doctor, Steve Hoefflin, who drove him to the hospital. They arrived at St. John's Hospital and Health Center at 9:00 pm. Jermaine arrived shortly after and stayed the night with Michael. He was listed in stable condition and was confined to bed while tests were administered to determine the cause of the pains.

Among the well wishers calling the hospital were President Bush, Liza Minnelli, Paul McCartney, Lionel Richie, and Elton John. Michael's mother visited him and LaToya, who was in London, sent him some black roses.

It wasn't until three days later that the findings of the tests were announced. Michael was suffering from costochondritis, inflammation of the cartilage at the front of the rib cage, suspected to be caused from over exertion and stress. The inflammation takes weeks to heal and if treated early leaves no lasting effects. The battery of tests performed showed no problems with his heart or lungs.

Some speculated the stress was due to Michael losing three very close people in his life within a short period of time. His maternal grandmother, Martha, Sammy Davis Jr., and Ryan White all died within weeks of each other, taking a large toll on him. Other sources speculated the stress Michael was under was due to his having to decide between two special projects. He was being forced to chose between his beloved Disney and the Universal Studios theme park in Florida. Disney Chairman Michael Eisner was working with Michael on a plan to lend his name to a new attraction. At the same time, David Geffin and Steven Spielberg wanted him to attend the opening of the Universal theme park in Florida. Eisner told Michael if he accepted the invitation from Universal, he could not in any way be associated with Disney ever again. This supposedly put enough pressure on Michael to cause his collapse.

Before being released on Friday, Michael visited with Elizabeth Taylor who was on the same floor of the hospital as he was, recovering from a long bout of pneumonia. A few weeks later, after her release, Elizabeth Taylor spent a few days recovering at Michael's ranch.

Michael was well enough by July to attend the wedding of Grace Eaton to Berry Gordy in Santa Barbara. Among the other wedding guests were Smokey Robinson and Diana Ross.

He was also well enough for some company. The Dream Street program in Los Angeles, an organization for children with life threatening diseases, held a camp in Santa Barbara for forty five children in July. They were camping near Michael's ranch when he invited them over. They were given a tour of his ranch, watched a movie and had lunch. The founders of the camp called the visit the perfect end to their week long stay in Santa Barbara.

A few weeks later, on August 18, 130 children from the YWCA Summer Program in Los Angeles and Santa Barbara were invited to Michael's ranch. They were treated to a barbecue, played video games, visited his zoo, and watch movies. Each child was given a free pair of sneakers, and you can bet they

weren't Reeboks! The children made him a banner reading, "We
Love You Michael" and made him an honorary member of the
28th St. YMCA in Los Angeles.

These were not the first instances in which he invited
children to his ranch. Earlier in the year, in January, he invited
eighty two children from Childhelp USA to his ranch. They too
were given a tour of the ranch, treated to lunch and watch two
movies, *The Little Mermaid* and *Back to the Future II*. Steven
Speilberg's *Back to the Future II* has a couple of references to
Speilberg's friend, Michael Jackson. The film's star, Michael J.
Fox, visits Cafe 80's in the next century where "Beat It" is being
played and Michael can be seen on a TV monitor. In another
scene, Fox startles a young girl in her bedroom in 1984, the walls
of which are covered with Michael Jackson posters.

Eighteen months after he fired Frank Dileo, on August 21,
1990, it was announced Michael Jackson had hired a new manager, Sandy Gallin. Whereas Michael's managing contract with
Frank Dileo precluded him taking any other clients, Gallin
manages several other artists including Neil Diamond, Dolly
Parton, and Whoopi Goldberg. One possible reason Michael
didn't require sole representation may be that he intends to
maintain more hands-on control of his managerial affairs, having
Gallin in an advisory capacity. Since taking on the new manager,
Gallin doesn't seem to be Michael's shadow like Dileo was,
attending every single public appearance and nearly always
speaking for Michael.

At the time Gallin signed on as his new manager, Michael
was in the process of, or at least rumored to be in the process of,
making two other unexpected, abrupt changes affecting his career.
He was rumored to be organizing a new legal staff to replace John
Branca. It was further rumored that Michael may be considering
leaving Epic Records for David Geffen's Geffen Records.

Hiring Gallin fueled both rumors. David Geffen was said
to be aiding Michael in organizing his new legal staff, made up
Bert Fields, Lee Phillips, and Allen Grubman. Gallin also has ties

with Geffen, giving reasonableness to a possible switch from Epic to Geffen.

It was speculated that Geffen could have easily swayed Michael from CBS to Geffen Records but he still owed CBS four more albums, and the cost to buy his remaining contract from CBS would "have been greater than the gross national product of Uganda."

David Geffen's new association with Michael Jackson and his advising Michael in building a new managerial and legal staff was reported to help trigger the departure of Walter Yetnikoff from CBS Records. Geffen advised Michael that he could negotiate better deals with other lawyers than John Branca because Branca was close friends with Yetnikoff. Yetnikoff and Geffen also clashed when Yetnikoff refused to allow Michael to contribute a song to the soundtrack album for *Days of Thunder,* which was released on Geffen Records. Yetnikoff further soured his relationship with Michael when he initially blocked Michael from contributing to *Listen Up! The Lives of Quincy Jones,* a documentary on, well, the life of Quincy Jones, because of a rivalry with Steve Ross, chairman of Time Warner. Ross' wife, Courtney served as producer of the film. Michael later did contribute to the film, doing an off camera interview. The film was released in September, 1990.

On September 4, 1990, Walter Yetnikoff stepped down as CEO and president of CBS Records. His decision was said to be due to allegations against him mentioned in Fredric Dannen's book, *Hit Men,* and to his deteriorating relationship with the label's biggest selling artist, Michael Jackson.

But this wasn't the first time it was rumored Michael was leaving Epic Records. A story had run on the front page of the Hollywood Reporter that Michael Jackson had signed a five year movie deal with Disney. The story reported further that Michael would design rides for Disney's theme parks and that he would be leaving Epic Records to join Disney's Hollywood Records. The story was found to be false and Disney began an investigation to find the source of the phony story. Michael Jackson's publicist told the press the next day, the story was "fraudulent and totally unofficial."

At the same time it was announced that Joe Jackson had started Jackson Records. A spokesman for the company claimed they would fund movie projects for both Michael and Janet Jackson. Michael and Janet each denied having any involvement with Jackson Records.

Aside from managerial concerns, Michael was still busy picking up awards. The Los Angeles council of Boy Scouts of America was the next organization to create an award named for Michael. Again Michael was the first recipient. The Michael Jackson Good Scout Humanitarian Award was presented to Michael on September 14, in recognition of his humanitarian efforts for all mankind through his fund raising efforts for the Make-A-Wish Foundation, The Prince's Trust, the United Negro College Fund, and Childhelp USA. Walt Disney Chairman Michael Eisner presented the award to Michael. Dressed in a gold and black military style jacket and sunglasses, Michael said only, "On behalf of the millions of past, present, and future Boy Scouts, I will try to abide by your motto of being prepared and always extending a hand to others."

Just before picking up this award, MTV compiled yet another countdown of the Top Dance Videos. Michael had five videos place on the countdown this time. "Bad" was ranked at number seventy seven, "The Way You Make Me Feel" placed at number forty three, "Beat It" at number twenty eight, "Billie Jean" at number fourteen and "Smooth Criminal" was ranked as the sixth best dance video.

In between collecting awards, entertaining various groups of children at his ranch, and re-constructing his legal and managerial staffs, Michael had some long awaited projects due for release. Originally scheduled for release in November, 1989, his greatest hits package, *Decade* was now a year late. *Decade* was to be a double album of Michael's greatest hits with three to five new songs included, among them his cover of the Beatles' "Come Together". Slated for release simultaneously was a *Decade* video cassette. This project was later scrapped in favor of releasing a whole new album, *Dangerous*. Of course, before its release, there would be the usual delays.

Also due out soon was a Moonwalker video game by Genesis/Sega. Michael aided in the game's design which is based on the Smooth Criminal story. The player attempts to defeat the bad guys with various dance moves. Three songs are included on the video game, "Beat It", "Bad", and "Smooth Criminal". The video game was introduced to video arcades and on game cartridges for use in home game systems.

Fall was once again time for *Forbes* magazine the publish their list of the highest paid entertainers. Michael Jackson placed at number two, behind Bill Cosby, with estimated two year earnings of $100 million. Michael earnings in 1989 totaled $65 million and the magazine estimated his 1990 earnings at $35 million.

At this same time, a lawsuit was dismissed that was filed in June, 1989, by George Mollases and John Griffen claiming Michael Jackson's video for "Man in the Mirror" infringed on their 1986 video, "All Over The World". The judge ruled the plaintiffs had no copyright interest in the video and they admitted there were no similarities between the songs' words or music.

In September, 1990, BET, the Black Entertainment Network, celebrated its tenth anniversary. A special section devoted to the network was featured in the September 22 issue of *Billboard,* composed of congratulatory messages. Michael Jackson was among those congratulating BET: " I am extremely appreciative of BET's support of my efforts. They have always provided a welcome home for my music."

My Family, The Jacksons, by Katherine Jackson and Robert Wiseman, was published in the United States in the fall of 1990. The book was previously only available in Japan. In the book she reveals Joe's many infidelities including one that produced a daughter, Joh'Vonnie, born August 30, 1974. She also discusses filing, then later withdrawing, a request for divorce from Joseph. He was served with the papers, but refused to move out of the house! Besides her relationship with Joseph, there is very little insight in her book concerning her children, especially Michael.

"A Tribute To John Lennon" aired in December. The tribute was a compilation of performances from several different artists performing John Lennon and Beatle songs. Included in the tribute was Michael Jackson's performance of "Come Together" taken from *Moonwalker.*

MTV's Martha Quinn chose her top ten favorite videos for *TV Guide's* January 19, 1991 issue. Listed among her picks was Michael Jackson's "Man in the Mirror".

Scheduled for release on January 15, 1991, the deadline President Bush gave Saddam Hussein to withdraw his troops from Kuwait, was a remake of John Lennon's "Give Peace a Chance". The song was rewritten by Sean Lennon and Lenny Kravits to better reflect current times. Several artists were contacted to participate in recording the song, including Michael Jackson, who is close friends with Sean. He did not, however, participate in the recording.

In February, Michael's publicist, Lee Solters, announced that 22 inch by 23 inch holograms reproducing Michael Jackson's face in 3-D would be displayed in galleries and museums. They would be sold for prices starting at $20,000. Smaller versions, 2 1/2" x 4" would be available in stores.

Also available in February by phone order only, was an audio tape about James Brown. Among the many contributors to the tape were Quincy Jones and Michael Jackson.

Another project Michael contributed to in 1991 was a solo album by former New Edition member Ralph Tresvant, *Sensitivity.* The CD format of the album featured a bonus track, "Alright Now", written by Michael Jackson and John Barnes.

During 1991 Michael Jackson and Sony, the new owner of CBS, were involved in contract renegotiations. Some speculated that Sony's negotiating power was significantly reduced due to the souring relationship between Michael and Walter Yetnikoff. Yetnikoff's replacement, Tommy Mottola had little room for negotiating; Sony was eager to please Michael and keep him from leaving for another record company. Besides Sony's seemingly reduced negotiating power, Michael Jackson is considered one of the most powerful people in the entertainment industry. He was even named so by *Entertainment Weekly* in their November 2, 1990 issue listing the 101 Most Influential Power People in Entertainment.

Among the items Michael wanted included in the contract were advances for each album of $18 million, and to split expenses and profits 50/50 with Sony. He also held out for starting his own record label. CBS is one the top bidders for the Motown Records Jobete Music catalog and some noted the company may have used its position as a possible buyer to entice Michael to re-sign.

Janet Jackson left A&M Records in March and signed a new recording contract with Virgin Records. Her new deal was worth an estimated $40 to $50 million. It was the largest recording contract in history. At least it was for a couple of days, then it was reported that Michael had finally resigned with Epic Records.

Michael's new contract with Sony eclipsed Janet's by millions and millions. Reports stated that it could potentially earn up to $1 billion for Michael. The deal was the first time a contract had been signed with a star for record, TV, and movie projects. The fifteen year contract provides for Michael to establish his own record label, deliver six albums to Epic, star in feature films, TV programs, and produce a series of short films from his upcoming album. Michael will also own 70% of all video rights. Under his new contract, he will receive a $5 to $10 million advance on each album and a 25% royalty rate based on the album's sales. His record label, Nation Records, will sign new and established acts and he will be paid a salary of $1 million per year as its CEO. He was scheduled to begin work on his first movie project with Columbia Pictures, also owned by Sony, by the end of 1991.

After the announcement that Michael's deal outpaced Janet's, her management noted that Janet's deal for recording did in fact surpass the recording portion of Michael's deal. Although it is difficult to put an exact value on the recording segment of the contract because Michael's profits depend largely on sales, *The Wall Street Journal* estimated Michael's record portion of the deal to be worth at least $60 million.

His new contract earned Michael another entry in the *Guiness Book of World Records*. The 1992 edition lists his deal with Sony as the largest contract ever at the more conservative estimate of $890 million.

Before it was announced that Michael Jackson's first movie under his new contract would be the musical action adventure, *Midknight,* speculation rose as to what movie would be his first. Both Michael Jackson and Eddie Murphy have expressed interest in portraying Little Richard in a movie of the legendary rocker's life. Little Richard has stated he would most like to see Michael portray him in the film. The movie project Michael did accept, *Midknight,* was written by Caroline Thompson, who wrote *Edward Scissorhands*, and Larry Wilson, author of *Beetlejuice.*

While speculation rose as to what role Michael would play, also being considered was who would play the role of Michael. A TV mini-series was in the works based on the lives of the Jacksons, "The Jacksons: An American Dream". The five hour long series follows their lives through the Victory tour and superstardom for Michael. The mini series was set to start filming in the summer of 1990 but was delayed. The series was supported by the entire family except LaToya who threatened legal action if her name or likeness was used. Katherine Jackson served as co-writer for the series and Jermaine co-produced it along with Suzanne de Passe. There was some interest in some of the grandchildren playing their parents, and Rebbie portraying her mother, Katherine, because of her close resemblance to her mother at the same age. In early 1992, a nationwide search began for twenty six youngsters to portray the Jacksons at three different ages. There were reports at this time that Michael suggested one actor to portray him in the movie. He could sing and dance, and was white. This story was later said to be false.

By the summer of 1992 casting was completed and production began on the project with Pittsburgh being substituted for Gary, Indiana. Jermaine Jr. portrays his father as a young teen, and three actors, Jason Weaver, Alex Burrall and Wylie Draper portray Michael at various ages. Each actor was approved by Michael. Lawrence Hilton Jacobs, Sweathog Freddie Washington of *Welcome Back Kotter,* was cast as Joseph Jackson, Katherine Jackson was played by Angela Bassett. Holly Robinson, known from *21 Jump Street*, was cast as Diana Ross and Berry Gordy was played by Billie Dee Williams. Vanessa Williams, who bears a remarkable resemblance to Motown executive Suzanne de Passe, plays de Passe in the movie.

Scheduled to coincide with and promote the mini-series was a soundtrack album made up of previously unreleased Jackson Five songs. A re-mix of Smokey Robinson's "Who's Lovin' You" was chosen as the first single. It was decided to include the single in the movie at the last minute, giving the cast only twenty fours hours to learn the song and new choreography. The choreographer for the Jackson Five mini-series was often time Michael Jackson associate, Michael Peters.

Another Jackson family project that was scheduled to open in August, 1992, is the first of ten Jackson's Main Events at the Mall of America near Minneapolis, Minnesota. The attraction will include a museum with a replica of their home in Gary, Indiana, videos of visitors performing with images of the Jacksons, and talent shows.

While still working on the upcoming and always delayed album, Michael and Madonna dined together at the Ivy Restaurant in Los Angeles. They left in separate cars. Madonna was dressed all in black, Michael wore a white satin jacket. On the 25th of

March, Michael accompanied Madonna to the 63rd Annual Academy Awards. Madonna was a scheduled performer, singing "Sooner or Later" nominated for Best Song from *Dick Tracy*. The song won the Oscar.

Michael could be spotted in the audience, seated next to Madonna in the front row on the isle. She was dressed in a strapless white sequined gown and boa, looking very much like Marilyn Monroe. Michael coordinated with his date wearing a white shirt and white sequined jacket and two black gloves.

Following the award presentations, Madonna and Michael headed to Spago's for an after Oscar bash. Seated at a table with Michael and Diandra Douglas, and Anjelica Huston with Robert Graham, Madonna and Michael seemed to attract the most attention. Others were surprised at how long Michael stayed at the party, being one to shy away from such events. They stayed well after midnight. Michael visited with Henry Fonda's widow, Shirlee, and Diana Ross while Madonna cozied up with her former boy toy Warren Beatty. Michael and Madonna then left together.

They were seen dining together again a couple of weeks later at another Los Angeles restaurant. They were rumored to be working together on a duet for Michael's upcoming album and possibly other projects as well. Becoming quite the social butterfly, he later dined with Brooke Shields at the Inn of the Seventh Ray in Topanga Canyon, California, just one week before the release of his new album.

In March, Michael's actor friend, Bubbles, guest starred in an episode of *Father Dowling Mysteries* as a murder suspect who had been framed. Bubbles was paid $800.00 per day for his role. Just after this job, Bubbles experienced a lack of interest in life. Michael consulted chimp expert Jane Goodall who suggested he get Bubbles two female companions, and a kinder trainer. Michael admires Goodall's work with chimps and later served as chairman of a tribute to her. Bubbles later starred with Bob Newhart as part of a vaudeville act in *The Entertainers*, a TV movie.

MTV counted down the 100 Greatest Video Hits of all Time in early 1991. Michael had five of the greatest hits. "The Way You Make Me Feel" was ranked at number ninety-four; "Man in the Mirror", number forty-four; "Billie Jean", twenty-eight; "Beat It", sixteen; and the number one greatest video hit of all time according to MTV was Michael Jackson's "Thriller".

An unauthorized biography of Michael was released in May, *Michael Jackson: The Magic and the Madness* by J. Randy Taraborrelli. The biography did not slam Michael as some assumed without even reading the book. He did, however, reveal some rather startling facts concerning Joseph Jackson and some of the brothers regarding their marital infidelities and financial problems. Taraborrelli did claim that Michael mislead the public in revealing he had romantic liaisons with Diana Ross, Brooke Shields and Tatum O'Neal. Taroborelli stated further that he believed Michael Jackson was still a virgin. He based this conclusion on the fact that he could find no one, who he believed, male or female, that had slept with Michael.

While Michael has frequently referred to Diana Ross as his mother-lover-friend, did say Tatum O'Neal was his first love, after Diana, and did reveal in *Moonwalk* that he and Brooke Shields were "romantically serious", he never claimed he had slept with any of them. "Romantically serious" can mean anything, Michael was no doubt being deliberately vague in discussing his romantic life. Taraborrelli's claim that Michael's statements were misleading is due to his own interpretation of what "romantically serious" is.

In response to claims that Motown cheated the Jackson 5 and other artists out of royalties due them, Berry Gordy filed a $100 million libel suit against J. Randy Taraborrelli. The author then filed a countersuit against Gordy. When the book was reissued in paperback in the spring of 1992, statements claiming Motown inflated expenses that artists had to pay to insure the artists owed Motown and not vice versa, were edited out.

Taraborrelli is also the author of an unauthorized biography of Diana Ross, *Call Her Miss Ross*. The biography infuriated fans so much the author was forced to do a Detroit television talk show by satellite from New York due to death threats from fans if he went to Detroit.

In June, David Ruffin of the Temptations died of a drug overdose. When it was revealed the former Motown singer was broke, Michael Jackson contacted Swanson Funeral Home in Detroit and made arrangements to pay the costs of his idol's funeral. He also sent a heart shaped arrangement of white carnations to the New Bethel Baptist Church in Detroit with a note, "With Love, from Michael Jackson". He did not attend the funeral services for fear his presence would turn the proceedings into a circus.

A dinner was held for Stevie Wonder to present him with the Nelson Mandella Award in June. The dinner was hosted by Bill Cosby. Michael served as co-chair of the event along with Quincy Jones, Harry Belafonte, Eddie Murphy, Lionel Richie, Denzel Washington, and Oprah Winfrey.

The Hollywood Arts Council announced in July, its intentions to construct a mural of Michael Jackson on the El Capitan Theater in Hollywood. The mural is said to have a 3-D extension of Michael's arm lit by strobe lights giving the illusion of movement. After the project was finally approved, Los Angeles City Councilman Michael Woo said, "We want to encourage a real pedestrian environment that appeals to the executive carrying the attache case as well as the kid with the boombox. It's hard for me to imagine a person who represents that popular appeal better than Michael Jackson."

A birthday party was held for Joe Jackson in August at Spago's in Los Angeles. Katherine and Joseph were joined by their children, including Janet and Michael.

Ebony magazine's August issue featured a series of articles on "How Black Creativity is Changing America". Michael was among several photos featured on the issue's cover. One of the articles in the series, "The Biggest Brother-Sister Stars in Show Business History" focused on the impact of Michael and Janet Jackson. "No individual or group has impacted the world of entertainment as have Michael and Janet Jackson, who both signed multimillion dollar contracts in recent months...Though the fast paced world of entertainment is forever changing, it's a safe bet that Michael and Janet Jackson will continue to exert their considerable influence on into the future."

At the 1991 MTV Music Video Awards, it was announced that the Video Vanguard Award had been given a new name. The annual award would now be known as The Michael Jackson Video Vanguard Award. The first recipient of the renamed honor was Bon Jovi. Janet Jackson had two nominations for the video awards, and one win, winning for Best Female Video for "Love Will Never Do Without You."

The Simpsons premiered its first episode of the fall season in September, featuring a huge white mental patient who was convinced he was Michael Jackson! Michael provided the voice of the imposter but it was credited to John Jay Smith. In the episode, Homer is institutionalized for wearing a pink shirt to work. His roommate is Leon, who thinks he's Michael. Michael sings a new version of "Ben", with the name Homer substituted for Ben. Michael later goes home with Homer where he helps Bart compose a birthday song for his sister Lisa.

Released in the fall by Geffen Records was an album entitled *The Simpsons Sing the Blues.* The album contains duets with members of the Simpsons with Rod Stewart and Jeff Healy. The co-executive producer of *The Simpsons,* James L. Brooks, asked Michael Jackson to contribute a song to the album, but he couldn't due to his schedule. He asked Bryan Loran to write the song which became, "Do The Bartman". The first single off the album contained many references to Michael: "If you can do the Bartman, you're bad like Michael Jackson", "I'm bad, I'm bad" and "Eat your heart out, Michael!"

September was time again for *Forbes* magazine to publish its annual list of the highest paid entertainers. Michael was listed at number five with combined two year earnings of $60 million. Ranked at number four was Madonna with two year estimated earnings of $63 million. Special attention seemed to be paid by the media to the fact that Madonna placed higher than Michael Jackson. What was conspicuously absent from many of the comments was the fact that Madonna earned relatively little more than Michael and that during the two year period being considered, she starred in *Dick Tracy,* released an accompanying soundtrack album, and a greatest hits compilation, *The Immaculate Collection,* an accompanying video cassette and a video cassette single for the roof-raising "Justify My Love". A tour documentary film, *Truth or Dare,* was also released documenting her Blond Ambition tour. Michael's new projects released during the same period totaled zero.

In October, 1991, a Michael Jackson fan visiting the Motown Museum in Detroit pryed open the glass showcase door in the Michael Jackson room and stole the sequined glove from the display. Museum officials asked that the glove be returned, and that no questions would be asked. They also attempted to contact Michael to try to get a replacement. Meanwhile, rapper M.C. Hammer offered a $50,000 reward to whoever returned the glove to him, saying, "Nobody can steal what I am going to take."

The glove was found two days later. Anonymous callers told police where the fan lived that stole the glove. Police went to the Flint home of Bruce Hayes who then took them to a friend's house in Grand Blanc where the glove was being kept in a video cassette box. It was returned to the museum and put back on display in February, 1992, with a new security system to protect it. Hayes was charged with larceny inside a building and sentenced in January to two years probation and twenty hours of community service.

A similar glove was auctioned off by Christies in December. It was purchased by Robert Earl of the Hard Rock Cafe restaurants for $27,000. It was said the glove would be put on display in Dublin. This set a record as the highest price ever paid for a piece of memorabilia. The record was short lived however. Six months later John Lennon's leather jacket sold for $43,100 at an auction in London.

The gesture on the part of Hammer fit in with his then upcoming single and video, "2 Legit 2 Quit", in which he fantasizes that he is able to compete with Michael Jackson and possibly "win" the single white glove as a symbol of his victory. He then supposedly intends to present the glove to James Brown. Hammer went so far as to issue a public dance challenge to Michael, which Michael ignored. Hammer evidently feels Michael has never given credit to James Brown for being an important influence on his career. Obviously if he had paid any attention, he would find otherwise. Michael has on numerous occasions cited Brown as one of his earliest influences, he has been an idol of Michael's since his childhood, when he studied his moves and often imitated Brown in his performances including the Jackson Five's audition for Motown. Michael mentions his admiration for Brown and his influence on his career in *Moonwalk*. He also paid tribute to the Godfather of Soul in his 1988 Grammy performance.

Taking time out from finally finishing the new album, Michael played host to the eighth wedding ceremony of Elizabeth Taylor. Michael gave away the bride to Larry Fortensky on October 5, 1991 on the grounds of his Neverland Valley ranch. A photo of the new couple and their host was featured on the next issue of *People* magazine. Later Michael was one of the organizers of Elizabeth Taylor's sixtieth birthday party. Disneyland closed for the evening to host the bash.

The first week of November, only two years late, the first single from the new album began to be aired on radio stations in New York and Los Angeles. "Black or White" was officially released one week later. The new single set a record when it was initially released, being added to 96% of 237 of the nation's top forty radio stations the first day of release. The previous record, of 94%, was held by Madonna's "Like a Prayer".

The single debuted on *Billboard's* Top Pop Singles Chart at number thirty five. It was estimated by the magazine that the single would have debuted much higher had the new automated system of ranking singles, Soundscan, due to begin the next week, had been in effect. The second week on the charts, it shot up to number three. The following week, December 7, 1991, the number one single in the country was Michael Jackson's "Black or White". It is the fastest rising single since the Beatles' "Let It Be" rose to number two in two weeks in 1970. It was the first single to reach number one in just three weeks since the Beatles' "Get Back" in 1969. It ended the year at number one, and stayed at the top of the singles chart into 1992, for a total of seven weeks, making Michael Jackson the first artist to earn number one pop hits in the 70's, 80's, and 90's.

"Black or White" reached number one in the U.S., U.K., Australia, Italy, Spain, Mexico, Sweden, Denmark, Norway, Switzerland, Finland, Israel, New Zealand, and the Euro Chart Hot 100. The single went platinum in the U.S., selling over one million copies.

Michael had made a deal with the Fox network giving the network exclusive right to air each video, or short film as Michael prefers to call them, released from *Dangerous*. On November 14, 1991, the video for "Black or White" premiered simultaneously on Fox, BET, and MTV. Coinciding with the television debut of the video, *TV Guide* featured Michael on its cover the week of November 2. Also to coincide with the release of the album, *Rolling Stone* featured Michael Jackson on its January 9, 1992 cover which was on newsstands in December. Fox cut short an episode of *The Simpsons* to air the video, which had been heavily promoted. BET, The Black Entertainment Network, aired a Michael Jackson special, *Armed and Dangerous*, featuring the video's premiere. MTV declared it "Michael Jackson Week" and aired Jackson videos and specials the entire week leading to the video's planetary debut, which they played twice, back to back. The next weekend was Michael Jackson Weekend on MTV. The music network began referring to Michael as "The King of Pop" in their ads for the video premiere. Supposedly this was due to Michael's request and one of the stipulations for being allowed to air the video. Regardless, the title more than fits.

The video was seen in twenty seven countries, by an estimated 500 million people. Approximately 14 million people watched the video in the United States. It was the first video to be shown on German national TV news. To say the video caused a stir would be an understatement. Michael sings and dances with different races from around the world, including Indians and Russians; using a morphing process, people of different races and sexes blend into each other. Using the same process, a black panther is transformed into Michael who then dances without music accompaniment, reportedly doing his interpretation of the animalistic behavior of the panther. Michael smashes the windows out of a parked car, and throws the steering wheel through a store window. Dancing on the roof of the car he not merely grabs at, but caresses, his crotch and zips up his fly, lighting up switch boards at Fox like a Christmas tree. Due to the many complaints that the second half of the video was too sexually explicit and too violent, Michael decided to edit out the last four minutes of the video from further broadcasts and issued a statement:

It upsets me to think that 'Black or White' could influence any child or adult to destructive behavior, either sexual or violent. I've always tried to be a good role model and therefore have made these changes to avoid any possibility of adversely affecting any individual's behavior. I deeply regret any pain or hurt that the final segment of 'Black or White' has caused children, their parents or other viewers.

It was the edited version of "Black or White" that was broadcast the following Sunday on MTV and Fox in the Michael

Jackson special, "Dangerous". The thirty minute special featured clips covering Michael's career, very little of which hadn't been shown before. The special then concluded with the new edited video which features George Wendt, Norm Peterson from *Cheers*, and Tess Harper as the parents of Macaulay Culkin. The panther in the video was actually two look-a-like panthers, Sasha and Ivory. In the rap segment of the video, Michael is surrounded by a group of children, made up of Culkin, and Dave Shelton and Mark Pugh, members of Another Bad Creation. The little girl on the steps looks like Brandi Jackson is working with Uncle Mike again.

Michael had become good friends with *Home Alone* star Macaulay Culkin. Following a trip to Bermuda in June, they visited Disney World. Michael was in Bermuda scouting movie locations and looking for a home and land on which to build studios. When a taxi driver told him the island was home to 58,000 people, he laughed saying he gets bigger crowds at his concerts. One of the attractions of Bermuda for famous people is that the natives tend to leave the famous visitors alone. This was not the case for Michael. During his stay, the island reportedly did lose its composure and quite a fuss was made. While staying in Hamilton, the country's capital, Michael was taken for a boat ride by H. Ross Perot.

Culkin spent his eleventh birthday at Neverland Valley where Michael, a big fan of water fights since his days on the road with the Jackson 5, was building a water balloon fort. The fort is stocked with ditches, water hoses and launchers that will shoot balloons sixty feet away. And of course, no water fight is complete without a selection of squirt guns. Michael visited Culkin on the set of *Home Alone 2* when filming began in early 1992 in Illinois.

Despite the enormous sales potential due to the widespread controversy, Epic officials decided not to release the unedited version of "Black or White" as a video single. Because of the overwhelming response to the video, the "Black or White" video was chosen by *TV Guide* at the end of the year as one of the 12 Most Mesmerizing TV Moments from the last 12 months.

Controversy over the video hit virtually every newspaper, news program, and morning radio show for the next few days. Speculation rose over if Michael had lost his mind or if it was all carefully orchestrated. The controversy certainly didn't seem to hurt promotion of the album. People who otherwise wouldn't have known that Michael Jackson had a new album and video, couldn't take their eyes off of it. There wasn't anybody who didn't know a new Michael Jackson album was due to hit stores soon. Michael Jackson or Sony couldn't have bought better, or more widespread, advertising. This coverage topped the thirty second commercials for the album directed by David Lynch that began airing in November. None of this hurt sales of the single either. It entered *Billboard's* Top Singles chart at number thirty five and in its second week on the chart, moved up to number three. This was also due to the publications new, more accurate, computerized method of tallying sales and airplay to rank singles that went into effect the single's second week on the chart. The single debuted at number ten on the Top 40 Radio Monitor chart, the highest debut ever for this chart compiled by monitoring a national sample of 125 top forty radio stations twenty four hours a day. The video received the heaviest airplay of any other video to date on MTV.

Along with the usual cassette and CD single, a special selection of mixes of "Black or White" was released with five versions of the song re-mixed by Robert Clivilles and David Cole, better known as the C&C of C&C Music Factory.

Just following the release of "Black or White" Genesis released a video for their single, "I Can't Dance" with Phil Collins doing a short spoof of Michael Jackson from "Black or White". Earlier in the summer, Rod Stewart released "The Motown Song". The song's video has animated images of himself, his pal Elton John, Madonna, and Michael Jackson, who moon-walks into an open manhole.

CHAPTER SIXTEEN

BRACE YOURSELF

Michael Jackson's long anticpated album was finally released in the United States on November 26, 1991. *Dangerous* was released on November 21 in Europe and on November 25 in Japan and Canada. Sales, to say the least, were staggering.

Record store owners and record industry executives hoped Michael Jackson's new release would revitalize the slumping record sales of the music industry. While this is a lot to place on one pair of shoulders, Michael had done it before in 1983 and 1984 with *Thriller*.

Dangerous was heavily promoted throughout the world. Billboards were displayed in France, made up of thin strips that continuously turned around, changing the picture. One side was solid black with only Michael's eyes. When the strips slowly turned around, the billboard now read, "Dangerous". In Holland, *Dangerous,* was advertised on milk cartons.

Jermaine also had high hopes for *Dangerous*. He hoped Michael's new release would boost sales of his own new album, *You Said*, anticipating fans of Michael's would pick up his album as well. This was not very likely for two reasons. The economy was in a recession, leaving little extra money for most people to impulsively buy a cassette or CD. Jermaine's new single wasn't going to help convince hard core Michael fans to buy his new album either. Jermaine's single, "Word to the Badd" , was a put down of Michael, criticizing him for losing touch with reality because of his superstar status:

> *Once you were made*
> *You changed your shade*
> *Was your color wrong?*
> *Could not turn back*
> *It's a known fact*
> *You were too far gone*

> *Reconstructed*
> *Been abducted*
> *Don't know who you are*
> *Think they love you*

They don't know you
Lonely superstar

While this version was released as a single, a cleaned up version appears on the album:

Once you were made
You changed your ways ...

Jermaine's hopes that his album sales would be helped by the release of *Dangerous* were soon dashed. *You Said* quickly peaked at number sixty on the R&B album chart, and it never made it to the pop chart. He would have done better to look to Michael as an example of professionalism and dedication, rather than trying to degrade his brother in public. Throughout his entire career, Michael has defended himself when he deemed it justified or necessary, but has never lashed out in anger against those who criticize or publically attack him, consistently choosing instead to stick to his own convictions. It has always paid off. Michael's unwavering status as an example for others, a role model for children, who he adores, makes those who attack him look foolish.

Beyond the feud between Michael and Jermaine, Randy was also in the news at this time. Randy was sentenced in November to a thirty day hospital stay for rehabilitation for domestic violence, to be followed by a one year program. He had been charged with abusing his wife, Eliza, and endangering their baby daughter, Steveanna. Randy was also accused of trying to steal some of Michael's thunder, turning himself into police one day after the release of *Dangerous*. The story received only minor news coverage.

Reviews of *Dangerous* were generally favorable. *Us* and *People* each gave the album a favorable review, and surprisingly, *Rolling Stone*, generally big MJ bashers, gave the album four and one half stars, a rating between excellent and a classic. *Billboard* also gave *Dangerous* a glowing review, "...artistically, it's one of Jackson's finest efforts."

A few reviewers slammed *Dangerous* for being too commercial, containing material that was in their opinion shallow and bland but what would probably be successful commercially. Michael was blamed repeatedly for catering to mass appeal, putting his true artistic feelings on the back burner to insure a commercially successful album. Others claimed if it didn't sell like *Thriller*, Michael's career would be considered in the music industry as being in decline. This absurd piece of logic means that *Dangerous* could sell 25 million copies worldwide and Michael would be considered as having lost "it", while having the top three best selling albums in music history. What a poor excuse for a music career! So, as far as a few critics were concerned, Michael was doomed in their eyes regardless of how well the album sold, if *Dangerous* sold like *Thriller* and *Bad,* he was purposely being too commercial, if *Dangerous* sold "only" a few million, his career would be in trouble.

Actually the tracks on *Dangerous* cover a variety of different styles, all of which Michael has no problem mastering. Catchy tunes like "Black or White", "Remember the Time", "In the Closet", "She Drives Me Wild" and "Who Is It" show he is indeed the King of Pop. "Jam" and "Give In To Me" have a more hard rock sound with "Jam" featuring a rap segment. Rap is also incorporated into "Black or White", "She Drives Me Wild" and "Dangerous". A "Man in the Mirror", gospel influenced sound delivers "Will You Be There" and the even better "Keep the Faith". The lyrics of "Gone Too Soon", dedicated to Ryan White, are a bit sappy but it is a perfect showcase for Michael's smooth, beautiful voice, reminiscent of "Ben". "Why You Wanna Trip On Me" is a sequel to "Leave Me Alone", sharing the same sentiment, why are people so concerned with his face, skin color, or supposed eccentricities? Interestingly, "Trip" was not written by Michael, but was penned by Teddy Riley and Bernard Bell.

One tradition Michael did keep was in featuring a well known rock and roll guitarist on the album. Eddie Van Halen was featured on "Beat It" from the *Thriller* album and Steve Stevens played on "Dirty Diana" from the *Bad* album. Playing on "Black or White" and "Give In To Me" on *Dangerous* is Guns and Roses guitarist, Slash.

Teddy Riley, who was suggested by Eddie Murphy, co-wrote and co-produced seven of the fourteen tracks on *Dangerous* with Michael. Bill Boutrell who wrote and performed the rap lyrics to "Black or White", co-wrote and co-produced three songs. Glen Ballard and Siedah Garrett, writers of "Man in the Mirror" wrote "Keep the Faith" with Michael. Michael's own compositions include "Will You Be There" and "Heal the World", a continuation of the "We Are The World" theme.

Dangerous was released on November 26, but a some may have gotten it a few days earlier when gunmen stole 30,000 copies of the album from a Los Angeles warehouse. The CD's and cassettes were worth $400,000.

Some radio stations were giving away copies of the album prior to its official release date. Record stores gave fans the opportunity to reserve their copy and gave away a package of three picture postcards. The album was released on the usual formats, cassette, compact disc, vinyl, and a special collectors CD which folds open with 3-D cutouts of figures from the album cover.

The cover art for *Dangerous* was done by Mark Ryden with some obvious input from Michael. It features only Michael's eyes with the rest of the cover containing many images of animals, skeletons, and statues. There are many references to Michael; a hand with the image of the world on the palm has white tape around three fingertips; one passenger in a tiny boat looks like Michael when he was about twelve years old; in another boat the passenger is a young blond boy with an "M" on his shirt, this is supposedly Macaulay Culkin. A figure at the bottom of the cover, who for some reason looks very much like actor Ed Asner, is wearing a lapel pin reading, "1998" with an arrow.

Sony restricted airplay of *Dangerous* on London stations to fifteen minutes in any one hour to prevent massive home tapings of the album. This was in response to one station's announcement that it would air the entire album the day before it hit record stores.

A few record stores in the states opened at midnight to begin selling the album as soon as possible. Tower Records in West Hollywood had a 20 foot by 150 foot replica of the album cover on the roof along with other oversized displays from the album cover. Tower Records had an impromptu midnight opening and sold over three hundred copies in two hours.

CBS Records initially shipped out four million copies of *Dangerous,* a new record. *Dangerous* is the first album to achieve advance orders of 50,000 units in the former Communist part of Germany. A spokesman for France's Virgin megastore said *Dangerous* was the quickest selling album the store has ever handled.

The cost to produce *Dangerous* probably also set new records, with an estimated cost of over $10 million. Seven recording studios were used to record the tracks. Michael had twenty four hour a day access for two years to Record One in Sherman Oaks, California at a cost of $4,000 per day. Three rooms at Larrabee Sound Studios in Los Angeles were reserved at three to four thousand dollars per day.

The "Black or White" video wasn't cheap to produce either. Estimates put the total cost of the video between 4 and $7 million. It certainly didn't help when Michael and director John Landis had a disagreement on the set. Michael stormed off to his trailer, holding up the crew for three and one half hours.

The expense seemed to all pay off when *Dangerous* debuted on *Billboard's* top album chart at number one. *Dangerous* also debuted at number one on the British album charts, the first album to do so on the strength of just three days of sales; it surpassed U2's new release, *Achtung Baby* which had a full week of sales. Michael's new album didn't do too shaby throughout the rest of the world either, debuting at number one in Australia, Spain, Switzerland, and Finland. The album entered the charts at number two in Sweden and Germany, and at number three in Italy. In Japan and the Netherlands, *Dangerous* debuted at number five on the album charts, and at number fourteen on the European chart.

The day following the release of *Dangerous*, Michael performed his new single on a TV special celebrating the tenth anniversary of MTV. The hour long special aired on ABC and featured some of the biggest names in pop and rock music. There were performances by Aerosmith, George Michael, REM, and a spoken tribute, of sorts, by Madonna. Each artist performed one song, except one.

The special concluded with Michael performing two songs from his brand new album. Guns and Roses guitarist Slash, who plays on two tracks on *Dangerous*, "Black or White" and "Give In To Me", joined Michael for "Black or White". Michael was dressed just as in the video, in black pants and white t-shirt underneath a opened white shirt. Michael's performance was energetic and fun, and he noticeably keep his hands off his crotch in the wake of the turmoil over the original video.

A gospel choir of various ages joined Michael for "Will You Be There", with an angel, performed by Angela Ice, flying down to Michael and putting her arms, or wings, around him symbolizing hope. Vincent Patterson choreographed the performance which was filmed in an airplane hanger in Los Angeles, with Michael Jackson fan club members being invited to attend the filming and make up the audience. The performance of "Black and White" was completed in six takes.

At the end of the song Slash tossed his guitar through the front windshield of a car that was parked on stage which then exploded. When the pyrotechnics used in "Black or White" were being tested Michael was careful to stand back saying, "I'm gonna get back, I was burned before by this kind of stuff."

During rehearsals, two of Michael's chimps visited the set, and MTV CEO Tom Freston presented Michael with a six foot version of the astronaut statue used as the network's music video award. While Freston spoke, the huge statue was lowered to the floor on cables. "We've made you this statue to show our appreciation for all you have done for music and MTV, and here it is. And it's rather large." Michael quietly said, "Thank you" and shook Freston's hand.

Soon there were stories of another romance for Michael. For the 1991 holidays, Michael spent a couple of days in Las Vegas where he reportedly met Las Vegas showgirl Shoshana Hawley. They spent a lot of time together in Michael's suite and took in the Excalibur Hotel's King Arthur's Tournament Pageant four times.

There were also stories that Michael had accepted an invitation from Sheikh Rashid Ahmed, the minister of culture and sports in Pakistan, to perform in the country's city of Lahore. A tentative date of April 14 had been set. It was hoped Michael's appearance would help portray the country in a more modern light. This report was immediately denied by Michael's publicist, saying he never accepted the invitation.

When "Black or White" finally gave up the top spot on the singles chart, the second single from *Dangerous*, "Remember the Time", was released, dedicated to an important lady in his life, Diana Ross. Its performance on the pop singles chart was unusual. After peaking at number three, for two weeks, it fell to number four only to bounce back to number three for two more weeks. "Remember the Time" spent two weeks at number one on the R&B singles chart. The short film for the second single debuted, just as "Black or White" had, simultaneously on Fox, BET, and MTV on February 2.

The video had an Egyptian theme with Eddie Murphy as Pharaoh Ramses and model Iman as Queen Nefertiti. When the queen becomes bored and wants to be entertained, a string of performers, announced by Magic Johnson, are led in front of the queen. With each being found unsatisfactory, she orders them to be thrown to the lions, or to be decapitated. A robed figure is next to be led out in front of the queen. Through some tricky special effects, the figure vanishes and reappears in a clear liquid and finally transforms into Michael in Egyptian garb. The queen becomes enchanted with him which angers Ramses, who immediately sends his guards after him. After eluding the guards and engaging in a Egyptian flavored dance routine, Michael meets up with Nefertiti. They embrace and kiss, Michael's first on screen kiss. Michael finally eludes Ramses by vanishing once again into a golden powder.

The "Remember the Time" video was directed by John Singleton, director of *Boyz N the Hood*. The choreographers of the short film, Fatima Robinson and Stretch, were also members of the video dance troupe. Singleton's next project was another movie, *Poetic Justice*, starring Janet Jackson. It was reported that Michael visited Janet on the set of the movie in disguise.

To return the favor of appearing in his video, Michael sang on Eddie Murphy's then upcoming album, *Love's Alright*. He contributed background vocals on two tracks, "Yeah" and "Whatzupwitu". Michael was one of many that contributed backing vocals on "Yeah". Also appearing on the record are Paul McCartney, Jon Bon Jovi, Elton John, Janet Jackson, and many others.

In less than two months sales of *Dangerous* exceed ten million copies worldwide. It was reported to be selling faster than *Thriller* and *Bad* did when they were first released. It had taken both albums over four months to achieve sales of ten million. *Billboard* carried an ad congratulating Michael on the success of the album and the first single:

*#1 around the world Dangerous. The global no. 1 smash album with sales over 10 million. Featuring the worldwide no. 1 single and short film, 'Black or White', and the new hit 'Remember the Time' on Epic. '**** 1/2 ' (Excellent/A Classic) Rolling Stone. Michael Jackson. Making the world a very Dangerous*

place. Don't miss the prime time national television debut of Michael's new short film, 'Remember the Time' February 2.

The ad featured a black and white photo of Michael with quite a different look. He was in black pants and a white under-shirt with his hair pulled tightly back in a ponytail. Sony Music Entertainment president Tommy Matolla presented Michael with an award marking sales of ten million copies for *Dangerous*.

It was probably this announcement that *Dangerous* was outselling *Bad* and *Thriller* that prompted the Cleveland Orchestra to demand a portion of the royalties from the sales of the album. In April, 1992, the Cleveland Orchestra filed a $7 million copyright infringement suit against Michael Jackson, MJJ Productions, Epic Records, and Sony Music Entertainment. The suit claimed Michael Jackson included a sixty seven second sample of a performance by the orchestra of Beethoven's Ninth Symphony at the beginning of "Will You Be There". The suit stated further that Michael Jackson claimed credit for writing the entire song, even the Beethoven portion. The orchestra and Michael both record for Sony who was negotiating with the orchestra for licensing fees.

Although Beethoven's work is now in the public domain, individual recordings of the material can be copyrighted. The piece in question was interpreted and conducted by George Szell. The lawsuit was settled in December. As part of the settlement, it was agreed that all future copies of *Dangerous* will carry a credit for Ludwig Van Beethoven.

A second lawsuit was filed in June by a songwriter from Denver, Colorado. Crystal Cartier sued Michael Jackson for $40 million claiming she first wrote and recorded the song "Dangerous" before Michael Jackson released his album. She wrote the song in 1985 and recorded it in 1990.

Confirming rumors that had been circulating since before the release of *Dangerous*, Michael held a press conference on February 3 in New York's Radio City Music Hall to announce his plans for a new world tour. Michael Jackson and Pepsi would be teaming up for the third time with sponsorship of the tour and a new set of Jackson Pepsi ads. The tour, to start in June, was announced to cover four continents, with no U.S. dates scheduled.

Michael, dressed in black, surprisingly did his own talking at the press conference. He announced he was touring to raise money for his "Heal the World" foundation, a charity he created for children:

The only reason I am going on tour is to raise funds for the newly formed Heal the World, an international children's charity that I am spearheading to assist children and the ecology. My goal is to gross $100 million by Christmas, 1993.

Heal the World will contribute to Pediatric AIDS, "in honor of my friend Ryan White", Camp Ronald McDonald, the Make A Wish Foundation, Juvenile Diabetes and the Minority AIDS Foundation.

The St. Thomas Boys Choir sang Michael's song, "Heal the World" and it touched Michael much the same way as the children's version of "We Are The World": "When I composed the song, it was my dream to hear it performed the way they just performed it, with such innocence and beauty. It took everything to keep me from crying".

No figures were released, but Pepsi said the new deal with Michael was the largest sponsorship deal ever between a corporation and a music entertainer. The first of the new ads, titled *Dreams,* is one of the most elaborate commercials in advertising history. It debuted in over 150 countries throughout the world, excluding the United States, in late July coinciding with the opening of the summer Olympic games in Barcelona, Spain.

Just two days after the press conference, Michael headed to Washington D.C. where he was honored with a lifetime achievement award by the National Association of Black Owned Broadcasters. He received the honor at their Eighth Annual Communications Awards Dinner held at the Sheraton Washington

Hotel which was attended by Jessie Jackson, Stevie Wonder, Muhammad Ali, and Spike Lee. Before accepting the award, video clips of Michael Jackson were shown as well as his entire performance from the 1988 Grammys. The trade organization represents 182 black owned radio stations and eighteen television stations.

"Black and White" and *Dangerous* were released late in 1991, so Michael was ineligible for American Music Award and Grammy consideration. However, eight hours before the Grammy telecast on February 25, 1992, Michael tried to get a performance spot on the show. Producer Pierre Cossette undoubtedly cost the show a few precious ratings points when he turned Michael down, saying it couldn't be arranged.

Michael had two nominations for the 1992 Soul Train Awards. "Black or White" was nominated for Best R&B Soul Single and Michael was nominated for Best R&B Soul Male Vocalist. He lost in both categories. The Sammy Davis Jr. Award, which Michael had taken home three years earlier, was presented this year by John Singleton to Janet Jackson.

On February 10, 1992, Michael left for a two week visit to Africa. The trip had been postponed from a year earlier due to the start of Operation Desert Storm. Each day he phoned the ranch to make sure the ranch and all his animals were safe from harm from the storms and floods that had been pounding California.

He was in Africa to visit Gabon, the Ivory Coast, Tanzania, Kenya, and Libreville and was reportedly interested in making a film, "Return to Africa" for his own video library. The Ivory Coast crowned Michael King of the Sanwis in an elaborate ceremony and in Gabon, he received the Medal of Honor from Gabon's President Omar Bongo. Michael Jackson is the first entertainer to receive this honor, it is usually reserved for heads of state and dignitaries.

When he was seen in public touching his nose people were offended, taking it as a sign he couldn't stand the smell. Michael's publicist explained the nose touching as nothing but a nervous habit. The nose touching incident gained enormous attention from the press who began labeling the trip as a pubic relations disaster. Michael then cut his trip short, missing a safari and a trip to Kenya, and flew to London. There he was mobbed, having a sweater ripped away from him that he was holding in front of him to protect his face.

While some said Michael left Africa to avoid the public nightmare over the offensive nose touching, others said he had to attend to urgent business related to his tour plans. He was also said to be castle shopping in Scotland and had become interested in two. Clish Castle in Perthshire has 80 rooms and was built in the 1400's. An Edwardian mansion near Dumfries is on 68 acres.

During his stay in London Michael visited with comic Benny Hill. Hill died a few months later. From the set of the video for "Jam", Michael released a statement to the press, "The world is suffering the great loss of a great talent."

One of the members of Michael's twenty six person entourage that travelled with him was *Ebony* and *Jet* magazine publisher Robert E. Johnson. Michael gave *Ebony* an interview, his first since September, 1987 when he appeared on the *Ebony/Jet Showcase* program just after the release of *Bad*. The interview, which appeared in *Ebony's* May, 1992 issue, focused on his trip to Africa and the *Dangerous* album. The issue's cover photo was of Michael wearing his crown he received when he was crowned king of the Sanwis. At the conclusion of the interview, which took only one page to print, Michael said, "You know, that's the most I've said in eight years...You know I don't give interviews. That's because I know you, and I trust you. You're the only one I trust to give interviews to."

Just before leaving for Africa Michael paid a visit to a storage facility in Oxnard, California. There items from a storage locker, belonging to the Jacksons were being auctioned off to cover unpaid storage costs. A sequined glove sold for $1,000. During his visit, before the auction, he visited with four children, singing "Man in the Mirror" for them when one child didn't believe it was really him.

Michael received two honors in February from the Pro-Set LA Music Awards. Michael was named Best Male Pop Vocalist and "Black or White" was named Video of the Year.

Premiering once again simultaneously on Fox, BET, and MTV, was the third video from *Dangerous* on April 23. Michael co-directed "In the Closet" with Herb Ritts, who had directed Madonna's "Cherish" video and Janet Jackson's "Love Will Never Do Without You." Rumors spread that the video was to include Madonna, but they were soon proven false as model Naomi Campbell was announced at Michael's co-star. The song and short film concerns a relationship in which the woman wants to stop hiding their love while the man wants to keep the relationship a secret, keeping it "in the closet". The gold band Michael sports on his finger seems to explain why he wishes to keep his new love "in the closet". What isn't clear is why he has the wedding band is on the wrong hand.

Naomi Campbell admitted to being a little nervous when she first met Michael. Things obviously became much more comfortable on the set for her quickly. Knowing Michael is a prankster, she hid a squirt gun under her very short skirt and planned a surprise attack on Michael. On the last day of shooting on the video, it was reported a whipped cream fight broke out.

Michael sports his new, healthier, physique in the video, dressed in black pants and a white t-shirt with the sleeves torn out. His arms, shoulders and chest are much more muscular than a couple of years earlier. During the Bad tour he became very thin; his ribs were noticeable beneath two layers of clothing.

"In the Closet" is certainly Michael's most sensuous video to date, with a courtship dance that has Naomi and Michael caressing themselves and each other while Michael sings, "There's something about you baby that makes me want to give it to you." It proved to be too sexy for some. A Fox affiliated television station in Syracuse, New York refused to air the film feeling it did not fit in with the family viewing time. The video was later banned by the government in South Africa because it was "of a very sensual nature which could offend viewers."

"In the Closet" premiered the next day on *Friday Night Videos* during yet another show devoted entirely to Michael Jackson. *Live and Dangerous* featured several songs performed live from the Bad tour along with footage of his trip to Africa and a look behind the scenes of "In the Closet".

"In the Closet" peaked at number six on *Billboard's* top singles chart and at number one on the black singles chart. The sexy single was the third consecutive number one hit from *Dangerous* on the black chart. Hot on its tail to the top ten on the pop singles chart was a single by Luther Vandross with Janet Jackson. "The Best Things in Life Are Free" is taken from the soundtrack of the movie, *Mo' Money*.

Coinciding with the filming of the "In the Closet" video was the culmination of a MTV contest. On Sunday, March 29, 1992, thirty five winners of a "Dinner With Michael" contest got to bring a guest to a dinner party with Michael Jackson on the set of his latest video.

Contest winners were treated to a reception at a hotel in West Hollywood before being taken by bus to the site of the party. A tent was pitched in the desert near Palm Springs, California and dinner was prepared by Michael's chef. A man on stilts and animals greeted the guests. For entertainment before the guest of honor arrived, there were games, a magician, a palm reader, and a caricature artist.

When Michael arrived, at 7:00 pm, the guests were told to put their cameras away. Michael spoke very little and ate dinner surrounded by bodyguards, but did briefly join his guests in a conga line. He was presented with a miniature model of the Eiffel Tower from a winner from France and was asked to verify his autograph on a fedora another winner had purchased at an auction. Michael was escorted away from the party in a van at 9:00 pm.

The winners of the contest were chosen over several weeks from 4.1 million callers to MTV during the network's *Most Wanted* program. "Dinner with Michael" had the largest response ever of any MTV contest.

On May 1, 1992, President Bush presented Michael Jackson with an award acknowledging him as "a point of light ambassador". The award was in recognition of Michael's efforts in inviting disadvantaged children to his ranch. Michael Jackson was the only entertainer of the twenty one recipients. Michael, dressed in black of course, wore sunglasses, but with light colored lenses that you could see his eyes through. "I wanted to come to lunch because I believe each person can make a difference in the life of someone in need. That is what a point of light is. I'm very, very happy to be here. I love you all. Thank you very much."

Before leaving Washington, Michael visited with Raynal Pope, a young girl who had been mauled by four dogs. He spent forty five minutes with the seven year old girl, her younger sister, Myja, and two of their cousins. They played hide and seek, wrestled, and danced. Michael posed for pictures and autographed a "Beat It" style jacket.

Almost immediately following the presentation of the Points of Light Awards, President Bush headed to Los Angeles to survey first hand the damage caused by several days of rioting in the city. The city had been under riot conditions as the result of racial tensions stemming from, among other things, the verdict in the carefully watched Rodney King police brutality trial. During the course of the next few days, several innocent people were killed including a nine year old boy from Watts. Ramon Sanchez Jr. was killed by a stray bullet in his home, he was in his kitchen drinking a glass of milk. After reading his parents couldn't afford to bury him, Michael Jackson offered to pay the funeral expenses. He paid for the funeral, mortuary and cemetery costs as well as a headstone, illustrating he genuinely is "a point of light" and that each person can make a difference in the life of someone in need.

The Sanchez family got the opportunity to thank Michael in person when it was arranged for them to visit the studio in Culver City where he was filming a Pepsi commercial. Mrs. Sanchez told Michael through an interpreter, "Ramon was one of your biggest fans. You have helped make a very tragic time for us more bearable. Your involvement was a pleasant surprise, and we are eternally grateful."

The fourth single from *Dangerous* was released in June with a remix of "Rock With You" as the B-side. The video debuted on Fox, BET, and MTV on June 19, and like all the videos before it, featured special appearances by some famous faces. For "Jam" Michael Jackson squares off against Chicago Bull champion Michael Jordan on the basketball court, and then on the dance floor. The King of the Court, Jordan, shows Jackson a few of his moves on the basketball court with Jackson going between Jordan's legs to get control of the ball, and failing that, jumping on his back to keep him from shooting. Jordan brings Jackson a step ladder so he too can stuff the ball into the net. Jackson, however, does get a couple of good shots in, throwing the ball through a window from next door right into the hoop. He also kicks the ball behind him with his heel with it going effortlessly into the basket.

Next it is Jordan's turn to be humiliated as Jackson shows him a few of his own tricky moves, including how to moonwalk. Michael ends up holding onto Jordan's ankles, pulling his feet backwards.

The video also has cameo appearances by rap duo Kris Kross and Heavy D, who performs the rap portion of the song as he does on the album. "Jam" is Heavy D's second appearance in a Jackson video, he was in Janet's video for "Alright" from her *Rhythm Nation* album. The video was filmed in Chicago and once again Michael worked with choreographer Vincent Patterson.

"Jam" is very entertaining and is another illustration of Michael Jackson's terrific sense of humor. It also delivers a serious message, that if you set your mind on doing something, you can do it whether it is basketball, dancing, singing, playing trumpet, or whatever, "It ain't too much for me to jam." A different version of "Jam" featuring footage of the Chicago Bulls was featured on a video cassette, *UntouchaBulls*, showcasing the world champion basketball team's drive to be the champions.

"Jam" was released on cassette single immediately but its release on the CD format was delayed for several weeks. This seemed to have a drastic effect on sales. Diehard fans will often collect albums and singles on all formats available and not having the CD readily available hurt the single's potential sales. This was evident in the single's performance on the pop singles chart, which is a composite of both airplay and sales. "Jam" stalled at number twenty six, giving Michael his lowest charting single since "Walk Right Now" from the Jackson's *Triumph* album more than ten years earlier. "Jam" did seem to find a bigger audience on the R&B charts, becoming his fourth consecutive top ten hit from the *Dangerous* album, peaking at number three.

At the time "Jam" was released in the United States, "Who Is It" was released in Europe. "Who Is It" was featured in his Pepsi commercials that were shown only in Europe.

Operation One to One honored Michael Jackson on June 3, 1992, with an award in recognition of his efforts in support of economically disadvantaged youth. The award was presented to Michael by the *Cosby Show's* Raven Symone in New York. After accepting the award, Michael toured Manhattan with friend Donald Trump and Marla Maples. They picked up Clint Eastwood along the way and headed to The Tavern on the Green where they met up with Elizabeth Taylor. Then Donald, Marla, and Michael visited the Plaza's Oak Bar for a nightcap. Michael had Evian water with lime, surrounded by bodyguards.

Just a couple days later it was announced that the National Football League was negotiating with Michael Jackson and Elton John to perform at halftime of the Super Bowl in January. Later it was announced Michael Jackson would be the only performer. The show's producer and directer, Don Mischer, must have known to expect something spectacular. He had worked with Michael before on *Motown 25.*

The next project due for Michael was a new book, *Dancing the Dream,* which hit book stores in June, 1992. It was published by Doubleday, who also published *Moonwalk.* The introduction was written by Elizabeth Taylor. It is dedicated to Katherine Jackson, "Dedicated to Mother with love." Again, there is no mention of his father.

Dancing the Dream was said to be filled with one hundred previously unpublished photographs with twenty poems and essays penned by Michael. Actually some of the photographs had been published before. Some were taken from the 1985 Michael Jackson calendar, and *Ebony* and *People* magazines. Others were still photographs from the videos for "Black or White" and "Remember the Time" or his performance from *MTV 10,* their anniversary special. As Michael releases so few pictures to the public, any new photos of him are always a treat. The photos included in *Dancing the Dream* are no exception.

The poems and reflections included in the volume concentrate mostly on, not surprisingly, children, and animals and the environment. Poems dealing with finding a sea gull feather coated with oil; seals wondering if they will be clubbed by hunters; and elephants refusing to lie down and die giving up their tusks for man's trinkets; illustrate the extent to which Michael is concerned with how man has treated animals. In "Mother Earth" he reflects on how man has mistreated the earth, "We've been treating Mother Earth the way some people treat a rental apartment. Just trash it and move on."

In "Ryan White" Michael writes of missing his friend and of how he suffered because of people's ignorance about his disease:

> *Ryan White, symbol of agony and pain*
> *Of ignorant fear gone insane...*

When Jeanne White, Ryan's mother, was a guest on the Maury Povich Show, Michael called the studio and recited his poem about Ryan on the air.

"Mother" is written for his own mother, to whom he has always been deeply devoted:

> *No matter where I go from here*
> *You're in my heart, my mother dear.*

Some of the poems have also been published before. "Mother" was included in Katherine Jackson's book, *My Family The Jacksons*. "Dancing the Dream", titled "The Dance", and "Planet Earth" are included in the liner notes of the *Dangerous* album. The lyrics to "Heal The World" and "Will You Be There" from the *Dangerous* album are also included in *Dancing the Dream*.

Children and the ecology are also the main concerns of Michael's new Heal the World Foundation which will receive proceeds from the Dangerous tour. Michael's goal is to raise $100 million from the tour for the foundation.

A peek at Michael's latest tour was given in a thirty minute special, *Michael Jackson: The Dangerous Tour,* which aired on Fox on July 2. It featured his entire live performance of "Billie Jean" and "Black or White" from the first stop on the tour on June 27, in Munich, Germany. Also shown in the special was the new video for "Jam" and a sneak preview of a video in the works for "Give In To Me" with a guest appearance by Slash. A similar, hour long, special aired the same night on MTV. *Live and Dangerous* included behind the scenes footage of "Jam" and footage of Michael arriving in Germany as well as the special live performances from the concert.

Just a few days before the kickoff of the tour, Slash joined Michael Jackson in Germany to film a new video for an upcoming single, "Give In To Me". It looks to be a performance video perhaps similar to "Dirty Diana". The songs share an aggressive sexual flavor except Diana is the aggressor in "Dirty Diana", and Michael is the aggressor in "Give In To Me":

> *Don't try to understand me*
> *Just simply do the things I say*
>
> *Love is a feeling*
> *Give it when I want it*
> *'Cause I'm on fire*
> *Quench my desire*

While Michael was in Europe with the Dangerous tour, London's tabloid, the *Daily Mirror*, following a popular trend of spreading rumors that Michael's face is a mess from the supposedly countless surgeries, printed a story on Michael referring to him as "Scarface". The tabloid claimed he is "a scarred phantom whose face is covered with scar tissues, with a hole in his nose, one cheek higher than the other and an oddly sagging chin." In response to the story, Michael immediately filed a libel suit against the publication, asking for a full apology and substantial damages. A few days later he won an injunction against the *Mirror* barring them from re-publishing a photograph, that they purported to prove his face is disfigured, until the case was heard. The tabloid then filed a countersuit against Michael Jackson claiming he defamed the publication in his remarks accusing them of publishing untruths about him and touching up photographs.

Still celebrating its tenth anniversary, MTV counted down the top ten biggest stars of their first ten years in July. Featured were videos, concert footage and interviews with the ten biggest acts of MTV's first ten years on the air, including Madonna, Def Leppard, George Michael, Aerosmith, Janet Jackson, U2, Guns and Roses, Prince, and REM. Capping off the countdown was tour footage, fan-mania, and the "Jam" video from Michael Jackson.

In July, it was announced in *Billboard* that the Second Annual Music Video Producers Association added "Beat It" and "Billie Jean" to their Hall of Fame. Sony presented Michael with yet another special award in September, this one commemorating his four albums with sales of over ten million copies each.

Michael received an honor of a different nature from psychologist Dr. Wayne Dyer. Dr. Dyer dedicated his book, *Real Magic* to Michael Jackson. Dr. Dyer, who had spent several days at Michael's ranch, felt Michael deserved the honor because of his commitment to world peace and helping children. He said further that he admired Michael Jackson for standing up to a lifetime of pressure from the tabloid press.

In September, MTV handed out its music video awards for the year. Michael's videos had two nominations, "Black or White" was nominated for Best Special Effects and "In the Closet" was nominated for Best Cinematography. Neither won an award. Michael did contribute a performance to the show, however. A filmed performance of "Black or White" was shown, taken from a concert at London's Wembley Stadium.

Premiering during the award telecast was a public service announcement made by Michael Jackson as part of the network's Choose or Lose campaign designed to encourage young adults to register to vote. Dressed in his gold and black concert costume, with large mirrored sunglasses, he encouraged others to help make a difference. "We live in a country where we have a chance to make a difference. To create a better way of life for ourselves and for our children. The future is now. Let's come together and express our freedom of choice. Choose or lose."

Though Michael's performance of "Black or White" shown on the MTV Music Video Awards was a treat for fans to see a bit of his Dangerous concerts, the whole tamale was later broadcast on HBO on October 10, 1992. Hyped as the only chance for U.S. fans to see Michael in concert, (he was still sticking to his story that he would not tour the U.S.), the show was widely publicized. Michael was reportedly paid $20 million by HBO for the rights to telecast the concert, though this was never confirmed by Jackson and was denied by HBO.

Every detail of the show was, of course, nothing short of mesmerizing. His stage entrance was no exception. Smoke machines hid the stage behind a curtain of smoke and as fireworks suddenly exploded, Michael jumped from beneath the stage amid the sparks and smoke dressed in black, gold and silver. There he stood, absolutely motionless for almost two minutes, as the crowd went wild. He slowly removed his oversized mirrored sunglasses, tossed them aside and began to "Jam", and his didn't stop jamming until two hours later with "Man in the Mirror".

"The Jacksons: An American Dream" aired on ABC on November 15, and concluded on November 18. While it wasn't the total whitewash of the Jackson family story that one might have expected, it did gloss over some areas and completely ignored others. It did depict Joe's strictness with the children though statements made by certain family members indicate he was actually much more abusive. Very little mention was made of Joe's infidelity, showing Katherine discovering just one instance when actually there were several. The legal action that ensued after the Jacksons left Motown and signed with CBS Records was never mentioned. Also omited is all of the controversy caused by the Victory tour planning and how vehemently Michael did not want to be a part of it.

There were a number of errors also. A scene from 1959 showing Joseph Jackson working in the steel mills of Gary, Indiana are followed by Katherine in the hospital thinking of a name for her new baby boy, Michael. However, Michael was born a year earlier, in 1958. Later, Michael is shown working in the studio recording "Human Nature" in 1983. The *Thriller* album, with "Human Nature" on it, was released in 1982.

Despite the errors and conspicuous omissions, Michael's *Off The Wall* album is never mentioned, "The Jacksons: An American Dream" was a surprisingly frank re-telling of the Jackson family story. Jackson 5 talent shows and later TV appearances were nearly perfectly re-created, duplicating the costumes, and especially Michael's moves and gestures. Wylie Draper did an exceptional job in re-creating Michael's unforgetable moves from the *Motown 25* performance of "Billie Jean", though the lip syncing needed work.

"The Jacksons: An American Dream" was the top rated show of the week and helped ABC win the all important November sweeps rating period for the first time in eleven years. The miniseries was watched by one third of all TV viewers, approximatley 22 million households tuned in for the conclusion of the two part movie. The movie was scheduled to be released on video cassette in February, 1993.

A soundtrack album was released by Motown to coincide with the mini-series, *The Jacksons: An American Dream*. The soundtrack wasn't as successful as the movie, however, peaking at number 137 on the pop album chart and never showing up on the R&B album chart. A single from the album, a live version of "Who's Lovin' You" never debuted on the pop singles chart, and peaked at number forty eight on the R&B singles charts.

In promoting the Jackson mini-series, and other of its programs, ABC featured a line from "ABC", in its programming ads. Michael could be heard singing in the background, "C'mon, C'mon, let me tell you what's its all about." Later, the network featured "Jam" in its programming ads.

Michael's Heal the World Foundation and AmeriCares joined together to fund a project sending relief supplies to Sarajevo, the capital city of Bosnia in which used to be Yugoslavia, where millions of civilians were suffering from starvation. Michael attended a brief press conference held at John F. Kennedy International Airport on November 24, 1992:

The mission of Heal the World, my mission, is healing. Pure and simple. To heal the world we must start by healing our children. Today we have come bearing gifts for the children of war torn Sarajevo. In 1992, Sarajevo has become a symbol of so much that is tragic, but avoidable in our world: prejudice and ethnic hatred, the destruction of the environment, the shattering of family and future of the whole community...

An AmeriCares cargo jet was then loaded with 93,700 pounds of medical supplies, blankets, heavy clothing and shoes.

The fifth single from *Dangerous* was "Heal the World". Unlike the previous singles, there was no highly publicized Fox televised debut for the song's video, which delivers the song's message with a compilation of footage of sick and needy children, including those Michael has visited and helped.

Although Michael performed the single on several TV specials and in concert, it had disappointing performance on the pop and R&B charts, never making it to the top forty. "Heal the World" stalled at number fifty two on the pop chart and number sixty two on the R&B chart. The single did much better on the adult contemporary chart, where it went to number nine. The single had much greater success in Europe where it quickly became a top five hit, peaking at number two in most countries.

On December 9, Billboard handed out its music awards for 1992. The awards were based on sales and airplay, the same factors that are used to compile the publication's weekly charts, so the winners could be easily be predicted by anyone who reguarly checks out the weekly music charts. Michael Jackson was among the top artists nominated for Top Pop Singles Artist, which ended up going to Boyz II Men, and for the Number One R&B Artist, which Jodeci took home. Michael didn't go home empty handed however. In 1992 the Billboard World Artist Award for the Number One World Single and Album belonged to the same artist. The Number One World Single was "Black or White" and the Number One World Album was *Dangerous*.

Before handing over the award, there was a short video tribute to Michael Jackson recognizing the worldwide success of "Black or White" and *Dangerous* and also celebrating the tenth anniversary of the release of the largest selling album in history,

Thriller. The award was presented to Michael by Phil Collins in a taped presentation: "Michael, on behalf of your millions of fans around the world, I am here to present to you the Billboard Award for the Number One World Album, *Dangerous,* and the Number One World Single, "Black or White". Michael, dressed in a red shirt and a black fedora, accepted the award graciously as always:

*I am honored to be recognized by **Billboard** which is considered to be the bible of the industry. Nothing would have prevented me from sharing this special occasion other than Heal the World and my commitment to tour on its behalf. My heartfelt thanks to **Billboard**, to the children, and to my fans in general. Your support over the years has been an inspiration. Thank you so much.*

Phil Collins then presented Michael with a second award:

*To commorate the tenth anniversary of **Thriller** and to recognize that in the past ten years you have basically outsold us all as the number one best selling artist in the world, we're very happy to present to you this special Billboard Award.*

Michael, now with his arms full of awards, accepted the honor and introduced his own performance:

*I am very touched by you saluting my efforts and more importantly that **Thriller** is remembered after a decade. I love you all. And now in my absence, here is a special performance of 'Black or White'.*

A taped, and edited, performance of "Black or White" from London was broadcast, the same performance that was featured on the MTV Music Video Awards in September.

HBO celebrated its twentieth anniversary in December with a special showcasing many of the events that have been broadcast by the cable channel over the last twenty years. Included was Michael's performance of "Beat It" from his Dangerous tour concert in Bucharest, Romania that was broadcast by HBO just two months earlier. That Dangerous tour telecast has since been named by Americans as one of the events of 1992 they most wish they would have recorded (provided they could figure out how to set their VCR's!). The concert was named along with coverage of the Olympics, the Presidential campaign, the Los Angeles riots, Johnny Carson's last *Tonight Show* appearance, and the Dan Quayle episodes of *Murphy Brown*.

Michael contributed a taped performance of "Heal the World" to Lou Rawls' UNCF telethon on December 26, 1992. The performance was taken from a Dangerous tour concert and was combined with footage of Michael's visit to Africa.

Michael started 1993 off with an unprecedented number of televison appearances. On January 19, he was among the stars to perform for President elect Bill Clinton at *An American Reunion: The 52nd Presidential Inaugural Gala*. He walked through the crowd to the stage dressed in black pants and a red military style shirt, with his hair pulled back in a ponytail. He first addressed the very soon to be new President on the need for continued and increased funding for AIDS research:

Thank you Mr. President elect for inviting me to your Inaugural gala. I would like to take a moment from this very public ceremony to speak of something very personal. It concerns a dear friend of mine who is no longer with us. His name is Ryan White. He was a hemophiliac who was diagnosed with the AIDS virus when he was eleven. He died shortly after turning eighteen, the very time most young people are beginning to explore life's wonderful possibilities. My friend Ryan was a very bright, very brave, and very normal young man who never wanted to be a symbol or a spokesperson for a deadly disease. Over the years I've shared many silly, happy, and painful moments with Ryan and I was with him at the end of his brief but eventful journey.

Ryan is gone and just as anyone who has lost a loved one to AIDS, I miss him deeply and constantly. He is gone but I want his life to have meaning beyond his passing. It is my hope President elect Clinton that you and your administration will commit the resources needed to eliminate this awful disease that took my friend and ended so many promising lives before their time. This song's for you Ryan."

Michael then performed his anthem to his friend Ryan White, "Gone Too Soon", his voice cracking with emotion at the last lines. Several children joined Michael on stage next for "Heal the World", which he dedicated to "all the children of the world". Michael later joined a specially reunited Fleetwood Mac and several other celebrities to sing "Don't Stop (Thinking About Tomorrow)".

The day before this Inaugural Gala, Michael made an unscheduled appearance an another pre-Inaugural celebration. He joined Diana Ross and several other celebrities on the steps of the Lincoln Memorial in a performance of "We Are the World", standing, dressed in black and gold, next to President elect Clinton, the soon to be new First Lady, and their daughter Chelsea.

While in the Washington D.C. area to attend the Inauguration galas, and to pick up some more awards, Michael stayed at the Madison Hotel. His only requests of the hotel staff was for clothes pressing service, and strawberry ice cream.

The number of social appearances he was making was unusual for Michael as well as the political involvment. Besides his plea for AIDS funding and Inaugural performances, a new video for "Man in the Mirror" showed up on MTV featuring footage of the Presidential campaign and some of the areas that most need change, such as poverty and homelessness, and the environment. The new version of the video was subtitled, "Portrait of Change".

Just prior to the Inaugural festivities, it was announced that Michael Jackson offered to perform for the new President but requested that the other ten to twelve scheduled balls be cancelled and that he be the sole performer. Also being circulated was a story that Michael had chosen a white boy to portray him in a new Pepsi commercial, this being a new version of the story that Michael requested a white child to play him in the Jackson television mini-series. That story was also shown to be false. After both stories circulated for several days, Michael's lawyer, Bert Fields, held a press conference on Michael's behalf to announce that both rumors were totally false and that Michael had indeed agreed to be a part of the Presidential Inauguration.

The same day Michael showed up at the Lincoln Memorial to perform "We Are the World", he was honored at the NAACP Image Awards. Michael's video for "Black or White" was honored as the Best Music Video over "Jump" by Kris Kross, "Tennessee" by Arrested Development, "End of the Road" by Boyz II Men, and "My Lovin'" by Envogue. The announcement of his win and the following standing ovation was a surprise to Michael:

I really wasn't expecting to win this. I love you all very, very much. Thank you to the NAACP, and all of you, you're very dear, sweet, loving people. Thank you so much.

Later Wesley Snipes presented the NAACP Image Award for Entertainer of the Year to Michael Jackson. Snipes narrated a tribute to Michael showcasing many of his video and live performances. Then Patti Labelle, with the Voices of Faith Choir, sang Michael's "Will You Be There". Raymon Symone, from *The Cosby Show,* and Bryton McClure, from *Family Matters* and who is a huge Michael Jackson fan, lead Michael from his front row seat, between his mother and Bill Bray, to the stage. In accepting the honor, Michael seemed very touched and gave an usually long and thoughtful speech:

First I'd like to say thank you to my mother who is here tonight, she's the one in blue. Thank you for giving me life. I really mean that, I love you. There are two things the NAACP stands for which are the most important things in my life, freedom and equality. In every person there is a secret song in their heart. It says I am free, it sings I am one. This is the natural feeling of every child, to be free as the wind, to be one with every other child. All the troubles in the world are caused by forgetting this feeling and when I perform my connection is with people. It's just to remind me of that, to be free and to be one. In this spirit the NAACP has done its cherished work. Thank you for having the faith to see that I share your work, for I deeply feel I do. I accept this award on behalf of the world's healing when all our brothers and sisters will be as free and equal as we are today. I love you so much and I am very honored. Thank you for this award. Thank you so much.

Patti Labelle then coaxed Michael into singing a couple lines of "Will You Be There" before leaving the stage.

Michael didn't win anymore awards until six days later at the American Music Awards. For the twentieh annual American Music Awards, presented on January 25, 1993, Michael Jackson had five nominations. But the audience got to see him before any winners were announced as he opened the award presentation with yet another dazzling performance. A man dropped to the floor from machine gun fire, revealing Michael standing directly behind him. Dressed in a black suit with spats and a fedora, Michael joined several dancers in a "Smooth Criminal" flavored performance of "Dangerous" featuring his usual facsinating choreography with plenty of crotch grabbing and carefully timed sound effects.

Michael won Favorite Soul/R&B Single for "Remember the Time". He came from back stage to accept the award, having taken his hair down, and removing his tie. In accepting the award, he acknowledged the fans in the balcony:

Thank you very much. I love you up there. I'd like to thank everyone at Sony Music, especially Mr. Morita, Mickey Schulhof, Tommy Mattola, Dave Glew, Bruce Swedian, Quincy Jones, Sandy Gallin, Jim Morey, and of course, all my fans. I love you.

Amidst the performances and award presentations, Elizabeth Taylor took the stage to announce the recipient of the first ever International Artist Award. She narrated a video tribute to Michael Jackson featuring footage from his videos and live performances from both the Bad and Dangerous tours. She then introduced a taped message from another of Michael's friends and fans, Eddie Murphy:

Hi, Michael. Knowing how uncomfortable you feel when someone says something nice to you right up in your face, I went 3,000 miles away to do this. Now, the inscription on your award says, 'In recognition of his record-breaking international concert tours, and his album sales, and his heartfelt efforts to make this world a better place, the American Music Awards presents its first International Artist Award to Michael Jackson January 25, 1993.' In addition the American Music Awards are proud to announce that when the award is given in the future, it will be known as 'The Michael Jackson International Artist Award.' So, congratulations Michael, I know you better be smiling from ear to ear. I know you better smile bigger than that, I want to see gums! Congratulations.

Elizabeth Taylor then called Michael to the stage from his front row seat at the Shrine Auditorium. He had now changed into a black leather jacket and removed his sunglasses before going on stage. The crowd was on their feet and cheering as Michael began to speak:

I love you very much, Elizabeth Taylor. Teddy Riley, you are a genius. Thank you Eddie, thank you all my friends. Travelling the world has been a great education for me and if there is one insight I've had it is this, wherever you go, in every country, on every continent, people yearn and hunger for only one thing, to love and be loved. Love transends international boundaries and it heals the wounds of hatred, racial predjudice, bigotry, and ignorance. It is the ultimate truth at the heart of all creation. I would also like to thank God, and my mother and father, Katherine and Joseph Jackson. Thank you once again, I love you all.

Michael's second nomination was for Favorite Soul/R&B Album for *Dangerous*. The award went to Envogue's *Funky Divas*. *Dangerous* did win, however, for Favorite Pop/Rock Album over *Totally Krossed Out* by Kris Kross, and U2's *Achtung Baby*. Michael, who had now removed the black leather jacket came from the wings and was brief in his acceptance. "I really wasn't expecting to win. Thank you again Teddy Riley, the public, I love you very much. Thank you."

Michael lost in his nominations as Favorite Soul/R&B Male Artist and Favorite Pop/Rock Male Artist. Bobby Brown won in the R&B category, and the Pop/Rock award went to Michael Bolton. Having won in two of the five categories in which he was nominated and being named the International Artist of the Year, Michael Jackson was the night's big winner.

Michael's recent appearances at the Inaugural festivities, the NAACP Image Awards, and the American Music Awards made him a big winner on the music charts too. The week following these events, *Dangerous* rose eighteen places on the R&B album charts, from fifty seven to thirty nine. The effect on the pop album charts was even greater, with a move up of forty three places, from number 131 to eighty eight.

The day following the American Music Awards, Michael was in Los Angeles at a press conference to accept donations to his

Heal the World Foundation. The National Football League (NFL) and Super Bowl XXVII halftime sponsor Frito Lay each donated $100,000 to Michael's charity. Michael's agreement to perform at halftime was contingent on it being a benefit for his charity. Michael spoke briefly, "I can't think of a better way to spread the message of world peace than by working with Radio City and the NFL and by being a part of Super Bowl XXVII."

He also used the opportunity to announce Heal LA, a project he will co-chair with former President Jimmy Carter. Heal LA will help disadvantaged children focusing on drug education, immunization, and mentor programs. Neil Austrian, president of the NFL, presented Michael with a custom made Super Bowl jacket that read on the back, "Super Bowl XXVII Radio City Halftime Show Michael Jackson." Michael accepted the donations, the jacket and made this thank yous all in fifteen minutes.

The January 29, 1993, issue of *Entertainment Weekly* magazine speculated on the value of current contacts of various superstars and decided whether or not the celebrity in question was worth the hefty price tag. Michael Jackson was among those being considered. The magazine put the estimated value of his contract at $65 million and declared Michael, "one of the most important artists on the planet." They also declared his latest effort, *Dangerous*, a dud compared to his earlier albums, selling only four million copies. What they didn't say was that not only is four million copies nothing to sneeze at, but also that this is only the U.S. sales of the album. Worldwide, *Dangerous,* had sold in excess of 16 million copies and wasn't even close to being finished. However, they did decide Michael Jackson was worth the price tag they put on him.

January 31, 1993 was Super Bowl Sunday. The Dallas Cowboys faced the Buffalo Bills for Super Bowl XXVII, but more important was halftime. The press had been barred from rehearsals, so no preview of the specutacular was included in any of the pre-game coverage. Expectations were high, and in fact the other networks didn't counter with any real competition for the Super

Bowl audience. It had been reported that Fox had made an offer to Madonna for a show opposite the halftime performance, but she refused, she didn't want to compete with Jackson. Michael didn't disappoint.

When the time finally came, a giant video screen counted down the last ten seconds and it was announced, "Ladies and gentlemen, Radio City Music Hall Productions and the National Football League are proud to present an unprecedented Super Bowl spectacular starring Michael Jackson."

Crowds of people gathered around the stage now set up on the middle of the field at the Rose Bowl. A giant video screen in the corner shows Michael dancing. There's an explosion and smoke rises from the top of the screen as Michael appears, dancing now on top of the screen. Just a few seconds later the video screen at the opposite side of the field shows Michael again. And again he appears on top of the screen. Following this, fireworks go off at center stage and Michael jumps from beneath the stage and stands motionless amidst the fireworks, smoke, and cheers from the 102,000 fans packed into the stadium. Dressed in black with gold bands across his chest, his right arm in a brace, and wearing sunglasses, he stands virtually motionless for over one minute before turning his head and slowly removing the glasses. More fireworks go off and dancers join Michael on stage for a very short version of "Jam".

He removes his jacket, having a white shirt and t-shirt on underneath. He reaches down for a black fedora that has been sitting on the edge of the stage, places it on his head and begins pumping his hips to "Billie Jean". He does a short performance of "Billie Jean" adding a crotch grab or two to his choreography from *Motown 25,* complete with the requisite moonwalk.

During the crowd's wild response to "Billie Jean", Michael reaches behind his head and undoes his ponytail, letting his hair down for "Black or White". Smoke and wind machines add great effects to the performance. More fireworks are set off at the song's conclusion.

While it is announced that, "Ladies and gentlemen, the children of Los Angeles have created their own personal drawings as a gift to the children of the world," Michael puts his hair back into a ponytail and is handed a long black wand. As he points the wand at the crowd, all the people in the stadium, section by section, hold up cards which together with the cards of the rest of the people seated in that same section make up a youngster's drawing of a child. Then Michael addressed the crowd, his voice sounding unusually deep:

Today we stand together all around the world joined in a common purpose, to remake the planet into a planet of joy and understanding and goodness. No one should have to suffer, especially the children. This time we must succeed. This is for the children of the world."

Thousands of young people lined the stage as Michael sang "Heal the World" and a huge inflatable globe rose from the center of the stage:

Heal the world
Make it a better place
for you and for me
and the entire human race

More fireworks ended the truly spectacular, and certainly unforgetable, halftime extravaganza. An ad for Michael's Heal the World Foundation and the newly created Heal LA followed the performance, the airtime for which was also donated by the NFL.

Reviews of the game the next day regularly mentioned halftime as being the most exciting part of the Super Bowl where Dallas beat the Bulls 52 to 17. There were approximately 133 million viewers in the United States, the largest audience in TV history. NBC recognized that Jackson was pivotal in making the game the biggest TV attraction in Super Bowl history. Dick Ebersol, NBC Sports President, said of Michael's performance, "He was better than our wildest dreams... He's an enormous name with crossover appeal from kids to grandparents, an enormous curiosity even for those for whom he is not a star." Some speculated that to top this halftime performance NBC would need to have Elvis Presley perform the next year!

Continuing momentum from the recent awards he had won, and his performance at the Super Bowl gave *Dangerous* another huge boost on *Billboard's* album charts. The R&B album chart had *Dangerous* moving up another sixteen places to number twenty three, and the pop album chart placed *Dangerous* at number forty one, up thirty seven places from the week before. The following week *Dangerous* moved up another fifteen places to number twenty six on the pop album chart.

After making more televison appearances in one month than he usually makes in a year, it was announced that Michael Jackson was to make another unprecedented television appearance. On February 10, Oprah Winfrey talked with the usually very shy and reclusive superstar during a live ninety minute interview from Neverland Valley that included a tour of the ranch and footage from his amazing career. It was revealed that the interview was Michael's idea and he agreed to discuss anything.

Michael Jackson was also the subject of Winfrey's regular daytime show that same day, with guests who have worked with Michael, and have known him for most of his life. Smokey Robinson, Suzanne de Passe, Gladys Knight were all guests who have known Michael since his very beginning in show business. Iman, his co-star for the "Remember the Time" video and Jeanne white, Ryan White's mother, were also guests on the program.

The special interview with Michael was heavily advertised, with commercials counting down the number of days until Michael speaks. There were even ads counting the minutes until the special was broadcast. All major news telecasts carried coverage of the special interview both before and after the special aired.

Winfrey began the interview with questions about Michael's childhood and his feeling that he missed out on a lot of normal childhood activities, and he attributed his attraction to children as his way of recapturing what he has missed. Michael also again confirmed that his father did in fact beat him as a child. He went on to explain that he does love his father, but doesn't really know him. There have been times when, both as a child and as an adult, Michael has become physically ill when having to face his father.

Probably the most anticipated portion of the interview had Michael answering, finally, all of the rumors, gossip, and outright garbage, that has been told about him over and over again, in some cases for many years. He said the areas on his face that he has had surgically alterated could be counted on two fingers, denying he had his cheekbones, eyes, or lips surgically altered in any way. He added that he is by far not the only person to ever have plastic surgery, "If all the people in Hollywood who have had plastic surgery took a vacation, there wouldn't be a person left in town."

He called both stories of him buying the elephant man's bones and of him sleeping in an oxygen chamber stupid and horrible, and he explained the chamber was actually a piece of equipment used to treat burn victims. He said nothing of the stories being originated by himself or by his manager.

Answering to the claims he has had his skin bleached, Michael replied emphatically, "As far as I know of, there is no such thing as skin bleaching. I have never seen it, I don't know what it is." He went on to disclose, "I have a skin disorder that destroys the pigmentation of the skin. It's something I cannot help. When people make up stories that I don't want to be who I am, it hurts me. It's a problem for me. I can't control it." He added that the disorder runs in his family, on his father's side and that he uses makeup to even out his skin tone. He then brought up a very interesting and significant point, "Why is that so important?" Michael's dermatologist later confirmed that he has diagnosed Michael as suffering from vitiligo, a disorder that causes discoloration of the skin.

Michael also responded to the more recent rumors being spread about him. Regarding his demands to be called "The King of Pop", he said he never proclaimed himself to be anything. Oprah added at this point in the interview that she did not contractually agree to call Michael "The King of Pop". Stories that he demanded to be the sole performer at the Inaugural Gala are quickly dismissed by Michael as being another crazy, completely made up story.

The story that he chose a white boy to play him as a child in a Pepsi commercial, and claims that he is ashamed of his race, were answered vehemently:

Why would I want a white child to play me? I am a black American. I am proud to be a black American. I am proud of my race. I am proud of who I am. I have a lot of pride and dignity in who I am.

Michael was surprisingly candid during the course of the interview, refusing to answer only two questions. He did not respond to any of LaToya's claims made in her book because he said he has not read the book. He also did not answer, and became embarrassed, when Oprah Winfrey asked if he is a virgin. He said only he is a gentleman and doesn't talk about such things. He did say later that he does date, and is currently dating Brooke Shields. He even answered a question concerning his constant crotch grabbing, which seems to have some parents upset. He said it is not always a conscious decision, that the music dictates how he moves.

Michael gave only a brief look at his outstanding talents as he demonstrated the moonwalk for Oprah and sang a few lines of "Who Is It" acappella, making the sounds of the instruments with his mouth. Near the conclusion of the interview came the world premiere video for his latest single, "Give In To Me".

Michael Jackson Talks...to Oprah was his first televised interview since 1987 when he appeared on the *Ebony/Jet Showcase* following the release of *Bad*. In that interview with the *Ebony/Jet Showcase,* Michael referred to the lyrics of "Man in the Mirror" and stated, "I always wish the world could be a better place. Hopefully, that's what I do with my music, bring happiness to people." You do, Michael. You do. Goodnight Michael, we all love you.

Lisa Campbell
Flint, Michigan
1993

PHOTOS

1. The Jackson home in Gary, Indiana (Lisa Campbell collection).

2. The Jackson estate in Encino, California. The grounds are protected by guards, a camera and an intercom system. (Lisa Campbell collection).

3. Solo albums recorded by Michael Jackson with Motown include *Got To Be There, Ben, Music & Me, and Forever, Michael* (Lisa Campbell collection).

4. Solo albums Michael recorded with Epic are *Off The Wall, Thriller, Bad,* and *Dangerous* (Lisa Campbell collection).

5. The Jackson's star on Hollywood's Walk of Fame. The Jacksons were presented with the star in September, 1980 (Lisa Campbell collection).

6. Michael Jackson's star on the Hollywood Walk of Fame. The star was awarded to Michael in November, 1984 and is located directly in front of Mann's Chinese Theater (Lisa Campbell collection).

7-8. Extensive security measures were taken for Michael Jackson's visit to the Motown Museum in Detroit on October 24, 1988. West Grand Blvd. was completely blocked off and police officers and mounted police awaited the arrival of Michael and Berry Gordy (Lisa Campbell collection).

9. Platinum Limited Editions issued 1,000 Artist of the Decade Awards honoring Michael Jackson. Each piece is numbered and signed by Michael (Lisa Campbell collection).

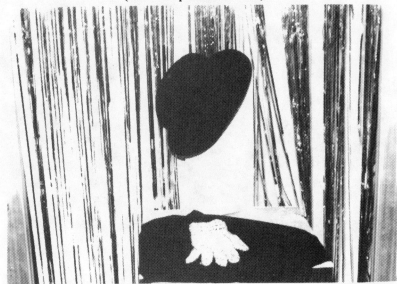

10. Michael's black fedora and sequined glove are on display at the Motown Museum in Detroit. A new security system has been installed since the theft of the glove (Lisa Campbell collection).

11-12. Just a small sample of the magazines to feature Michael Jackson on their covers in the past few years (Lisa Campbell collection).

13. Gold copies of singles from *Thriller* are housed in Chicago's Hard Rock Café along with a note of thanks signed by Michael (Lisa Campbell collection).

14. The Hard Rock Café in Chicago also houses 38 platinum copies of *Thriller* (Lisa Campbell collection).

15. The L.A. Gear Press Conference, September 13, 1989 (Photo courtesy of Starworld).

16. The Dedication of the Michael Jackson Auditorium at Gardner Elementary School, October 10, 1989 (Photo courtesy of Starworld).

17. The Artist of the Decade at the American Cinema Awards, January 27, 1990 (Photo courtesy of Starworld).

18. *Smooth Criminal* on stage--The Bad tour in Los Angeles, January, 1989 (Photo courtesy of Starworld).

19. Michael Jackson
at the circus, fall
1989 (Photo courtesy
of Starworld).

20. The Bad tour
in Los Angeles,
January, 1989
(Photo courtesy
of Starworld).

21. Unveiling of *The Book* by Brett Livingstone Strong, January 26, 1990
(Photo courtesy of Starworld).

22. An L.A. Gear
Promotional Shot,
1989 (Photo
courtesy of
Starworld).

23-24. Disney Chairman Michael Eisner presents the first Michael
Jackson Good Scout Humanitarian Award, September 14, 1990
(Photo courtesy of Gayle Stever).

25-26. Michael Jackson accepting the first Michael Jackson Good Scout
Humanitarian Award, September 14, 1990
(Photo courtesy of Gayle Stever).

27. Bob Jones (left) and Bill Bray (far right) join Michael Jackson
at the presentation of the first ever BMI Michael Jackson Award,
May 8, 1990 (Photo courtesy of Starworld in Hollywood, California.
(213) 469-0757).

28. Michael at the presentation of the Lifetime Achievement Award from the National Association of Black Owned Broadcasters 8th Annual Communications Awards Dinner, March 5, 1992 (Photo courtesy of David Manley).

29-31. Michael accepts the NABOB Lifetime Achievement Award with Al Jarreau and Jesse Jackson also in attendance. (Photo courtesy of Lori Byler).

APPENDIX A

MICHAEL JACKSON AND JACKSON
5 ALBUM DISCOGRAPHY

MOTOWN		12/69	DIANA ROSS PRESENTS THE JACKSON 5
MOTOWN		05/70	ABC
MOTOWN		09/70	THIRD ALBUM
MOTOWN		10/70	THE JACKSON 5 CHRISTMAS ALBUM
MOTOWN		04/71	MAYBE TOMORROW
MOTOWN		09/71	GOIN' BACK TO INDIANA
MOTOWN		12/71	THE JACKSON 5IVE'S GREATEST HITS
MOTOWN		05/72	LOOKIN' THROUGH THE WINDOWS
MOTOWN	(SOLO)	01/72	GOT TO BE THERE
MOTOWN	(SOLO)	08/72	BEN
MOTOWN		03/72	SKYWRITER
MOTOWN	(SOLO)	04/73	FOREVER MICHAEL
MOTOWN		09/73	GET IT TOGETHER
MOTOWN		09/74	DANCING MACHINE
MOTOWN	(SOLO)	01/75	MUSIC AND ME
MOTOWN		05/75	MOVING VIOLATION
MOTOWN	(SOLO)	08/75	THE BEST OF MICHAEL JACKSON
MOTOWN		06/76	THE JACKSON 5 ANTHOLOGY
MOTOWN		10/76	JOYFUL JUKEBOX MUSIC
EPIC		11/76	THE JACKSONS
EPIC		10/77	GOIN' PLACES
EPIC		12/78	DESTINY
MOTOWN		01/79	BOOGIE
EPIC	(SOLO)	08/79	OFF THE WALL
EPIC		10/80	TRIUMPH
EPIC		11/81	THE JACKSONS LIVE!

MCA	(SOLO)	11/82	ET: THE EXTRA TERRESTRIAL
EPIC	(SOLO)	12/82	THRILLER
EPIC		07/84	VICTORY
EPIC	(SOLO)	08/87	BAD
EPIC		06/89	2300 JACKSON ST.
EPIC	(SOLO)	11/91	DANGEROUS
MOTOWN		11/92	THE JACKSONS: AN AMERICAN DREAM

MICHAEL JACKSON VIDEOGRAPHY

1978 "BLAME IT ON THE BOOGIE" (THE JACKSONS)
1979 "DON'T STOP 'TIL YOU GET ENOUGH"
1979 "ROCK WITH YOU"
1980 "THE TRIUMPH" (THE JACKSONS)
1983 "BILLIE JEAN"
1983 "BEAT IT"
1983 "SAY SAY SAY" (DUET WITH PAUL MCCARTNEY)
1983 "THRILLER"
1984 "BILLIE JEAN" (LIVE FROM THE VICTORY TOUR)
1985 "WE ARE THE WORLD" (USA FOR AFRICA)
1987 "BAD"
1987 "THE WAY YOU MAKE ME FEEL"
1988 "MAN IN THE MIRROR"
1988 "DIRTY DIANA"
1988 "SMOOTH CRIMINAL"
1989 "LEAVE ME ALONE"
1989 "LIBERIAN GIRL"
1991 "BLACK OR WHITE"
1992 "REMEMBER THE TIME"
1992 "IN THE CLOSET"
1992 "JAM"
1992 "HEAL THE WORLD"
1993 "GIVE IN TO ME"

VIDEOCASSETTES

1983 MAKING MICHAEL JACKSON'S THRILLER
1985 WE ARE THE WORLD: THE VIDEO EVENT (USA
FOR AFRICA)

1985 MOTOWN 25: YESTERDAY, TODAY, AND
FOREVER (ORIGINALLY BROADCAST IN MAY,
1983. FEATURING A JACKSON REUNION AND
MICHAEL'S PERFORMANCE OF "BILLIE JEAN")
1989 MOONWALKER
1989 MICHAEL JACKSON:
THE LEGEND CONTINUES

MICHAEL JACKSON BILLBOARD CHART HISTORY

TITLE	HIGHEST POP CHART POSITION	
	Album	Single
DIANA ROSS PRESENTS THE JACKSON 5	5	
"I WANT YOU BACK"		1
ABC	4	
"ABC"		1
"THE LOVE YOU SAVE"		1
THIRD ALBUM	4	
"I'LL BE THERE"		1
"MAMA'S PEARL"		2
MAYBE TOMORROW	11	
"NEVER CAN SAY GOODBYE"		2
"MAYBE TOMORROW"		20
GOIN' BACK TO INDIANA	16	
JACKSON 5 GREATEST HITS	12	
"SUGAR DADDY"		10
GOT TO BE THERE (SOLO)	14	
"GOT TO BE THERE"		4
"ROCKIN' ROBIN"		2
"I WANNA BE WHERE YOU ARE"		16
LOOKIN' THROUGH THE WINDOWS	7	
"LITTLE BITTY PRETTY ONE"		13
"LOOKIN' THROUGH THE WINDOWS"		16
BEN (SOLO)	5	
"BEN"		1
SKYWRITER	44	
"CORNER OF THE SKY"		18
"HALLELUJAH DAY"		28
MUSIC & ME (SOLO)	92	

TITLE	HIGHEST POP CHART POSITION	
	Album	Single
"WITH A CHILD'S HEART"		50
GET IT TOGETHER	100	
"GET IT TOGETHER"		28
"DANCING MACHINE"		2
DANCING MACHINE	16	
"WHATEVER YOU GOT, I WANT"		38
"I AM LOVE" (PARTS 1 & 2)		15
FOREVER MICHAEL (SOLO)	101	
"WE'RE ALMOST THERE"		54
"JUST A LITTLE BIT OF YOU"		23
MOVING VIOLATION	36	
"FOREVER CAME TODAY"		60
THE BEST OF		
MICHAEL JACKSON (SOLO)	156	
THE JACKSON 5 ANTHOLOGY	84	
THE JACKSONS	36	
"ENJOY YOURSELF"		6
"SHOW YOU THE WAY TO GO"		28
GOIN' PLACES	63	
"GOIN' PLACES"		52
THE WIZ SOUNDTRACK		
"EASE ON DOWN THE ROAD"		
(DUET WITH DIANA ROSS)		41
DESTINY	12	
"BLAME IT ON THE BOOGIE"		54
"SHAKE YOUR BODY		
(DOWN TO THE GROUND)"		7
"YOU CAN'T WIN" (1) (SOLO)		81
OFF THE WALL (SOLO)	3	
"DON'T STOP 'TIL		
YOU GET ENOUGH"		1

TITLE	HIGHEST POP CHART POSITION	
	Album	Single
"ROCK WITH YOU"		1
"OFF THE WALL"		10
"SHE'S OUT OF MY LIFE"		10
TRIUMPH	10	
"LOVELY ONE"		12
"HEARTBREAK HOTEL"		22
"CAN YOU FEEL IT"		77
"WALK RIGHT NOW"		73
ONE DAY IN YOUR LIFE (SOLO)	144	
(ALL SELECTIONS		
PREVIOUSLY RELEASED)		
"ONE DAY IN YOUR LIFE"		55
LIVE	30	
THRILLER	1	
"THE GIRL IS MINE" (DUET		
WITH PAUL McCARTNEY)		2
"BILLIE JEAN"		1
"BEAT IT"		1
"WANNA BE STARTIN' SOMETHIN'"		5
"HUMAN NATURE"		7
"P.Y.T.(PRETTY YOUNG THING)"		10
"THRILLER"	4	
PIPES OF PEACE (PAUL McCARTNEY)		
"SAY SAY SAY" (DUET WITH PAUL		
McCARTNEY)		1
VICTORY	4	
"STATE OF SHOCK"		3
"TORTURE"		17
"BODY"		47
WE ARE THE WORLD (USA FOR AFRICA)		
"WE ARE THE WORLD" USA		
FOR AFRICA		1

TITLE	HIGHEST POP CHART POSITION	
	Album	Single
BAD	1	
"I JUST CAN'T STOP LOVING YOU"		1
"BAD"		1
"THE WAY YOU MAKE ME FEEL"		1
"MAN IN THE MIRROR"		1
"DIRTY DIANA"		1
"ANOTHER PART OF ME"		11
"SMOOTH CRIMINAL"		7
2300 JACKSON ST	59	
DANGEROUS	1	
"BLACK OR WHITE"		1
"REMEMBER THE TIME"		3
"IN THE CLOSET"		6
"JAM"		26
"HEAL THE WORLD"		52

APPENDIX D

MICHAEL JACKSON'S NUMBER ONE SINGLES

"I WANT YOU BACK"	01/31/70	1 WEEK
"ABC"	04/25/70	2 WEEKS
"THE LOVE YOU SAVE"	06/27/70	2 WEEKS
"I'LL BE THERE"	10/17/70	5 WEEKS
"BEN"	10/14/72	1 WEEK
"DON'T STOP 'TIL YOU GET ENOUGH"	10/13/79	1 WEEK
"ROCK WITH YOU"	01/19/80	4 WEEKS
"BILLIE JEAN"	03/15/83	7 WEEKS
"BEAT IT"	04/03/83	3 WEEKS
"SAY SAY SAY"	12/10/83	6 WEEKS
"I JUST CAN'T STOP LOVING YOU"	09/19/87	1 WEEK
"BAD"	10/24/87	2 WEEKS
"THE WAY YOU MAKE ME FEEL"	01/23/88	1 WEEK
"MAN IN THE MIRROR"	03/26/88	2 WEEKS
"DIRTY DIANA"	07/02/88	1 WEEK
"BLACK OR WHITE"	12/02/91	7 WEEKS

ACKNOWLEDGMENTS

Thanks to my wonderful husband, John, who encouraged me and lent his technical and design expertise,

to Michele, my research assistant, who helped tremendously in gathering information and without whom this could not have been written,

to my parents who never doubted my dreams, ambitions, or abilities,

and to Michael Joseph Jackson, who has served as a constant source of inspiration, motivation, and enjoyment.

Thank you and I love you all.

INDEX